New Public Managers in Europe

Public Servants in Transition

Edited by

David Farnham

Sylvia Horton

John Barlow

and

Annie Hondeghem

MACMILLAN
Business

First published 1996 by
MACMILLAN PRESS LTD
Houndmills, Basingstoke, Hampshire RG21 6XS
and London
Companies and representatives
throughout the world

ISBN 0–333–65082–4

A catalogue record for this book is available
from the British Library.

10   9   8 7 6 5 4 3 2 1
05   04   03 02 01 00 99 98 97 96

Typeset by EXPO Holdings, Malaysia

Printed and bound in Great Britain by
Antony Rowe Ltd
Chippenham, Wiltshire

Contents

List of Figures and Tables

Figures

Tables

vi

Notes on the Contributors

Manzoor Alam is currently working as a management consultant in the Delta Business International, Helsinki, Finland. His publications include *Civil Service Training and Development* and *Public Management in Europe: The Quest for Efficiency and Effectiveness.*

John Barlow is Co-ordinator for Government and Politics in the Department of Politics and European Studies, University of Central Lancashire, United Kingdom. His research interests are public policy and public-sector management. He has published in the areas of central–local government relations, local authority finance and the politics of 'hung' councils. He is currently working on a project on the impact of competition on local government and on developments in local government in Germany and Eastern Europe.

Jean-Luc Bodiguel is Director of Research at the *Centre de Recherches Administratives de la Fondation Nationale des Sciences Politiques*, Paris, France. He has researched widely on the French public service and has some 130 publications. These include *Les magistrats, un corps sans ame? La fonctionnaire detrone?* (with Luc Rouban) and *Les fonctions publiques dans l'Europe des Douze.*

Mary Coolahan is Registrar of the Institute of Public Administration, Dublin, Ireland. She was a serving civil servant before entering higher education.

Roger Depré is Professor of Public Management at the Public Management Centre of the Catholic University of Leuven, Belgium. He specializes in local government and personnel policy and trains civil servants. His publications include *Motivation of Civil Servants* (with Annie Hondeghem).

Sean Dooney is a Senior Lecturer in Government at the Institute of Public Administration, Dublin, Ireland. He was formerly an assistant secretary in the Irish Civil Service. He writes extensively on public service issues and his publications include *The Irish Civil Service, Irish Agriculture* and *Irish Government Today* (joint author).

Carlo D'Orta is the Secretary of the Justice Affairs Commission of the Italian Chamber of Deputies. In 1992–93 he was consultant to the Italian Government on the reform of public employment. He also teaches administrative law at the University of Rome, Italy. His publications include *Il Pubblico Impiego* (*Public Employment*), *La Dirigenza Militare* (*The Military Management Corps*) (with S. Cassese), *La Riforma della Dirigenza Pubblica* (*The Reform of Public Management Corps*) (with C. Meoli) and *La Riforma del Pubblico Impiego* (*The Reform of Public Employment*) (with G. Cecoza).

David Farnham is Professor of Employment Relations at the University of Portsmouth, United Kingdom. He has published widely in the areas of industrial relations and personnel management, with a special interest in higher education. His latest books include *Understanding Industrial Relations* (with John Pimlott), *Employee Relations*, *The Corporate Environment*, *Managing the New Public Services* (co-edited with Sylvia Horton) and *Managing People in the Public Services* (with Sylvia Horton).

Annie Hondeghem is Senior Researcher at the Public Management Centre of the Catholic University of Leuven and Professor in Public Administration in the Faculty of Political and Social Science at the Catholic University of Brussels, Belgium. She trains civil servants and her research interests are in personnel policy, public-service ethics and motivation. Her publications include *The Careers of Civil Servants* and *The Public Manager: New Developments in Public Management* (with G. Bouckaert and R. Maes).

Sylvia Horton is Principal Lecturer in Public Sector Studies at the University of Portsmouth, United Kingdom. Her research interests include the civil service and people management in public organizations. Her recent books include *Managing the New Public Services* (co-edited with David Farnham) and *Managing People in the Public Services* (with David Farnham).

Gerd Oosterhuis is Associate Professor in Sociology and Human Resources Management at the Royal Netherlands Naval Academy in Den Helder. His current research interests are focused on Human Resources Management in the Royal Netherlands Navy.

Manfred Röber is Professor of Public Administration at the *Fachhochschule fuer Verwaltung und Rechtspflege* and Lecturer at the

Free University in Berlin, Germany. He has published widely on organization theory, public management and public administration. He has also worked as a consultant for the German Foundation for Economic Development (DSE) and the German Agency for Technical Co-operation (GTZ) in Asian, African and Eastern European countries.

Luc Rouban is a researcher in the *Centre National de la Recherche Scientifique de la Fondation Nationale des Sciences Politiques, Centre de Recherches Administratives*, Paris. His research interests are public administration, the civil service and state theory. His most recent publications include *Les cadres superieurs de la fonction publique et la politique de modernisation administrative* and *Le Pouvoir anonymé – Les mutations de l'etat à la francaise.*

Markku Kiviniemi is Research Manager in the Department of Political Science, University of Helsinki, Finland. He has written *The Improvement of the Public Services* and *Perspectives on Structure, Culture and Action: Studies in the Public Administration of the Welfare State*, in English, as well as several books in Finnish. He is currently conducting research on recent developments in the Finnish public sector.

Theo van der Krogt is Associate Professor in Organizational Sociology and Director of the Public Management Training Centre in the Faculty of Public Administration and Public Policy at the University of Twente in Enschede, the Netherlands. He publishes mainly on the management of public organization, especially local government.

Salvador Parrado teaches human resources management at the University of Carlos III in Madrid, Spain. His main research interests are personnel policies at top levels of central bureaucracies. He is also interested in public policy and privatization. He has been visiting researcher at De Montfort University, England, Bamberg University, Germany, the Free University of Berlin, Germany, and the University of Central England, United Kingdom.

F. F. Ridley is Professor of Politics Emeritus at the Liverpool Institute of Public Administration and Management, University of Liverpool, United Kingdom. He is a founder member of the European Group for Public Administration, Vice-President of *Rencontres Europeennes des Fonctions Publiques*, member of the advisory committee of the Research Institute for Administrative Sciences, Speyer, Germany, and editor of

Parliamentary Affairs. His publications include *Policies and Politics in Western Europe* and *Specialists and Generalists*.

Valerio Talamo is currently undertaking research into environmental impact evaluation with the Italian National Research Council. His publications include 'Collective bargaining and trade union rights' in L. Fiorillo and C. Russo (eds) *Il Rapporto di Pubblico Impiego (The Public Employment Relationship)* and *Lavoratori Communitari e Pubblici Imieghi (The EEC, Workers and Public Employment)* (forthcoming).

Turo Virtanen is Associate Professor of Administrative Science at the University of Helsinki, Finland. He has written widely in Finnish on Human Resources Management. His on-going research projects include new public management in Finnish universities, and performance, public management and organization culture, a follow-up study of managing cultural change in 15 public agencies.

Preface

In 1992 the European Group of Public Administration (EGPA), which is a section of the International Institute of Administrative Sciences, set up a Study Group on Personnel Policy, under the joint chairmanship of Jean-Luc Bodiguel and Roger Depré. The focus of the Study Group was 'new' public managers in Europe. The main purpose of the Study Group was to obtain answers to a series of questions within nine countries – Belgium, Britain, Finland, France, Germany, Ireland, Italy, the Netherlands and Spain. The questions were:

- Why is there a shift towards new public managers?
- How many public managers are there?
- Where are they located?
- What are their social and professional characteristics?
- For what are they responsible and to whom are they accountable?
- What is their relationship with politicians and political institutions?

This book is the outcome of research on this topic by 19 contributors drawn from universities and other institutions throughout Europe. The central aim of the book is to provide an important source of information on the growing importance of the public manager, on a comparative basis, through national studies in nine member states of the European Union (EU).

The emergence of New Public Management (NPM) and new public managers is one of the most important developments in governmental systems of the Western world. Although managerialization has gone furthest amongst the Anglophone countries of the United States of America (USA), Britain, Australia, Canada and New Zealand, it is increasingly taking root in all countries of the EU. Studies by the Organization for Economic Co-operation and Development confirm that it is a phenomenon of all advanced industrial societies and, although there are significant differences in the speed of change and the particular forms that NPM is taking, new public managers are replacing traditional public administrators throughout a wide variety of public organizations. Their numbers, location and composition are contingent, however, upon the political, legal, administrative and cultural contexts of the countries concerned.

The book is divided into three parts. Part I provides the background to the study of public managers in Europe and some theoretical ideas underpinning comparative studies in this area. It addresses three themes. First, Barlow, Farnham, Horton and Ridley set the scene. They examine the problems of defining public managers, the difficulties associated with comparative studies and some of the similarities and differences in the national studies reported in the book (Chapter 1). Farnham and Horton then discuss the extent to which managing can be seen as a generic set of activities, common to both public and private organizations. Using a contingency analysis, they argue that although there is growing convergence of managerial activity in the two sectors, public managers ultimately operate not in a market context but in a political one, hence their behaviour is likely to be different (Chapter 2). Third, Virtanen makes an original, theoretical contribution to an understanding of the role of new public managers and the competencies they need to perform effectively. He questions the emphasis on instrumental competencies and the relative neglect of value competencies which, he argues, are the key to effective management and a responsive, democratic polity (Chapter 3).

Part II sets out nine national studies of public managers in Europe. These provide a wealth of detail on specific developments throughout the mid-1990s, enabling analyses of the trends, similarities and differences amongst states to be made. Depré and Hondeghem start by examining recent changes in Belgium and, by using an ideal typology of the public manager, they identify six organizations in which public managers are found. They give biographical details of 32 new public managers and their contracts of employment. They conclude that Belgium's public sector is in transition, but point to evidence that NPM and public managers are spreading to other parts of the public sector (Chapter 4).

The radical changes which have taken place in the managing of Britain's public services since 1979 are identified by Barlow, Farnham and Horton. They focus specifically on the civil service and local government, where the transition from an administrative to a managerialist culture, reflecting many of the values and attitudes of private-sector businesses, has taken root. Public managers are now in place throughout both sectors, functioning as active agents of political changes imposed in Britain by a series of reforming Governments over four Parliaments (Chapter 5).

An interesting account of the changes taking place in Finland, including new orientations towards clients, shedding of governmental activities and tighter control over financial and human resources, is presented by Manzoor and Kiviniemi. They identify public managers in 134 organizations, which have varying degrees of financial autonomy. Biographical data on the new public managers is analysed and their recruitment and training discussed. The authors conclude that the introduction of modern management techniques is resulting in a division of authority and responsibility between politicians and managers, with the latter being responsible for the delivery of politically determined outputs (Chapter 6).

Rouban argues that France is a special case in the transition towards NPM. A modernization programme, introduced by earlier Socialist Governments, has resulted in the utilization of new management techniques and processes, but so far there have been no major structural changes. His survey of some 500 civil servants indicates that new public managers, defined as those supporting and implementing the modernization programme, are concentrated in field administrations and lower *corps*. The *grand corps* and civil servants in central ministries display more negative dispositions towards modernization than do officials in quasi-commercial and technical fields. The outlook for NPM in France is favourable, however, given the recent election to power of a rightist President and Government. Nevertheless, the situation is likely to proceed slowly, because of the institutional barriers to change and the legal context of the administrative system (Chapter 7).

Röber demonstrates that the development of the NPM in Germany has not been uniform, largely because of the complex federal system and the legal and political barriers to change. The term public manager is only used in state-owned enterprises, although public officials performing many of the functions of managers are found in all levels of government. The main impetus for managerial reform has come from local government, where the pressures of financial restraint, changing consumer expectations and the need to respond to new economic and social factors are greatest. Changes at federal and state level have been slower but a shift is taking place from public administration to public management. These are reflected in developments in training, personnel systems and rewards. Germany, however, remains at the minimalist end of the reformist spectrum (Chapter 8).

The advent of NPM in Ireland and the gradual movement away from classic public administration to a more performance-oriented approach, ensuring continuing improvements in service delivery and efficiency and effectiveness in using resources, is traced by Coolahan and Dooley. At present, public managers are mainly found in market-driven public enterprises, but senior public officials are aware of developments taking place in other countries. The Strategic Management Initiative, introduced in 1994, is leading to major innovations throughout the whole Irish public sector (Chapter 9).

D'Orta and Talamo identify core elements in the intensive administrative reforms recently introduced in Italy. Important changes are occurring in relationships between political and administrative institutions, whilst a new business-management approach is being injected into public administration. Amendments to the law are enabling the employment contracts of public officials to be changed, thus facilitating the emergence of new public managers. The authors analyse them in terms of sex, age, geographic origin and education and training. Whilst it is too early to assess the lasting effects of managerialization on Italian public administration, D'Orta and Talamo conclude that the ultimate test must be its consistency with two fundamental constitutional principles: respect for the law and administrative effectiveness (Chapter 10).

The study of the Netherlands by Oosterhuis and van der Krogt suggests that reform of the administrative system started in the late 1970s, in response to serious budgetary problems. To some extent, the pattern of change mirrored the British experience, which has greatly influenced developments in the Netherlands. Although few public officials meet the full criteria of the model public manager, a survey indicates that about 30 per cent of senior ranks in the civil service are public managers. They are also found at top levels in provincial and local government. Public managers are concerned with the same issues as private managers, including cost-based accounting, performance budgets, performance indicators and quality management. The authors conclude that whilst the NPM is irreversible, politicians will not leave policy implementation solely to public managers, because they are not politically sensitive enough (Chapter 11).

In the case of Spain, the 'old' public administration has not yet given way to NPM, although there is evidence of change. Parrado argues that a modernization programme, launched in the late 1980s, designed to introduce a 'new managerialism' and 'new public managers' into administration, has had only limited results. The first phase involved enhancing communications with citizens, improving service quality and modernizing internal management. The second phase, beginning in 1994, is focusing on cost reductions and increased productivity. There is some evidence of a new managerial culture amongst civil servants delivering public services, but failure to create autonomous units means that they have no control over the deploying of resources. New public managers are found only in areas where a new type of agency has been created, operating under private commercial law. Paredo explains the failure of the modernization programme in Spain in terms of the administrative law tradition and the power of the *corps* (Chapter 12).

Part III draws conclusions from the national studies. Depré, Hondeghem and Bodiguel argue, on the basis of the national reports provided, that a transition from traditional public servants to public managers is taking place within Europe. The rate of change is not uniform, however, with some countries, such as Britain, exhibiting higher degrees of transition than others. Germany and Spain, in particular, demonstrate much lower degrees of change. Depré and his colleagues argue that shifts towards public management depend upon social, political, legal and cultural factors and the ability, or not, of major institutions, such as public-service *corps*, to resist change. They conclude that public management cannot be reduced to private management, and that effective management alone cannot solve the political problems of complex modern societies (Chapter 13).

The completion of a book like this would not have been possible without the involvement and co-operation of a large number of people. First, the editors would like to thank EGPA for supporting this project and facilitating the participation of the contributors in the Personnel Policy Study Group over the past three years. Second, we would like to thank all the contributors for meeting the tight deadlines required to get this book to press on time, despite all their other professional commitments. Third, our thanks are also due to June Burnham, Middlesex University, for assistance in translating French into English text. Fourth, we thank Mike Meredith, Analyst/Programmer, and Phil Brown, Senior Technician, University of Portsmouth, for their technical assistance in co-ordinating, integrating and harmonizing the variety of disks provided by our contributors from across Europe. Without their help, we might still be struggling with the arcane mysteries of the variety of software used to produce the text. Fifth, we would like to thank Stephen Rutt, Publishing Director, Macmillan Press, for commissioning this book and supporting us throughout its production.

Finally, as editors, we have been heavily interventionist throughout and appreciate our colleagues' tolerance of our approach. This was necessary to clarify the text, ensure as much consistency as possible amongst chapters and contain the size of the book. We hope that our readers will find the resulting volume crisp, informative and reflective, in an exciting area of policy change.

DAVID FARNHAM
SYLVIA HORTON
JOHN BARLOW
ANNIE HONDEGHEM

Part I
Background

1 Comparing Public Managers

John Barlow, David Farnham
Sylvia Horton and F.F. Ridley

Recent study of public administration has been dominated by the emergence of 'the new public management' (NPM). Yet whilst the NPM phenomenon is being discussed, analysed and evaluated across Europe and countries of the Organization for Economic Co-operation and Development (OECD, 1990, 1992, 1993), relatively little is known about the people actually handling the transition from classical public administration to NPM – 'the new public managers'. Even in Britain, where NPM is most firmly rooted, an impressionistic survey of 20 or so leading texts on public administration or public management reveals numerous references to NPM and managerialism but only one to the 'new public manager' (Farnham and Horton, 1993, pp. 111–12).

This book seeks to remedy this omission, by focusing on the new public managers in a European context. It seeks to identify who the new public managers are, where they are found, what their functions are and to what extent they are replacing traditional public administrators, on a comparative, international basis. Inevitably this involves examining the extent to which countries have moved towards NPM, since new public managers are a corollary of this process. Comparing both phenomena in different countries, however, raises problems of cross-national comparisons, whilst the European Group of Public Administration (EGPA) Study Group's research strategy of undertaking national case studies is only one approach to a complex issue. Nevertheless in presenting nine studies offering 'focused comparisons' (Hague, *et al.*, 1992) around the theme of public managers, this book enables some systematic comparisons to be made. Further, though the national studies do not test any particular theory, they can be seen as 'hypothesis generating' cases (Lipjhart, 1971) about the phenomenon of new public managers and the transformation process leading towards NPM.

THE INTERNATIONAL CONTEXT

The 1980s have been described as a tumultuous decade for public bureaucracies across the developed world, as governments faced new financial problems and sought to limit public expenditure growth. Economic recession and the apparent end of sustained economic expansion meant limits to public revenue, as did voter resistance to increased taxation. Governmental costs continued to rise in many fields, such as pensions and health-care, due to socio-demographic factors, and social security due to high levels of unemployment. Containing public expenditure became a priority for governments of all political persuasions in western Europe and beyond. Most resorted to curbing welfare redistributive spending programmes or reducing levels of service provision. The cost of government itself also came under scrutiny and savings were and still are being sought, though with varying degrees of enthusiasm and success. These include cutbacks in the size and remuneration of the bureaucracy and reduction of costs through greater efficiency in the work of public administration.

Pursuit of the three E's – economy, efficiency and effectiveness – has produced a host of administrative reforms across the world, independent of the economic climate. There has been growing public dissatisfaction with government, as well as a growing literature on waste in administration (Chapman, 1978; Miller, 1984; Grace, 1984). It was the economic climate, however, that focused politicians' attention on reform proposals in a way that critics alone could not have achieved. As emphasis on economy replaced the more traditional concerns of top bureaucrats, there was an almost irresistible shift in style from an administrative to a managerialist mode of operating. Senior public officials were forced to become public managers, albeit to a greater or lesser degree depending on the national systems within which they operated.

That is the standard explanation of the rise of managerialism in public administration, the emergence of NPM and the creation of new public managers: economic pressures. If one looks at the countries of western Europe, however, the environmental factors leading to reform of governmental bureaucracy are more complex and combine differently in different countries: they do not all lead inevitably to convergence. Particularly important has been the coming to power in some countries of New Right politicians who blamed the bureaucratic state for many of the problems their societies faced (Kaufman, 1979). Their critiques included: bad policy advice by overpowerful, top officials; poor administration by officials without managerial skills; and resistance to change by entrenched public-service unions. In President Reagan's phrase, 'Government is the problem, not the solution'. In other words, even without any fiscal crisis, political leaders came to office in some countries, such as the United States of America (USA), Britain, Canada and New Zealand, committed to rolling back the frontiers of the state, cutting public-service personnel, making what remained more business-like and bringing business people as well as business practices into the public services. If one looks at political developments it is clear that ideology was as strong a force as economic need in the development of NPM.

The extent to which Conservative parties moved to this neo-liberal extreme, however, can be exaggerated. Thatcher, Reagan and Mulroney, as its arch proponents, represent something of an Anglophone phenomenon. Continental European conservative parties, such as the German Christian Democratic Union (CDU) and the Gaullist *Rassemblement Pour la Republique* (RPR) in France, have rather different philosophies and, of course, some European countries have had socialist governments during this period, such as Spain and Finland. Although the search for economy and efficiency has led all governments some way along the same path, continental European states seem to have gone nothing like as far as Britain, and none seem anxious to 'reinvent government' to the extent of Britain, Canada, New Zealand and the USA (Aucoin, 1988; Boston *et al.*, 1991; Codd, 1988; Massey, 1993; Zifcak, 1994).

Another factor influencing NPM is social change. Populations are generally becoming more educated and individually better off, despite serious problems of the unemployed and underprivileged in all countries. They are also increasingly accustomed to being wooed as 'customers' by politicians. Ordinary citizens have become more self-confident in dealing with public authorities and expect better treatment than before. As a result, all countries of western Europe seem to have initiated reforms giving the public better services, even if no more money can be spent, by delivering what is available in a more user-friendly way. This can be seen as a by-product of managerialism, in that managerialism takes account of market expectations as well as production costs. But the changing mood in the citizen market is itself a force that encourages the managerialization of public administration.

In some countries the development of self-confidence and the revolution of rising expectation is greater than in others. Some societies are clearly further along the road to consumer modernism than those retaining elements of more traditional social structures. Reforms have also gone furthest where politicians have picked this up and integrated it in an articulated ideology. One can point again to Britain where consumerism appears to have gone furthest and where citizens have become the customers of public authorities, even of their tax offices. The language is now so pervasive that it affects the way officials think. France took longer to move from the once common *administrateur et administre* (administrator and administered person) to *administrateur et usager* (user) which has nothing like the same force. It tried to make officials more friendly by a smile campaign (*operation sourire*), though with limited success. In other countries, where society is not as modern and is more deferential, clientelistic or rural, the marketization of public administration and the emergence of a consumer orientation by new public managers seem less evident. This raises the question of whether there are causal links between these factors.

A different movement which is sweeping across the world is that of new management theory. Many years of cutting or curbing public expenditure have increased the receptiveness of governments, public organizations and senior public officials to 'how to do more with less'. Attractively simplistic economic solutions to economic problems, like monetarist theory, have been tried by governments. At the more practical level of management, one finds not only an unquestioned belief in the ability of managers to solve social problems (Pollitt, 1993) but a constant flow of formulae promising success to their adherents: Management by Objectives, Cost-Benefit Analysis, Total Quality Management, Market Testing, Performance Related Pay, Value for Money and Process Re-engineering. Theories encapsulated in catch phrases and abbreviated to initials become a way of thinking.

The rapid movement of management ideas across national frontiers owes something to the structures of transmission, notably the ever-growing influence of international consultancy firms, together with messages from the OECD or, in the developing world, the World Bank. Again, national cultures affect the reception of 'new' ideas. It is significant that the new managerial ideas, with all the buzz words, have been most readily accepted in the Anglophone world and in those parts of Europe where English is usually the second language, where there are intellectual links with America, American-style texts are read by students, and management consultants are used by public organizations. In Britain, for example, it is estimated that Conservative governments spent nearly £320 million on consultants' advice on privatization and market testing between 1979 and 1995 (Smithers, 1995).

In contrast, French reluctance to embrace managerialism may be seen as an aversion to accepting foreign concepts or even more crudely as part of an anti-American tradition (Servan-Schreiber, 1969). French governments have rules against the use of English words and, since 'manager' is hard to translate, the concept of public managers is hard to nationalize.

We have mentioned economic constraints, New Right ideology, growing citizen expectations and the management theory industry as international factors. There are also country-specific factors which, because they drive in similar directions, also suggest a universal rise of managers in European administration. In Spain, for example, there have been reforms of the state after Franco's authoritarianism, followed by adaptation to entry of the European Union (EU). Attempts to modernize administration, as an escape from administrative weakness, particularist interests and blocked societies are relevant in Greece and Italy, though they depend on political opportunities as well. Post-unification Germany's need to modernize the economy of the former German Democratic Republic and democratize its administration, albeit largely on traditional West German lines, can also also be cited as a specific national factor.

DEFINING PUBLIC MANAGERS

Identifying public managers presents a number of problems, not least of which are the ways that jobs are labelled and how different titles are used in different languages. The EGPA Study Group, therefore, decided to define the public manager in terms of functions and other criteria which would enable them to be identified cross-nationally, irrespective of what public officials were called. Using the EGPA framework, outlined in the Preface, public managers are those meeting all or most of the following criteria:

- they have responsibility for the execution of a programme or the realization of a product or service;
- they are evaluated on their results according to well defined criteria and management objectives;
- they are appointed to post and often have limited contracts of employment;
- they are accountable directly or indirectly to a public body;
- they have an important degree of autonomy in decision-making;
- they have freedom of action over the use of resources: both financial and human;
- they are essentially line managers: that is, they achieve objectives and results through people; they are not advisers or consultants.

In short, public managers are different from 'classic' civil servants operating in traditional bureaucracies. The classical public administrator is constrained by requirements of political accountability and must operate in a hierarchy governed by rules, regulations and standard operating procedures. Their career prospects are not linked to performance and they are not typically responsible for a discrete output of government.

Using this definition there may not be many managers fulfilling all aspects of the model. However, it is possible to identify key components of the model or recognize a shift in the direction of meeting most of these criteria. We started out with a number of propositions about where the new public managers might be found. These propositions guided our approach and later provided a basis for explaining what was found.

First, public managers were more likely to be located in commercial and industrial activities rather than in structures delivering classical state functions. For example, we did not expect to find them where the role of the public official was to advise on policy, or diplomacy, or where the role was to represent the state and exercise state authority, as amongst German *Beamte*, described as 'bearers of state sovereignty', or amongst French *fonctionaires* performing 'acts of public authority'.

Second, public managers are less likely to flourish where the density of rules and procedures is greatest. In particular, where the organization of state services and their procedures are generally prescribed in detail in admistrative law, the scope for public managers to manage their offices and take decisions on the use of human and financial resources is likely to be very limited.

Third, proximity of public officials to the delivery of services, and hence the customers of that service, provides a milieu suited to the development of public managers.

Fourth, specialists or technically trained professionals, operating at middle to senior levels, are likely to be receptive to ideas of NPM and its practices. Conversely, their professional training, however, may identify them too much with traditional practices and make them resistant to NPM.

Fifth, within state organizations, public managers may be found at strategic level rather than operational level. This is because where strategic decisions are involved fewer rules are found, even in administrative law countries. It may therefore be easier to introduce new management techniques at this level than lower down, say, at the level of office management.

THE NEW PUBLIC MANAGEMENT

Though our concern is primarily with the new public managers, it is important to look at the different ways in which managerialism and NPM are being integrated into governmental systems of the countries studied here. This helps situate managers and identify how far countries have gone in establishing managerial posts and in appointing people designated as managers. It also indicates how far different countries have focused merely on introducing managerial techniques within existing administrative structures, rather than on reorganizing institutions. One way to approach these questions is to examine changes in systems, structures and culture as three elements within the managerialization process.

Systems refer to the techniques and procedures used within the administrative process. They include information systems, financial systems and personnel systems, within which techniques for controlling the efficient use of resources can be used. The introduction of the Financial Management Initiative and Management Information Systems are examples of new systems introduced in Britain in the early 1980s. Both these laid the foundations for identifying cost centres and introducing devolved budgeting, with named managers responsible for achieving financial objectives. In addition a range of management techniques including output budgeting, performance management, staff appraisal and performance-related pay have subsequently been adopted. Such new methods of working are easiest to introduce when they complement traditional administrative procedures. They are harder to introduce if they replace existing practices or where they involve the creation of new posts or new institutions.

Structures refer to both institutional arrangements generally and the designation of specific posts. Where public management is seen as concerned essentially with executing and implementing governmental policies, there is a tendency to create separate agencies to provide services. This distinction between policy-making (politics) and policy execution (administration) was long discredited in Britain on both theoretical and practical grounds (Thomas, 1978). But such an institutional split has been a major feature of its structural reorganization policy, known as 'Next Steps' (Jenkins *et al.*, 1988).

In most continental European countries, at least for the levels actually responsible for administrative decisions affecting citizens, the interface at which 'services' are delivered, a policy/implementation distinction has always been assumed. In Germany, for example, much of the work of administration is thought of as a quasi-autonomous, quasi-judicial activity, although it does not apply at the highest levels in ministries, as in France, where such top posts are defined as involving work of '*conception et direction*'.

The question is whether structural reforms have occurred, leading to organizations which have managers at their head rather than civil servants in a traditional ministerial hierarchy. There seem to be relatively few reforms abroad that have gone as far as Britain's 'Next Steps' Executive Agencies (Goldsworthy, 1991), though Sweden, of course, went as far long before this. What one can see in some countries is the transfer of commercial/industrial services from central or local government to public corporations of one sort or another. In countries where this has been long accomplished, privatization now tends to be the trend. Finally, another structural response is 'quasi-agencification', which takes various forms, some of which allow heads of agencies some managerial freedoms but where law, political control or both constrain managerial autonomy.

Another aspect of structural change is whether new posts are actually created for managers, designated as such, or whether new responsibilities are simply given to officials in established hierarchies. The chief executives of British agencies are an example of new titles and new job descriptions. Much earlier, during the 1970s, reorganization of local government in Britain produced chief executives, and Irish local government, following the USA, has long used the title 'manager' for its senior officials. Elsewhere in Europe, however, it is hard to find such changes. There may be new, managerially oriented officials in some top posts, with managerial-type powers in certain respects, but it is hard to distinguish them in formal organization charts.

Turning to culture, we do not mean the administrative traditions embodied in procedural rules and formal institutions but ways of thinking and ways of behaving in public organizations. Have they altered? NPM is identified with a managerial culture which is economistic, rationalist and generic (Farnham and Horton, 1993). The evidence of the dominance of NPM is reflected in a preoccupation with 'value for money', driven by objectives and performance indicators and by general managers committed to change, 'excellence' and quality. A changing culture may, of course, make it difficult to distinguish public managers from other senior civil servants if it becomes pervasive. In Britain, for example, permanent secretaries and their deputies, the top two grades in the civil service, describe themselves as managers. Indeed, all higher and middle-ranking civil servants are now continually told that they are managers. This is not a common feature of continental Europe.

THE NATIONAL STUDIES

This study of public managers is based on nine national studies of member states of the EU. It includes the four largest countries, Britain, France,

Germany and Italy, smaller countries such as Belgium and the Netherlands and a broad geographical distribution from Finland in the north, Ireland in the west and Spain in the south. The inclusion of some countries and the exclusion of others were shaped by pragmatic considerations but in this instance the results provide a usefully representative sample for analysis: 75 per cent of EU member states. It is possible to group the countries in a variety of ways. On the one hand, there is a group of northern European countries (Germany, the Netherlands, Finland and Britain) with their own patterns and traditions of government and administration. These can be contrasted with the Mediterranean countries of the south (France, Spain and Italy). On the other hand, one can distinguish between Catholic and Protestant countries, federal and unitary ones and large and small ones: issues we return to later in this chapter.

As a group, they share many broad political similarities. They are all western European states which are pluralist, liberal democracies. They all have multi-party competition in parliamentary systems of representation and all feature a distribution of power across a range of national, regional and local institutions of government. Their bureaucracies have long been founded on rational-legal principles influenced by the key models of France (Napoleon) and Prussia (von Stein-Hardenberg), with the exception of Britain where administration has traditionally been viewed as an art and rooted in the philosophy established by Northcote-Trevelyan in 1854 (Dyson, 1980). Also, as Meny (1990, p. 242) comments:

> There are many similarities between the Western bureaucracies, despite all the differences caused by history or by the particular position of each administration within the framework of its country's system as a whole. And today they are complemented by yet another unifying factor: Western democracies all face the same problems, are all subject to similar constraints and are all engaged in continual interactions which lead them to seek similar solutions. By reason of these common constraints and experiences there exists today a veritable market in methods of administrative reform, in which ideas are exchanged about new structures, new methods, and new modes of management.

However there are also differences, not least in their relative progress – or lack of it – on administrative reforms.

These national studies clearly demonstrate different rates of change in the acceptance of NPM and development of public managers. In looking for explanations, one is confronted with a vast array of factors influencing the ways countries are likely to respond to pressures for change. These include a country's system of government, its constitution and legislative process, its politics, the power base of government and the commitment of politicians to reform. Administrative traditions, the role of administrative law, administrative organizations and staff associations able to resist change are also significant. Administrative culture and the self-image of officials are further variables. Finally one must take into consideration the structure of society, its stage of economic development and its wider political culture.

TRANSFORMATIONS AND CHANGE

The transformation of national administrative and state systems from a bureaucratic to a post-bureaucratic paradigm (Overman and Boyd, 1994) has been occurring at different rates and in different ways throughout Europe. One explanation of the differential changes and rates of change amongst countries is the views of the key actors involved. In other words, there is always a personal element in reforms, depending on who is making policy at the time. This 'chance' element is often overlooked in cross-cultural analyses of policy change. Though it is not the most significant factor, the personality, style and conviction of Margaret Thatcher were all important factors in introducing NPM into Britain. The starting point for our comparisons is Britain, because Britain has gone much further along the road of reinventing government (Osborne and Gaebler, 1992) and embracing the NPM than the rest of Europe, and has been looked to by many of the European states as in part a model to follow. Top French, Dutch, German and Spanish officials have studied the processes of privatization, deregulation and agencification in the British civil service and in one case produced an important report upon which the British Government has acted (Trosa, 1994).

Why has the managerial revolution been so much easier to achieve in Britain than abroad? In answering this question some major contextual variables can be identified which influence the way in which and the speed with which such changes can come about. First, Britain has no written constitution. More important, it has no constitutional law which is entrenched and difficult to amend. All statute law has the same legal status. Parliament is said to be sovereign, which means that it can pass any legislation and repeal any previous legislation using the same legislative process. No aspect of public administration is protected. This is not true elsewhere.

In other countries, the constitution places legal constraints upon governments. In Germany, for example, the constitution states that the civil service is to be organized according to traditional principles. Civil service rights are entrenched, as is the administrative independence of sub-national governments. In France, the *Conseil d'Etat*, composed of civil servants, scrutinizes all draft laws and can declare them unconstitutional. All European member states have written constitutions and special procedures for amending their constitutions except Britain.

Second, Britain has an electoral system which generally leads to a single party having a majority in the House of Commons, where party discipline is strong. The Government can rely on a majority for its proposals in all but the rarest circumstances. There are no countervailing centres of power, as in coalition governments, systems with less disciplined parties, systems with a powerful second chamber or those which are federalist. Determined governments can get their projects through Parliament – if not in a day, as in New Zealand, forerunner of many managerial reforms – at least without serious problems. Nothing so easy can be found in continental Europe, where legislation concerning administrative reform has often run into difficulties.

Furthermore, reform of central government administration, including the organization of ministries and the civil service, do not usually require legislation in Britain where such matters are regulated by government using Crown Prerogative, that is its executive powers. Major reforms, including the establishment of agencies with their managerial chief executives and the managerialization of the civil service through the opening of top posts to outsiders and changing contracts of employment, were introduced by Orders, which require no prior parliamentary involvement or even debate. In other countries, such reforms would usually involve legislation.

Third, in Britain a strong Prime Minister, ideologically determined to de-bureaucratize the civil service, privatize major public industries and impose markets on local government, was able to use her disciplined parliamentary majority and executive powers to do so. Other constraints were ignored, notably civil service unions whose influence, like that of other unions, was much diminished under her leadership, in part through legislation and in part by adopting a strident and confrontational strategy towards them. She had the will as well as the power to start a movement of radical reforms. She intervened in senior civil service appointments and, suspicious of the traditional culture of senior officials, 'the Mandarins', she selected 'hands on' managers rather than policy-makers. Nowhere else in Europe can one point to political leaders with quite the same spirit or determination. Though her successor, John Major, could not match that strength, he made further administrative reforms, with the *Citizen's*

Charter and market testing, as central parts of his programme. No other European country has displayed such centrality of power at least in the post-war period.

What other factors explain why managerialism was more likely to fit British patterns of administration than those of continental Europe? Britain does not have administrative law in the sense that the term is used elsewhere. Though the ordinary courts have extended the possibilities of judicial reviews of ministerial decisions, on the grounds, for example, that they are contrary to natural justice, there is no special body of law which administrators apply in their dealings with citizens. All law regulating relations between the state and the individual is part of civil and criminal law. Indeed, comparatively little of the routine work of civil servants is regulated by law. In managerial terms, the routine work that needs managing does not differ that much from work in many other large organizations. That is why the British civil service does not recruit law students or train its staff in law. Administration has traditionally been described as an art learnt in practice, with extensive discretion in decision-making and little supervision through the courts.

In most continental European countries, on the other hand, administration is seen as the application of laws. What many administrators do, at least in non-technical services, is make individual decisions, on tax liability, benefit entitlement, building permits and so on. They do this by applying the law to the facts of the case in a quasi-judicial fashion, objectively, impartially, in a legal-rational manner. Such decisions are subject to appeal in administrative courts, at the rate, in the larger countries, of several hundred thousand a year. Whilst the legalistic philosophy is perhaps strongest in Germany, it is found in all EU countries and lies at the core of the difference between Britain and the rest of Europe. It imposes limits on managerialism and the power of managers.

In fact, the role of law in continental European countries goes further than that suggested above. Many procedures that could be regarded as 'office management' in Britain are regulated by administrative law, a point made already. In France, for example, personnel management is constrained by special laws regulating the civil service, and public money is handled according to complex legalistic controls. The same applies to public contracts. This may be dismissed as antiquated bureaucracy by American-style new public managers but such procedures are more than Weberian formalized bureaucracy. They are an integral part of the traditional theory of the state in continental Europe. Public laws impose limits on the roles of public officials, including managers, and place constraints on their personal discretion.

Laws regulating the public service itself, on recruitment, training, promotion and remuneration, also constrain the development of public managers. Thus the requirement for training in law in Germany does not easily allow space in the curriculum for management topics, which is currently being fiercely contested. But in Britain there is wide flexibility in the training of public administrators (Bischoff and Wendt, 1992).

The lack of a single unified public service in Britain also increases the scope for a variety of responses to change, and increases the capacity for innovation. Individual local authorities, for example, enjoy considerable freedom to create their own management structures and designate their own management posts. Most European countries have more unified services, found at several levels of government and, given that they are rooted in public law, this constrains innovation. Although the distinction drawn in Germany between *Beamte* (civil servants) and *Angestellte* (public employees) suggests that in theory the latter may be more open to ideas of public management; in practice, differences between the two groups is minimal (Johnson, 1983).

More speculatively perhaps, the distinction between Britain's generalist tradition of recruitment to the higher civil service and the more specialized backgrounds found elsewhere may help to explain the seemingly readier acceptance of managerialism in the British civil service compared particularly with France, Germany and Spain. Civil servants in the latter have studied administrative science, administrative law and other relevant subjects such as economics or engineering, so they see themselves as specially qualified for the posts they occupy. The arts graduates that still dominate Britain's higher civil service, intelligent though they may be, skilled in the writing of papers, and knowledgeable about the way their ministries work, do not carry the status of professional experts. To that extent they may well find it easier to adapt to the new managerialist culture. Indeed, they may welcome a new, not to mention fashionable, professionalism where they had none before.

The question of culture is also important. Some bureaucratic cultures may be more resistant to managerialism than others. Also, as a result of social change, the values and attitudes of entrants to the civil service have changed over time. The values and lifestyle of British graduates today are different from those of the Oxbridge mandarins of the past. They are also different from the *Enarques* of France, the one socialized into a more diverse peer group than the other and thus perhaps more open to the values of other professional groups. The degree to which public employees are insulated from the private sector has diminished in both central and local government in Britain, thus increasing receptivity to the central tenets of NPM (Dunleavy and Hood, 1994).

The above is obviously an over-simplification of national administrative cultures. There are considerable variations amongst the civil services of continental Europe and the same applies to different branches of the civil service in one country. In France, for example, it is said that members of the élite technical *corps* such as the *Ponts et Chausséés* are more receptive to managerialism than members of the non-technical élite, the famous *Enarques* (see Chapter 7). That may reflect a greater interest in management on the part of engineers than of lawyers or economists but the real reason is probably that members of the technical corps spend periods in the field services actually managing operations. In Germany, the Netherlands and Spain, local government staff seem more open to managerialism than those in ministries and there are more likely to be posts designated as managers in local authorities. Perhaps this is because they are more in touch with the public and feel the need for user-friendly, market-oriented organizations. Other factors are harder to explain, particularly when they are attributed to national character, as sometimes the more managerialist approach of Flemish (Dutch-speaking) civil servants in Belgium compared with their Francophone Walloon counterparts.

RESISTING CHANGE

The creation of public managers and other aspects of NPM clearly threaten established interests but also offer opportunities for some to increase their power. The introduction of public managers in some instances is an overt attempt at limiting the power of other professional groups, such as the medical profession in the National Health Service in Britain. These reforms have had the effect of redistributing power away from the doctors towards the nursing profession on the one hand and the new managers on the other.

Resistance within the administration to the changes which public managers bring about can also come from staff organizations protecting the interests of their members, either against the usurpation of promotion prospects or against the flexibilization of employment conditions that new public managers can facilitate. An example of the former is the role of the French civil service corps protecting their fiefs against 'outsiders', such as other corps. Examples of the latter are trade union actions to protect existing employment rights. Public-service unions remain relatively strong in most European countries. Even in Britain, where governments have sought to reduce the power of public sector unions, trade union membership and collective bargaining are still the dominant orthodoxy in industrial relations in most of the public sector (Farnham and Horton, 1996). Additionally, pressure against legislative change can be brought to bear where a large number of parliamentarians come from the civil service (Aberbach *et al.*, 1981). In President Mitterrand's first government, the Communist Minister for Administrative Reform was an *administrateur civil*, a non-élite civil servant, who was a traditionalist in defence of civil service rights and the special role of civil servants as representatives of the state.

Political interests may equally be served or threatened by administrative reform. Some politicians may be reluctant to relinquish their ability to supervise day-to-day administration, because this is important to them in terms of votes as well as enabling them to influence policy. The British tradition of clear lines of demarcation between the 'political' and 'official', in contrast with the overlapping and blurred distinction at the top of the executive in many continental European countries may provide another explanatory variable. If, as in the case of Germany, large percentages of elected politicians are civil servants, where does the political will for change come from? The point has been made already that in Britain a strong ideologically driven Government had no fear in attacking the civil service, particularly when the backgrounds of the politicians were predominantly from business.

Finally, drawing on Greek experience, although it is probably true of other southern European states too, it is usual to think of Weber's classical bureaucratic, hierarchical, formalized, impersonal, legal-rational model of administration as the antithesis of managerialism and thus harder to shift to NPM than other organizations. However, it requires strong hierarchical organization to implement reforms. If new rules are not obeyed, new procedures not used and management post-holders carry on as before, reforms remain on paper and nothing really changes. In societies where public administration shows high levels of particularism, fragmentation, clientelism and some corruption – sometimes described as a low degree of institutionalization – laws and orders from above are too easily ignored. One can only infer that a well-organized bureaucracy is necessary before managerialism can be imposed and public managers can exercise their new-found powers and authority.

DISCUSSION

One must beware of drawing the wrong conclusions about the reasons for any similarities and differences in approach to NPM in the nine country studies in this book. But clearly some variables do provide explanations of variations in the degrees to which European countries have transformed their administrative systems into the NPM mode and the extent to which public managers are replacing traditional public officials.

Explaining and Classifying Change

The concept of the state and the administrative law tradition offers a sharp distinction between Britain, and other Anglophone/Commonwealth countries, and the rest of Europe which were all influenced by either Napoleonic or Prussian traditions of the state. Britain does not have 'a state' as an institution in law: civil servants are servants of the Crown and orders are made in the name of ministers. Elsewhere public officials represent the state and exercise state authority. As stated earlier, German civil servants are the 'bearers of state sovereignty', whilst French civil servants perform 'acts of public authority'. Theirs is clearly an administrative-political role and not one so susceptible to managerialism as those which are not grounded in the law.

Public managers are more likely to be found in the commercial and industrial sectors of state activity than in structures delivering classical state functions. Moreover, as noted earlier, the organization of state services and their procedures are generally prescribed in considerable detail through administrative law. That is an essential part of the *'Rechtsstaat'*, the state based on law, which has a different meaning from Britain's 'Rule of Law'. In the Rechtsstaat, the scope for public managers to manage their offices, by using human and financial resources flexibly, is often limited.

Alternatively, it may be useful to develop a classification into those countries with a northern tradition, centring around Britain and Germany, and those of the southern Mediterranean tradition based upon the French model. Some application of the two is likely to be the most fruitful in unravelling the political, economic and social factors influencing the trend towards NPM in Europe. They were identified earlier in terms of public expenditure restraint, political ideology, changing citizen expectations and the influence of management theory.

Whilst all the national-study countries have experienced degrees of fiscal pressure and demands for tax cuts, that pressure is likely to be greatest in countries which have either the highest ratios of public expenditure to gross domestic product (GDP), the largest workforces in the public sector, or the greatest relative economic decline. A crude ratio of public expenditure to GDP is inadequate as a measure. There is a need also to compare the size and functions of the public sector. This may be indicative of resistance to

NPM. The sheer size of employment in the public sector is both a reflection of state traditions and the extent of state intervention in the economy. A large public sector providing secure employment may be isolated from and impervious to the private sector. The distribution of employment between central, regional and local governments may in itself be a significant factor explaining resistance to public management. These measures must in turn be supplemented by a measure of direct provision by the state, contrasting it with indirect provision by the private or voluntary sectors.

The extent to which the state is directly responsible for delivering services, as opposed to providing the finance and managing a network of providers, is certain to have an impact on management tasks (Hood and Schuppert, 1988). In countries with a mixed economy of welfare, the pressures for change may be less than in one with a strong tradition of direct and more costly state provision.

Political ideology has been an important factor in debates about the role of the state. Conservative or right of centre governments have distrusted extensive state intervention, preferring individual welfare provision or collective provision through non-state organizations such as the voluntary sector in Britain or church organizations in the continental European christian democratic tradition. The emergence of the New Right has given further emphasis to privatization and development of managerialism in the public services.

Throughout much of the 1980s and 1990s, centre right parties have been in government across much of Europe. Their willingness to espouse New Right ideas has varied and been restrained by lack of continuity in office or the need to form coalitions with other political parties to remain in power. Thus, NPM and public managers are likely to emerge where there are rightist governments, whose ideology has not been tempered by the need to form coalitions and where the right has dominated for long enough to implement its political and social agenda.

On that basis Britain meets all these criteria, with the Conservatives in power continuously since 1979. Centre right parties have dominated this period in both Ireland (*Fianna Fail* since 1979) and Germany (CDU since 1982) but without sharing the radical vision of the New Right in Britain. At the same time, they have had to rule in coalition for all (Germany) or part (Ireland) of this period. In the Netherlands, the Christian Democrats have been in government since 1977 but in a variety of coalitions. The same can be said of the Christian Democrats in Italy, although there was a socialist-led coalition from 1983 to 1987. The instability of coalitions in Italy, however, mitigates against a period of sustained administrative reform.

Belgium has also been characterized by government by unstable coalition, with power fluctuating between left and right of centre parties.

Moving further along the spectrum, Finland was governed by a Social Democratic-led coalition from 1977 to 1987, though the Conservative KOK (the National Coalition Party) has had power since then. At the far end of the right-to-left spectrum is France, governed for the most part by the *Partie Socialiste*, apart from brief periods of 'cohabitation' with a socialist President and a rightist government during 1986–88 and 1993–95. Spain, in turn, has had a socialist government since 1982. The danger with assigning countries along different parts of a spectrum of transformation based on political control can overlook the capacity of local and regional governments to effect their own independent decisions in the acceptance of NPM. It also begs the question regarding the willingness of social democratic parties to modernize and embrace administrative reform.

Citizen demands and expectations are rising everywhere, especially in industrialized high income nations. It is here that pressures to deliver high quality services have been greatest and where the shift to public management is most obvious. Conversely, where there is traditionally greater deference to hierarchy and authority, pressures for change are likely to be weaker. Thus deference to the Catholic Church, with its own strong traditions of welfare provision, suggests, other things being equal, that the move towards public managers is likely to be relatively low in predominantly Catholic countries.

An initial rank ordering of the nine countries against these four variables is suggestive of two distinct groupings: one in the agrarian south and the other in the northern industrialized 'golden triangle', with Ireland in the former rather than the latter group. Thus the proportion of the population in agriculture may be another indicator.

Since the spread of new ideas in management thinking has been dominated by North American literature, it follows that the reception of these ideas is likely to be greatest in English-speaking countries or those which are more open to the English language. Thus the impact of management literature is likely to be high in Britain and Ireland, moderate to high in the Netherlands, moderate in Germany and Belgium, and positively low in France, Italy and Spain.

Combining the seven sets of variables, as in Table 1.1, it is clear that Britain is identified as the most receptive to NPM ideas and public managers. The Netherlands, Belgium and Finland have similar profiles to Germany and are predicted to be slightly less receptive, whilst the southern Catholic countries – France, Italy and Spain – are predicted to be the least receptive to the introduction of public managers.

Clearly, Table 1.1 gives only an impressionistic framework for locating public managers. Nevertheless, it indicates that it is useful to develop dis-

Table 1.1 Socio-economic indicators identifying public managers

Country	Public expenditure as percentage of GDP [1]	Public employment as percentage of total population [2]	Influence of new right ideology on politics [3]	Percentage of workforce in agriculture [4]	GDP per capita [5]	Catholics as percentage of population [6]	Influence of English language [7]
Belgium	44.2	9.1	Lo	3	$8212	88	Mod
Britain	40.0	6.7	Hi	2	$8070	<20	Hi
Finland	34.2	3.0	Lo	11	$11026	<10	Hi
France	41.1	11.0	Lo	7	$9236	90	Lo
Germany	41.7	8.2	Lo	7	$10290	45	Mod
Ireland	23.0	7.5	Mod	14	$5074	95	Hi
Italy	39.8	5.3	Lo	10	$6269	90	Lo
Netherlands	51.4	3.4	Mod	5	$8631	38	Hi
Spain	25.1	5.8	Lo	15	$4376	95	Lo

Key: Hi   indicates high influence
          Mod indicates moderate influence
          Lo   indicates low influence
SOURCES: [1] OECD National Accounts
         [2] Information in case studies
         [3]–[6] J. and I., Derbyshire, *Political Systems of the World* (Edinburgh: Chambers) (1989)

tinct northern and southern models of public-manager penetration which have been used elsewhere as, for example, in describing decentralized state systems (Page and Goldsmith, 1989) or categorizing different modes of welfare provision (Abrahamson, 1991). Abrahamson's thesis is that there is a convergence of welfare provision in Europe as northern countries reduce emphasis on welfare delivered through state agencies ('commodification'), by integrating family and community sources of welfare, which have been the dominant mode of provision in southern states. They, in turn, are modernizing their welfare provision by turning both to more state provision and the market (Baldock, 1993).

Models of Public Service

There are a number of models of the 'public service' with different philosophies about the role of civil servants in the modern state. They suggest different ways in which civil servants perceive their roles, reflecting in part the different historical experiences of different countries. It is hard to identify them with particular countries, since a mixture of models is generally found, and this varies across countries. First, there is the idea that civil servants are the servants of a democratically chosen government which is answerable for administration to an elected parliament. Their overriding duty is to ministers or elected representatives. At top level, this means helping ministers of whatever party is in office to work out their policies, and implementing these wholeheartedly. All administrative decisions are in principle those of a minister who is answerable either politically or before the courts. In this, the traditional British model, there is little space for a self-image with other responsibilities such as to the 'national interest' or 'the state'.

A second model, essentially a German one, tries to separate policy-making from implementation, meaning the application of laws by the administration. Administration is the responsibility of a professional civil service, making decisions that are legal, rational, objective and impartial. This is a formalized activity, where files may be reviewed by an administrative court, and hence is an activity relatively independent of politicians.

A third model, reflecting the French tradition, sees the civil service as having an independent view of the national interest, above party politics and sectional interests, a self-image of responsibility, not just to government but as independent guardians of the state and qualified judges of policy. Coupled with this, there may be a self-image of subject-expertise, in not only administrative law but also the technical fields that government regulates. It is technocrats who know best what should be done.

A fourth and newly emerging model is the managerialist one, which is based on a mixture of management and political expertise. Where there has been an institutional separation of policy-making and the delivery of services, as in Britain's executive agencies, this leads to the public manager's approach. The self-perception here is of seeking to implement the policies of the government as efficiently and as effectively as possible within the resources made available. This necessitates both political and market accountabilities by public servants. The skills and competencies needed to perform that role are a mixture of political and general management aptitudes (see Chapter 3).

Some Concluding Issues

The notion of the 'public manager' is both a contestable one and one open to change. The studies in this volume seek to begin mapping out the territory, but there is more research needed before we can begin to make definitive statements about a new type of public manager. Some things, however, are becoming evident. The rapid transmission of ideas is producing some common responses on how to implement the NPM, with some evidence of a growing European convergence, assisted by the EU and the OECD. However, there is also counter evidence of a Euro-spectrum, with variations which may remain or increase over time.

There is also some evidence of managerial convergence between the public and the private sectors. In some countries, such as Britain, a greater permeability across the public–private divide arises when governments appoint non-civil-servants as public managers. In contrast, in France the movement is still in the opposite direction, with the *pantouflage* of élite civil servants to top posts in the private sector. In the one case managerialism is entering the civil service, in the other public-service values are permeating private enterprise.

The debate about the distinctiveness or otherwise between public or private management continues and the view that management is generic and managers can transfer effortlessly from one sector to the other is still hotly contested, especially in Britain, where the opportunities for such flows are greatest. However, perhaps it is more fruitful to ask whether there is a new hybrid type of public manager emerging, whose contexts, competencies and accountabilities differ from those of private managers but also from traditional public administrators (Perry and Kraemer, 1983).

This book makes a contribution to these discussions and seeks to encourage its readers to participate in the debate. It provides a useful source of information about new public managers in Europe, where they can be found, who they are and how they differ from traditional public administrators. It also demonstrates that personnel working in the public sector are increasingly required to be more flexible in the ways that they work and the work that they do. They are having to tailor their expectations according to the ever-rapid rate of change. The impact of this 'flexibilization' on the delivery of public services, in an increasingly globalized market place, presents a major research project for the future.

References

Aberbach, J., Putnam, R. and Rockman, B. (1981) *Bureaucrats and Politicians in Western Democracies*, Cambridge, Mass.: Harvard University Press.

Abrahamson, P. (1991) 'Welfare and poverty in the Europe of the 1990s: social progress or social dumping?', *International Journal of Health Science*, 21(2).

Aucoin, P. (1988) 'Contraction, managerialism and decentralization in Canadian government', *Governance*, 1.

Baldock, J. (1993) 'Patterns of change in the delivery of welfare in Europe' in P. Taylor-Goodby and R. Lawson, *New Issues in the Delivery of Welfare*, Buckinghamshire: Open University Press.

Bischoff, D. and Wendt, H. (1992) *Europa als Herausforderung fur den offentlichen Dienst*, Berlin: Hitit Verlag.

Boston, J., Martin, J., Pallot, P. and Walsh, P. (1991) *Reshaping the State*, Auckland: Oxford.

Chapman, L. (1978) *Your Disobedient Servant,* London: Chatto & Windus.

Codd, M. (1988) 'Recent changes in machinery of government', *Canberra Bulletin of Public Administration*, 54 (May).

Dunleavy, P. and Hood, C. (1994) 'From Old Public Administration to New Public Management', *Public Money and Management,* July/Sept.

Dyson, K. (1980) *The State Tradition in Western Europe*, London: Martin Robinson.

Eliasson, K. and Kooiman, J. (eds) (1993) *Managing Public Organizations*, London: Sage.

Farnham, D. and Horton, S. (eds) (1993) *Managing the New Public Services*, London: Macmillan.

Farnham, D. and Horton, S. (1996) *Managing People in the Public Services*, London: Macmillan.

Goldsworthy, D. (1991) *Setting Up Next Steps*, London: HMSO.

Grace, P. (1984) *Report of the President's Private Sector Survey on Cost Control*, Washington: White House.

Hague, R., Harrop, K. and Breslin, S. (1992) *Comparative Government and Politics*, 3rd edn, London: Macmillan.

Hood, C. and Schuppert, G. (1988) *Delivering Public Services in Europe*, London: Sage.

Jenkins, K., Caines, J. and Jackson, A. (1988) *Improving Management in Government: The Next Steps*, London: HMSO.

Johnson, N. (1983) *State and Government in the Federal Republic of Germany*, Oxford: Pergamon

Kaufman, H. (1979) 'Fear of bureaucracy: a raging pandemic?', *Public Administration Review.*

Lipjhart, A. (1971) 'Comparative politics and the comparative method', *American Political Science Review*, 65.

Massey, A. (1993) *Managing the Public Sector: A Comparative Analysis of the UK and the USA*, Aldershot: Edward Elgar.

Meny, Y. (1990) *Government and Politics in Western Europe*, Oxford: Oxford University Press.

Miller, T. (ed.) (1984) *Public Sector Performance: A Conceptual Turning Point*, Baltimore and London: Johns Hopkins University Press.

OECD (1990) *Public Management Developments Survey*, Paris: OECD.

OECD (1992) *PUMA Public Management Development Update 1992*, Paris: OECD.

OECD (1993) *Pay Flexibility in the Public Sector*, Paris: OECD.

Osborne, D. and Gaebler, T. (1992) *Reinventing Government*, Wokingham: Addison Wesley.

Overman, E. and Boyd, K. (1994) 'Best practices research and post-bureaucratic reform', *Journal of Public Administration Theory and Research*, 4.

Page, E. and Goldsmith, M. (1989) *Central and Local Government Relations: A Comparative Analysis of West European States*, London: Sage.

Perry, J. and Kraemer K. (1983) *Public Management: Private and Public Perspectives*, New York: Harper & Row.

Pollitt, C. (1993) *Managerialism and the Public Services: The Anglo-American Experience*, Oxford: Blackwell.

Savoie, D. (1994) *Thatcher, Reagan and Mulroney: In Search of a New Bureaucracy*, Toronto: University of Toronto Press.

Servan-Schreiber, J. (1969) *The American Challenge*, Harmondsworth: Penguin.

Smithers, R. (1995) 'Sell-off advice bill nears £300m', *The Guardian*, 18 September.

Thomas, R. (1978) *The British Philosophy of Administration* , London: Longman.

Trosa, S. (1994) *Next Steps, Moving On*, London: OPSS.

Zifcak, S. (1994) *New Managerialism: Administrative Reform in Whitehall and Canberra*, Buckingham: Open University Press.

2 Public Managers and Private Managers: Towards a Professional Synthesis?

David Farnham and Sylvia Horton

Growing academic and practical interest in the emergence of the public manager stems from changes taking place in the structures of the state in Western, liberal democratic societies. These changes derive from fundamental economic, social, demographic and political forces, which have led all western governments to reflect on the nature of the post-war state and its political settlement after 1945 (Farnham and Horton, 1993; Pollitt, 1993; Kooiman and Eliassen, 1987). Governmental reforms have focused on the need to cut and contain public expenditure and to reduce the state's share of gross national product. The role of the public manager – and the 'new public management' (NPM) – have been critical in implementing such policies. Indeed, the central thrusts of NPM are: public resources must be used efficiently; public managers must be held accountable for the use of the resources they consume; and public organizations must be responsive to the growing demands of their 'clients' and 'customers' for high quality services in the 'market place'.

Given the increasing penetration and importance of public management, and its growing reliance on the methods and techniques of private management, this chapter seeks to address the extent to which the managerial function is converging in the public and private sectors. This is a daunting task when focusing on a single, national system, let alone if the comparison is international. This is because public and private organizations are so diverse in their characteristics and qualities, whilst their environmental contexts are so varied. This chapter is, therefore, a tentative, first step towards providing an analytical framework within which the respective roles of public managers and private managers might be analysed and compared.

THE MANAGERIAL FUNCTION AND THE CONTINGENCIES OF MANAGEMENT

One of the problems in examining any similarities and/or differences between the roles of public and private managers is a semantic one: there is no agreed definition of either term. Hence, in the public sector, the phrases 'public manager', 'public administrator' and 'public official' are sometimes used interchangeably. In the private sector, including 'not-for-profit' organizations, the title manager is sometimes given to people, such as functional specialists, who are not strictly managers. It is possible, however, to identify some essential elements in any managerial job. Thus managers:

- are appointed as agents for achieving the goals of the organization in which they work;
- create policies, with subordinate managers being responsible for implementing and monitoring them;
- have authority for taking and executing decisions in their own areas of responsibility;
- are subordinate to higher managers or higher authorities, such as governing bodies, and are accountable to these authorities for what they do and their job results;
- attempt to control, co-ordinate and deploy organizational resources, whether physical, financial or human, in the best interests of goal effectiveness and efficiency;
- can only achieve their purposes, and those of the organization in which they work, through people as individuals and groups;
- ultimately have collective responsibility for organizational success, howsoever this is measured.

Using these broad criteria, managers can be loosely defined as those individuals, in generalist or specialist posts, in any hierarchically structured organization, who undertake these sorts of responsibilities.

Managers as a group, then, are located within systems of corporate authority and are collectively responsible for the success and efficiency of the organizations employing them. Those at the top have responsibility for the enterprise; those in the middle for a section or functional activity; and those who supervise for ensuring that operational work gets done.

Top managers are involved in making strategic choices and strategic decisions about goals and translating these into policies and decisions for implementation. In particular, top managers are involved in the organization's interaction with its external environment, seeking to ensure that it responds effectively to the multiplicity of forces acting on it. Middle managers are primarily concerned with implementing policy, coordinating activities and providing links between operational units and top management. First-line managers are directly responsible for allocating work and monitoring daily outputs.

In the Anglo-American context, at least, the division amongst these levels of management is not always a clear one. Most research into what managers do (Mintzberg, 1973, 1979 and 1983; Stewart, 1967 and 1988; Kotter, 1990) concludes that there is a wide variety of activities – depending on the type and size of the organization, its structure, technology and managerial levels – in which managers are involved. It is the direction and leadership given by top managers, however, and the dominant culture of the organization, which appear to fashion people's behaviour at lower levels. It is the impact of these and other organizational contingencies, we contend, especially on top managers, which largely determine the nature of the managerial function, and its related practices, in both public and private organizations.

Public organizations are created by governments for primarily political purposes. They exist to satisfy citizen need for goods or services, irrespective of the ability of individuals to pay for them at the point of use. Private, for-profit organizations, or businesses, on the other hand, are created by individuals and groups for the purposes of satisfying consumer demand in the market place and of making a profit. Private, not-for-profit organizations, or voluntary bodies, such as charities, trade unions and professional associations, exist for welfare or interest-group purposes. They are judged by their ability to achieve the non-economic goals for which they are created on behalf of those whose interests they represent.

There is a vast literature (see, for example, Friedman, 1962; Hayek, 1944 and 1976; Lindblom, 1977; Seldon, 1990) debating the case for and against politics or markets determining production, distribution and exchange decisions in societies. But ultimately, the configuration of public and private organizations reflects political choices and priorities, not economic ones. The pattern is relative to time and place, although common environmental factors may lead to similar trends across different countries and national cultures at any one time. What is becoming evident is that distinctions between public and private organizations are becoming less clear (Tomkins, 1987). It is within this contextual dynamic that the respective functions of public and private managers need to be identified and located.

Figure 2.1 identifies the principal organizational contingencies confronting managers in public and private organizations. Our basic argument is that these contingencies are major influences on managerial behaviour. We also contend that, at the extremes, the contingencies facing public and private managers differ. There are, therefore, differences in substantive and procedural behaviour between the two managerial groups but there are also similarities. However, as distinctions between public and private organizations blur, their managerial roles converge, with the balance between their differences and similarities changing. Further, as the managerial hierarchy is descended, management practices and behaviour are more alike, since lower-level managers lack discretion in the ways they perform their jobs, being constrained by the decisions of higher-level managers.

MANAGERS, MISSIONS AND GOALS

All organizations have a mission and goals, whether explicitly or implicitly stated. A mission provides the overall purpose of an organization and establishes the rationale for its existence. Its formal goals are set by those governing it and can be tangible outputs, or throughputs, which can be

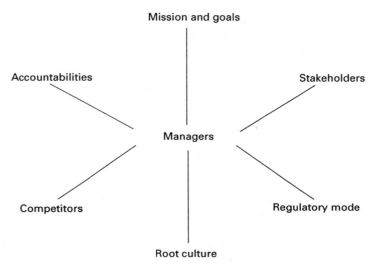

Figure 2.1 *The organizational contingencies of public and private managers*

measured. Formal goals act as guidelines for decision-making and reference points for evaluating the success and effectiveness of an organization. Formal goals, in turn, are translated by senior managers into organizational objectives and policies which provide the parameters within which middle and operational managers are expected to carry out their tasks and activities.

An organization's formal mission, goals, objectives and policies, however, may not be fully internalized by all those working in it or by its other stakeholders – whether they are customers, citizens, suppliers or members of the organization – or by the general public. It is also clear that what is espoused policy by senior managers may or may not be operationalized by subordinate managers. There may be multiple, covert goals and objectives within an organization which are either congruent or incongruent with the formal ones.

The formal mission and goals of public organizations are set by the law and politicians. Their missions are normally welfare and socially oriented, whilst their goals may be influenced by people who are not elected politicians, such as public officials, lobbyists and external experts. Policy decisions, however, are taken by elected representatives or their agents. In contrast to private organizations, the goals of public bodies are complex, vague and might even be unattainable (Simon, 1957; Wildavsky, 1979; Gunn, 1987). Pollitt (1990, p. 121) identifies three pressures resulting in the vagueness and ambiguity of goals in public organizations.

First, there is the need to build and maintain coalitions of support .... Second, a broadly-based objective is less likely to give immediate hostages to fortune ... and it is easier to argue that it has been, at least in part, successful .... Third, vague wording ... [or] 'woolly wording' is ... attractive in the sense that it provides endless opportunities for the defence, evasion and apparent innovation during the process of political debate.

Another feature of public organizations is that it is not uncommon for one level of government to set goals which another level has to implement. Formal goals may be implemented by regions, localities or other public or private agencies which inhibit the ability of central government to control the implementation of its overall goals (Page, 1992).

For-profit organizations, in contrast, tend to have more easily stated and less disputed missions and goals. Put crudely, private businesses have the economic mission of making a profit. This is for redistribution as dividends to shareholders and for reinvestment purposes. They also have second-order goals set by senior managers, such as growth, market domination, product diversification and brand leadership, satisfying consumer demand and complying with government regulators or laws. The common element is that these goals are market-driven. Profit is therefore the bottom line in for-profit organizations and is the main measure of their efficiency and success.

The missions of not-for-profit organizations focus on mutual self-help, members' interests or the welfare of others. Their goals are concerned with services to members, protection of group interests and getting recognition from those outside them. Their survival depends on the willingness of appointed managers and members or supporters to work cohesively and co-operatively together.

ACCOUNTABILITIES AND STAKEHOLDERS

All organizations are accountable to a variety of stakeholders. Accountabilities are the *de facto* and *de jure* obligations that managers have to take into account when making decisions, whilst stakeholders are the parties with interests in the processes and outcomes of managerial decisions. Table 2.1 shows the main stakeholders in public and private organizations.

Table 2.1   *Main stakeholders in public and private organizations*

	Public organizations	Private organizations
External	Taxpayers/users	Customers
	Suppliers	Suppliers
	Communities	Communities
	State authorities	Shareholders
Internal	Employees	Employees
	Professional staff	Managers
	Managers	[Members]

Conflicts can arise amongst stakeholders including between: state authorities and their employees; citizens as taxpayers and citizens as users of public services; shareholders and employees; and members and officials of voluntary associations. It is one of the roles of senior managers to balance these conflicting interests, to avoid them becoming dysfunctional for the organization.

Public Organizations

The ultimate external accountability of public organizations is to taxpayers and users of public goods and services. They are interested parties in what public organizations do because, first, public bodies are often monopolistic providers, leaving the public no choice but to take what is supplied. Second, public bodies exercise power to ensure compliance with public laws and regulations, by fining people or even depriving them of their liberty. Third, they provide merit and public goods which directly affect the quality of people's lives. Fourth, they levy compulsory taxation to fund governmental activities. Fifth, they regulate many areas of social life from licensing drinking, driving and entertainment to controlling building design, allocating land use and protecting the ecological environment. It is this exercise of public power that necessitates public organizations being held politically accountable in a democratic society. Public managers are expected to act as stewards of the public interest and public purse, as well as being formulators and advisers on policy and facilitating the provision of goods and services.

In practice, the external accountability of public organizations is largely legal. All public bodies operate within a strict legal framework which is national, local and increasingly international. Unlike private organizations, which can do anything which the law does not specifically forbid, public ones are more constrained. In the UK, for example, public bodies can only do as the law prescribes. This legal rule, known as *ultra vires*, means that public officials must be able to point to legal authority for all their actions. Failure to do so can be mandated and restrained by the courts.

Unlike most other western European countries, however, there is no system of public courts in the UK. It is ordinary courts that hold public organizations to account, for their actions and the procedures used. Public officials are required to demonstrate that they have complied with the substantive law, procedural law and natural justice. In other countries, with written constitutions, legal empowerment and legal constraints are limited by constitutional rights, embedded in the basic law and enforced through constitutional and public courts. Public officials are far more constrained in the exercise of discretion which affects their ability to manage (see Chapter 1).

Political accountability manifests itself in a number of ways. All public officials are directly or indirectly accountable to a political person or body. Civil servants are accountable to a minister and elected assemblies, local government officials to elected councillors and managers of public enterprises to sponsoring departments. In the UK, the model assumes that powers are invested in ministers who are responsible for what public servants do and are accountable, in turn, to Parliament for those actions. Although constitutional procedures vary in Europe, the basic principle of bureaucratic accountability to democratic institutions applies. *Beamte* in Germany and *fonctionnaires* in France are answerable to, and controlled by, political executives accountable to elected assemblies. Even in the USA, with its separation of powers, public managers are accountable to political executives and committees of Congress. The constraints of political accountablity are probably greater in the USA than in Europe, because of the greater powers that the assembly has (Page, 1992).

External accountability to users, clients and consumers of public goods or services is through complaints and grievance procedures. Administrative courts and tribunals deal with appeals against administrative decisions, whilst other complaints are determined by Ombudsmen. Other public bodies have internal complaints procedures and, in the UK, *The Citizen's Charter* (Prime Minister's Office, 1991) resulted in radical changes in accountability including limited statutory rights for consumers, thus taking accountability to consumers from the administrative and political realms into the legal one (Farnham, 1992).

Public organizations also seek to be internally accountable to those whom they employ, by acting as responsible, good employers able to attract, recruit and retain committed and qualified staff. Public employers normally seek to provide terms and conditions of employment, job security and rewards – such as promotion on merit – which compare favourably with those of private employers (Beaumont, 1992; Fredman and Morris, 1989). Public officials, in turn, sometimes accept loss of civil rights and some restrictions of their civil liberties, although this varies amongst countries (Bamber and Lansbury, 1993).

The accountability of public bodies to professional groups is particular to them, since public authorities generally employ large numbers of professional workers such as doctors, nurses, lawyers, teachers and social workers. Professionals often claim professional autonomy, clinical freedom or academic freedom from the state authorities. To facilitate effective working amongst professional groups, politicians and senior managers, attempts are made to maintain formal contacts between the professions and the authorities, through consultative and communication channels.

Private Organizations

Accountability in private organizations is less complex than in public ones. A major external accountability is to their customers or consumers –

or to those individuals or organizations buying the business's goods or services. Ultimately, unless for-profit organizations are able to sell their products or services in the market place, they are unable to survive. The final arbiter of private-sector accountability is the market. Businesses are also accountable to their customers through consumer protection legislation and fair trading agencies, created by the state. This makes private organizations accountable to their consumers, by providing legal remedies to anyone whose interests are infringed where businesses act unscrupulously, unreasonably or unfairly.

Private businesses are also accountable to their suppliers. This is embodied in 'good business practice' and by trust and goodwill between purchasers and suppliers in the market place. Fair businesses pay their accounts on time, do not exploit their market position and deal with supplier complaints quickly and efficiently. These activities are underwritten by laws around which businesses build their trading and exchange activities.

The accountability of private businesses to the communities in which they are located incorporates a variety of measures. These relate largely to legal controls over health and safety, land use and development, pollution control and noise abatement. These measures are designed to achieve a balance between the interests of those living within the community and those of business enterprises themselves. Since private businesses do not generally incur the direct social costs associated with damage to the environment, pollution or resource depletion, the state requires them to constrain their activities where such social costs are involved. Where organizations fail to do this, the state penalizes them financially or by other means, such as by withdrawing their licences to do business.

The social and moral accountabilities of businesses are becoming more important, as businesses have steadily accepted that they have ethical responsibilities to the wider community. These have to be taken into account when senior managers take decisions about production, pricing, resource utilization and the distribution of profits. Companies are, therefore, becoming increasingly socially aware and conscious of their external accountability to the wider community.

Another external accountability of private businesses is to their shareholders. Shareholders are sources of corporate funds and companies are legally accountable to them, whether they are individual or institutional shareholders.

Private organizations are also accountable to their employees. This is partly fulfilled in terms of good employment practices, fair dealing with employees and, where they are recognized by employers, through trade union organization. But corporate accountablity to employees is embodied in law too. In the UK, for example, employees have a set of statutory employment rights, although they do not have a legal status as a collectivity within the business enterprise, as in Germany with its works councils and in France with its enterprise committees (Bercusson, 1986). Where employers fail to conform with the minimum standards required by the law, dissatisfied employees may seek the redress of the law to obtain their rights.

Not-for-profit organizations also have key accountabilities but these are largely to their members or the community generally. They too are accountable to the law, such as trade union law, employment law and health and safety law, and to their constitutions, articles of association or internal rules. In the case of professional bodies, there may be, additionally, codes of conduct, or good practice, regulating relations between members and clients and between members and the wider community.

COMPETITORS

Since organizations are rarely absolute monopolies, they are constrained by other enterprises competing with them for resources, staff and customers. Public organizations approximate most closely to monopolies where the state is the sole provider of a particular good or service, such as national defence, policing and judicial services. Yet, even in these monopolies, there is competition amongst them for labour, other resources and finance and, in the UK, some of these former state monopolies are increasingly faced with competition from the private sector.

Many public organizations compete in product markets, either with one another or with private organizations. National railways compete with alternative forms of transport, both public and private. National electricity companies compete with coal and gas suppliers as alternative sources of energy. Publicly owned car manufacturers compete with private and public manufacturers in national and international markets. In the welfare sector, public hospitals compete with private and voluntary ones, public schools and universities with private establishments and public job centres operate alongside private employment agencies.

Since the early 1980s, there has been a tendency for competition between the public and private sectors – and within the public sector – to increase. This has been the result of privatization and the creation of internal or quasi-markets. This trend has been most marked in the UK, where the sale of public assets and the break-up of the former nationalized industries have re-drawn the boundaries of the public/private domains, although the systems of regulation imposed on the privatized industries leaves them far from the fully private end of the organizational spectrum.Organizations remaining in the UK public sector have been exposed to policies of compulsory competitive tendering (CCT) and market testing, which exposes them to competition from private companies and other public bodies. Finally, where it has not been possible to transfer activities to the private market, internal or pseudo-markets have been created such as in the UK's National Health Service.

This mixed economy of provision is not new to continental Europe, or to the USA, where public and private organizations have always co-existed. The existence of competition inevitably affects the behaviour of public managers, and requires skills and responses different from those associated with managing bureaucratic monopolies.

Competition is the norm for private organizations, although the extent varies in different product markets. Some organizations are in near-perfect markets, where access is open and prices are taken by producers. Others operate in monopolistic or oligopolistic markets, where price and quality competition is managed through cartels and price-fixing arrangements. Research into how businesses and firms take decisions in these varying market conditions illustrates a range of high risk to low risk responses (Cyert and March, 1992). Anticipating competitors' reactions is an essential element in corporate decision-making.

Not-for-profit organizations often operate in competitive markets for members, volunteers, funds and, in some instances, for contracts funded by public agencies. They are increasingly faced with the need to improve their competitiveness and to counteract their competitors in their respective markets for members and resources (Drucker, 1990).

REGULATORY MODES

The regulatory mode of an organization mediates relations between it and its stakeholders, with major differences between the ways in which public and private organizations are regulated. The regulatory mode determining relations between public organizations and taxpayers, state authorities, users of and suppliers to public organizations, and their public officials, is a combination of public law, legal interpretation through the courts, intervention through public agencies and the political process. Internally, the regulatory mode is traditionally bureaucratic and rooted in hierarchy, rules and delineation of competencies.

Public law directs and circumscribes what public officials can do. Countries such as France and Germany, which are characterized by legal codes and the *Rechtstaat* respectively, are the most legalistic systems. All countries, however, are increasingly bound by thousands of new laws and regulations, enacted annually. Politics, or the political process, is clearly a crucial, fundamental feature of the regulation of public bodies, where goal setting, resourcing issues and managerial priorities are determined by high-ranking politicians, whilst their decisions, in turn, are the responsibility of senior public officials to execute and administer.

Ultimately, politicians have to justify their policies and the actions of their officials to the electorate and their representatives who can replace ministers, councillors and elected officials through the ballot box at periodic elections, (or between elections by votes of censure or withdrawal of support) thereby changing the direction in which public policy moves and is implemented. The relationships between governments and assemblies varies from the pervasive influence of the American Congress to the relatively weak assemblies of Europe (Page, 1992). However, assemblies have the ability to ensure that there is some accountability between elections. Legislative, budgetary and scrutinizing procedures constitute important elements in the regulatory modes of public bodies.

Public bodies are also open to pressures from interest groups, which use a variety of mechanisms to influence these organizations to act in ways benefiting them. Public bodies, in turn, may wish to cultivate links with particular interest groups to elicit their support and co-operation. Political systems vary in the extent to which links between public bodies and interest groups are institutionalized but to a greater or lesser degree all liberal democratic states are pluralistic and incorporate different interests. Page (1992) observes that the role of interest groups in the regulatory mode of the four countries he studied was very similar. Interests were ubiquitously consulted and the closer one looked into policy implementation, the more pervasive their presence was. Schmitter and Lehmbruch (1978), Schmitter and Lehmbruch (1979), Cawson (1985) and Hood and Schuppert (1987) have all contributed to a clearer understanding of the interdependencies between public and private organizations in the regulatory mode of both sectors.

In taking account of the occupational interests of those employed in public organizations, politicians and public managers often deal with trade unions and other employee organizations, although some senior public officials are excluded from union membership and collective bargaining. In some states, civil servants are forbidden by law to strike or take part in any form of industrial action, since the consequences of industrial action can be more far-reaching in public organizations than in their private counterparts. Industrial democracy in public organizations has to be managed carefully, if it is not to conflict with the principle of political democracy and political accountability. The situation regarding public employees is not very different from that in private organizations where unions are recognized. But the potential conflict in private organizations is not between industrial and political democracy but between the principles of industrial and shareholder democracy.

One feature of public employment differing significantly from employment in the private sector is the large number of professional workers. Public employers have to find constitutional mechanisms to manage relations between themselves and their workers sensitively and responsively. This means involving them in policy-making and decision-taking, where their professional interests are concerned.

The regulatory mode determining relations between businesses and their customers, suppliers, shareholders and employees is dominated by the market. The law, particularly contract law, is of secondary but significant importance, since it normally tries to uphold the principles of fair, reasonable and agreed exchanges between the parties in an organization's product, commodity, capital and labour markets. Alternatively, the role of the law is a prescriptive but limited one in those areas seeking to prevent organizations creating unhealthy and unsafe working conditions, polluting the environment or discriminating against minority groups of workers or consumers.

It is the market, then, underpinned by contract law, which is the basic regulatory device in business organizations. Ultimately, it is 'meeting the bottom line' which counts. Unless, over time, private organizations are able to satisfy customer demand in the market place, to provide a surplus of revenues over costs and to ensure capital investment for the future, they cease to operate as viable economic units. Private organizations, in short, must be economically efficient, sufficiently profitable and able to sustain steady growth, if they are to survive in a dynamic market environment.

Increasingly, private businesses and especially large corporations, like public organizations, are becoming constrained by regulatory bodies and interest groups, with a growth in both in recent years (Veljanovski, 1991; Peacock, 1984; Coase, 1988). Activist groups challenging 'big business' interests have become important catalysts in its regulatory mode. Their views have to be increasingly taken account of and this brings private businesses into the political rather than the economic arena (Pattakos, 1992). This involvement in politics is most prominent for those businesses engaged in public contracts. To the extent that they are reliant on state contracts, their regulatory mode comes closer to that of public organizations.

The regulatory mode in not-for-profit organizations, which determines relations amongst members and between members and the external community, is fashioned by their rules and articles of association. Another feature is their use of 'codes of conduct' or standards of ethical behaviour to be maintained by members. Since these bodies are not driven primarily by the market, they tend to act like political bodies, with networks of cliques or power where ultimate organizational authority is concentrated and key decisions taken.

ROOT CULTURE

The root culture of an organization is the dominant set of values, ideas and beliefs which underpin decision-making and behaviour within it. 'It is what is typical of the organization, the habits, the prevailing attitudes, the grown up pattern of accepted and expected behaviour' (Drennan, 1992, p. 3).

The root culture of public organizations is embodied in the principles of 'bureaucracy', 'public service' and 'citizen need'. Bureaucracy rests on the underlying belief that public organizations need to be governed by fixed rules and mechanistically administered, in accordance with established hierarchies and agreed rules and procedures. This is to ensure clear lines of authority and accountability and to limit the discretion of public officials. It is also justified in the interests of procedural fairness, standardization, predictability, decision-making objectivity and substantive effectiveness. Belief in the value of public service implies that those working for public organizations are dedicated to the public interest and to ensuring good standards of service to those using them. It also implies that public organizations and public servants are committed to satisfying the demand for public services from all citizens wanting them, irrespective of the ability of individual citizens to pay for them.

The root culture of private organizations is embodied, in its most pure form, in the principles of 'free enterprise', 'free markets' and 'free trade', though in reality these are more often ideological totems of aspiration rather than practical norms of business behaviour, depending upon the extent to which the state accepts or rejects these behavioural norms. Free enterprise is the belief that private business organizations are more efficient and adept in responding to people's demand for goods and services than public organizations are. They are more likely to provide choice and to maximize social welfare by supplying what people want in the market place. Private enterprise should therefore be promoted, if necessary at the expense of the public sector which is seen to be wasteful, uncompetitive, monopolistic and unresponsive to public needs (Bacon and Eltis, 1976).

The belief in free markets posits that economic efficiency is best facilitated, and profitability best promoted, by unregulated market conditions. This is where the free interplay of supply and demand determines prices and the amount bought and sold in each market. In practice, most large-scale businesses are price-makers, not price-takers, but corporatist arguments for free, unmanaged markets predominate over those for regulated or state-controlled ones.

Belief in the virtues of free trade, in turn, asserts that free markets promote fair competition, the efficient allocation of scarce, limited resources and the maximization of economic welfare. The implication is that government intervention in the market, and the imposition of bureaucratic rules which interfere with the freedoms of firms to take their own production, investment and market decisions, is both inefficient and ineffective. Underlying the principles of free markets and free trade is the belief that competition is beneficial to all parties and that those who are successful should be rewarded and those who fail should incur costs. Risks are inherent in competition and there will always be winners and losers in free-market, free-trading systems.

The root culture of not-for-profit organizations is embodied in the principles of 'self-government' and 'voluntary self-help'. An underpinning belief is that, as democratic or ethical organizations, voluntary bodies should involve their members or supporters in taking key decisions. Another is that voluntary self-help is deemed to be morally and ethically superior to political or market regulation in determining and protecting the sectional or specialist interests of such groups.

ORGANIZATIONAL CONTINGENCIES AND THE IMPLICATIONS FOR MANAGEMENT PRACTICE

In our view, how managers in public and private organizations carry out their managerial tasks derives from the organizational contingencies, outlined above. The contingent factors constrain and prescribe the limits within which both public and private managers are able to act. If, as Reed (1989, p. 177) asserts, managing is 'a set of diverse and interrelated social practices concerned with assembling and controlling the dispersed pattern of social relations within which work is performed and reviewed', then the contingencies within which senior management operate are crucial to effective management practice.

Administrative or Management Systems?

In public organizations, with their emphases on political choice, the law, citizen rights and multiple accountabilities, and in not-for-profit ones too, it is primarily administrative systems, rather than managerial ones, which have traditionally dominated management practice. The overall task of senior managers within traditional public bodies has basically been an administrative one, with limited scope for strategic, entrepreneurial and innovatory interventions. This is in part historical, because public organizations emerged as administrative bodies, supporting policy-makers and law-makers to ensure that the law was administered fairly, consistently and justly. Traditional administrative culture is also a consequence of public systems of financial accountability. Since public bodies have monies appropriated by a legislative assembly or a local authority annually, they are required to account for their expenditures each year. This provokes a cautious attitude to the use of funds and close scrutiny over each commitment of resources. Any decision to change the use of funds has had to be approved by the finance department.

Formalized administrative systems are also in part a consequence of the relatively large size of public bodies, their dispersion throughout a country and the need to ensure standard and uniform provision of service within them. The law requires that all those entitled to social or welfare rights should receive equal treatment, and it sets down the rules and procedures to be followed for doing this. Only routinized systems can ensure this happens.

Systems which are primarily administrative tend to be concerned only with resource utilization, in so far as limited resources constrain what can be done by those running public bodies. They do not evaluate success in terms of a narrow economic definition of efficiency – the ratio of resource inputs to product/service outputs – but in terms of goal effectiveness. Although public organizations have to achieve a balance between resource efficiency and goal effectiveness, Self (1971) argues that only those public agencies operating in the market can use 'resource tests' of efficiency. Those not operating in the market have to use 'goal tests' and those operating in the market, but committed to political goals, employ mixes of policy and resource tests. Policy tests are qualitative and judgmental, implying reflections about organizational goals and their relative priorities.

In public organizations, it is politicians who decide the goals and resources to be used in pursuing them, although they may be influenced by officials and other political actors. There is, in short, no objective way of determining what are the 'right' policies or the 'right' amount of resources to be allocated in public bodies. In the public domain, it is political choice and political judgement which decide this.

In private, for-profit organizations, in contrast, it is management systems, rather than administrative systems, that have tended to dominate decision-making and management practice. The overall task of senior managers is, therefore, basically a 'systems management' one. Tight management systems are necessary, since private organizations are predominantly economically and market-driven, whilst their primary goals and accountabilities, which are largely to shareholders and customers, are also market-centred and more narrow than those of public organizations. Keeling (1972) summarizes the characteristics of management systems as follows:

- Organizational goals and objectives are clearly identified, with specific time scales and targets being set for achieving them.
- The criteria for success are the achieving of 'hard' targets, normally expressed quantitatively.
- The efficient use of resources is of prime importance.
- Task cultures are the norm, with relatively short organizational hierarchies.
- There is a willingness of senior managers to delegate authority so that certain decisions are taken locally.
- Managers are opportunists, continually seeking new openings, fighting for resources and taking initiatives.

Public Management Practice

Since classical public organizations are primarily administratively driven, and because of the largely political nature of their goals, accountabilities, regulatory mode, root culture and wide-ranging stakeholders, management decision-making and management practice within them tend to be 'bureaucratic', 'incrementalist' and 'particularist' (Farnham and Horton, 1993). The characteristic features of bureaucratic management are specialization, hierarchy, impersonality of decision-making and functional expertise. Those in managerial positions have clearly defined roles within a vertical and horizontal division of labour. Responsibilities are narrowly defined and circumscribed by rules, which senior management have little discretion in modifying. The implications are that individual managers do not control the resources used to carry out managerial tasks and responsibilities. Managers cannot vary the mix of resources and are bound by human resources allocations determined centrally. Bureaucratic management leads to narrow spans of control, and policy decisions are taken at the top of the organization. Decision-taking is slow and there are delays in responding to the demands made upon managers, including the demands of the public as consumers and citizens.

The impersonal nature of bureaucratic management practice is reflected in the ways that managerial tasks are executed. This is done according to prescribed rules, non-arbitrarily and without favouritism, with written records being kept of each transaction. Public officials are expected to ensure that members of the public, suppliers and employees are treated fairly, equitably and 'within the rules'. This results in predictability and standardization of procedures and outcomes, although it can produce inflexibility, unresponsiveness to particular needs and lags in implementation.

The functional expertise of traditional public administrators derives from their skills as either 'generalists' or 'professional specialists', with experience in a career structure. The British Civil Service, for example, has been dominated at the top by administrative generalists. Their skills lie in understanding the machinery of government and the political process, skills acquired through experience in various parts of the service as their careers progress. Middle managers have also tended to be generalists, though managers of specialist groups, such as lawyers, economists and statisticians, in contrast, have usually been professional specialists. However, in British local government and the National Health Service (NHS), top jobs have traditionally been occupied by professional specialists, with their particular expertise rooted in knowledge of their technical fields.

Recruitment patterns of senior managers in public bureaucracies vary (Lane, 1993). In Britain and France, career officials dominate. In the USA, political appointees come to the fore, whilst in Germany merit and politics converge. The route to selection also varies. France with its *grands corps* selects top managers from amongst a range of technocrats, Germany from legally trained experts often with political affiliations, and the USA from state administrators, political office-holders, private-sector managers and federal civil servants. In the UK, the route is predominantly from career administrators or specialists. Middle managers in all these systems are usually recruited from within established career structures.

The incrementalist nature of public management practice reflects the fact that the perspectives of senior public managers are generally short-term ones. Planning takes place through small changes and limited adjustments to existing policies (Hogwood and Gunn, 1984). Financial planning tends to be based on the annual budget cycle or on short-term expenditure plans which are little more than forecasts and not binding. External changes of policy and intra-organizational changes of priorities constantly confront senior public managers in the ways they work.

Changes in political leadership often mean substantial changes in public policies and social programmes. Although there have been attempts by some public authorities to adopt rational decision-making strategies and longer-term plans, these have generally been short-lived and unsuccessful. The introduction of planned, programme, budgeting and policy analysis in the USA in the 1960s, and in the British civil service in the early 1970s, for example, fell victim to changes of government and the practicalities of implementation (Gray and Jenkins, 1985; Heclo and Wildavsky, 1974; Hogwood and Gunn, 1984). The problem of long-term planning is greatest where the processes of strategic choice and strategic implementation are separated. In consequence, strategic managers tend to adopt consensual policies which are likely to survive changes in political control (Elcock, 1993).

Public management practice is particularist in the sense that there has traditionally been an absence of general managers in public organizations. Although managerial structures in public enterprises or nationalized industries, which sell goods or services in the market place, bear a closer resemblance to those of the private sector, this characteristic is limited to these more market-oriented public enterprises. Management in the British civil service, local government and the NHS is particular to these organizations: senior managers within them rarely transfer across sectors. Specialist management structures, based on particularist traditions, as in British local government, make coordination, planning and rational use of resources difficult to achieve, resulting in managerial fragmentation. Further, professional bureaucracies tend to prioritize services to clients, rather than focusing on resource considerations, whilst resisting external controls infringing their autonomy, such as amongst doctors, teachers and social workers. These features are less pronounced in European countries, where mobility between different parts of the public sector is greater and institutions, such as the French *Préfecture*, act as integrating forces. Traditional public organizations, we contend, reflect these bureaucratic, incrementalist and particularist characteristics.

Private Management Practice

Since private organizations are primarily financially and systems driven, and because of the market nature of their goals, accountabilities, regulatory mode, root culture and more limited range of stakeholders, decision-making within them tends to be 'economistic', 'rationalist' and 'generic' (Farnham and Horton, 1993).

The economistic nature of private management practice is reflected in the market goals and accountabilities of private organizations and the dominance of economic efficiency as the main criterion measuring their success. It also explains why the 'value-added' areas of functional management, such as finance, production and marketing, have such high status and standing. They provide the keys to: profitabity; cost control; productivity; innovation; growth; and market share. The rationalist nature of private management practice emerged out of the ideas of 'scientific management' and classical management theory (Taylor, 1911; Urwick, 1944; Fayol, 1949). Rationalist management practices are seen to be essential if private-sector managers are to run successful enterprises, using techniques such as planning, organizing, staffing, directing, coordinating and budgeting. Rationalistic management also rests on the belief that there is a corpus of received management knowledge, techniques and skills which all managers need to develop. This corpus of knowledge seeks to enable senior managers to determine appropriate organizational structures, technical systems and work design to make their businesses profitable and capable of growth. Senior managers also are responsible for creating effective communication and control systems and providing measures of corporate success. As Drucker (1989) writes, management as a system 'expresses the belief in the possibility of controlling [humankind's] livelihood through systematic organization of economic resources'.

The view that management practice is a generic set of tasks, activities and skills, common to all organizations, had its origins amongst classical management theorists before the Second World War. By the 1950s, a body of modern classical management principles had been created which, it was claimed, had relevance to both the private and public sectors (Drucker, 1954 and 1974; Herzberg *et al.*, 1959; McGregor, 1960; Rice, 1963; Lawrence and Lorsch, 1969; Mintzberg, 1973). These writers on management insisted that although there was 'no one right way', managing is a universal activity which uses a mixture of rational decision-making techniques, problem-solving routines and intuitive judgements. This generic approach to management was very influential in North America and the

UK. Although it had less impact in mainland Europe, Thurley and Wirdenhuis (1989, p. 16) nevertheless concede that 'Europeans have recognised American expertise in management for nearly 100 years.' But it was Marshall Aid, followed by influxes of management consultants and American academics into Europe in the 1960s, which first exposed western Europe to generic management ideas and practices. This was reinforced by the penetration of multinational, American companies into Europe, using generic techniques, processes and systems within their organizations.

A 'new wave' school of generic management thinking emerged in the USA in the 1980s, finding its way into some leading-edge companies in the UK and Europe. It argued the need for managing culture, quality and excellence. These ideas were generated by a group of largely north American management gurus who sought to provide prescriptive, model solutions to current managerial problems (Peters and Waterman, 1982; Peters and Austin, 1989; Peters, 1987; Moss Kanter, 1983 and 1989; Porter, 1980, 1985 and 1990). What managers appeared to be looking for were means for achieving corporate success in increasingly competitive, cut-throat, global product markets. These new generic approaches to management stressed the central importance of strategic management, culture management, customer care and 'searching for excellence', as the essential tools for business survival.

For the first time, other generic ideas and practices, outside the dominant Anglo-American paradigm, became current, especially from Japan. Japanese management ideas, such as 'just in time' management, 'enterprise unions' and 'total quality management', are based on quite different principles from those of Europe and the USA. They tend, in essence, to be focused on managing quality, facilitating teamwork and providing continuous training, linked to paternalist employment practices (Wickens, 1987). These ideas have been imported into European-based, Japanese-owned companies and copied by some indigenous firms, thus challenging the hegemony of more traditional rationalist and generic ideas in management (Ohmae, 1982, 1985 and 1990; Whitehill, 1991; Deming, 1986; Juran, 1989).

Management practices in private, not-for-profit organizations have been less well studied, partly because, as Drucker (1990, p. 9) states, 'they were generally seen as marginal to a ... Society dominated by government and big business'. Although their importance has been greater in continental Europe, their missions are less contentious. They tend to be small organizations, with low institutional profiles. Management practices within them appear to be more democratically based and less market-centred than those in for-profit enterprises. However, the number of not-for-profit agencies is increasing in the western world and they are becoming, as Handy suggests, one of the distinguishing features of modern society (Handy, 1988).

PUBLIC MANAGEMENT AND THE LEGACY OF HISTORY

Perry and Kraemer (1983) were amongst the first to claim that a new public management was emerging, which was not identical with private management but integrated traditional public administration with the more instrumental orientation of business management. If one accepts this integrative model of management, it reflects the unique nature of the managerial function in the public sector, stemming from the fundamentally political nature of public organizations and the dynamic organizational contingencies facing public officials since the 1980s. These contingencies have resulted, *inter alia*, in:

- more commercially and financially focused missions and goals, driven by politicians and top managers;
- more emphasis on the public as 'customers', 'clients' and 'consumers' of public services;
- growing involvement of public managers with internal markets, pseudo-markets and quality issues;
- the opening-up of public organizations to competition, CCT, contracting and market testing;
- a modified root culture, which is shifting from an administrative to a managerialist one and is focused on target-setting, performance management systems and performance indicators.

The NPM that has developed is also underpinned by a managerialist ideology, distinctly economistic, rationalist and generic in nature. It is reticulist too, with strategic managers 'assisting individuals and organisations to communicate and negotiate with one another' to achieve their objectives (Elcock, 1993, p. 61).

In Europe, the NPM has penetrated deepest in the UK. Here generic managers have been appointed across the public services, sometimes from the private sector, either to run reformed public organizations resource-effectively and cost-efficiently or to advise them how to increase efficiency, reduce costs, raise productivity and cut back waste. Public managers are increasingly operating in a milieu where meeting the 'bottom line' and providing 'value for money' structures their behaviour. It is no exaggeration to say that the efficient use of resources dominates the activities of UK public managers today. CCT and market testing have exposed public managers to markets, whilst the introduction of internal markets has forced them, like their private-sector counterparts, to balance costs, quality and service standards in tendering for contracts. These moves towards economism and rationalism are coinciding with changes in the USA and other parts of Europe.

There has also been a weakening of bureaucratic control strategies in public organizations, which have been superseded by new management control systems. Public management practice is following the example of the private sector in moving away from large, centralized monolithic structures to more decentralized, tight–loose systems with devolved managerial authority and responsibilities. This has been made possible by developments in information technology and the introduction of new management and financial information systems. But, at the same time, central direction has increased, with top management tightening its grip on the managing of strategy, culture and performance.

The creation of over a hundred 'Next Steps' agencies in the British civil service, the break-up of the NHS into autonomous trusts and the creation of locally managed schools have been accompanied by emphases on management by objectives, performance indicators and new reward structures. Performance-related pay is being used as an incentive for improving management performance and facilitating added value, whilst the introduction of new staff appraisal systems has been directed at reinforcing organizational change strategies. Another feature of the NPM is the move away from permanent to more flexible employment.

These developments have been accompanied by intensive management training programmes designed to improve the skills of public managers and inculcate the culture of managerialism into public organizations. Public managers thereby become leaders of the new managerial techniques, 'heroes' of the managerialist ethic and orchestrators of continuous change.

From the evidence available, therefore, it appears that the role of the public manager is shifting towards that of the private manager. The organizational contingencies of both public and private managers are changing, with the result that classical public administration has been weakened and, in response to government attempts to control public spending and seek greater efficiency, public managers are taking on some of the features of their private-sector counterparts (Richards, 1992). Private managers, in turn, are having to adapt to a wider range of accountabilities, such as the environmentalist lobby, public regulators and legislation. This requires increasing sensitivity to the social costs of business and its ethical responsibilities to the wider community. To this extent, then, a synthesis between the roles of public managers and private managers is taking place, in both directions. Significant changes are also taking place in not-for-profit voluntary organizations, which are growing in the mixed economy of welfare provision. Managers are being appointed to negotiate contracts, attract funding and compete for shares of the market for welfare.

There remain significant differences between public and private organizations, however, to constrain the behaviour of public managers. And these strictly limit their roles as managers of resources. For example:

- Private managers are constantly striving to expand demand, whilst public managers have to suppress it, with public budgets effectively rationing the provision of public services rather than increasing them.
- Public managers work in organizations with missions and goals which continue to address issues of welfare, redistribution and social provision. Using economic efficiency as the prime criterion of decision-making is neither viable nor possible.
- The stakeholders of public organizations are far more diverse than those of private organizations. They cannot be ignored or permanently excluded within a democracy which provides relatively open access to public agencies, state enterprises and political representatives. In this sense, the role of public managers, as agents balancing the interests of multiple stakeholders, is increasing rather than diminishing in importance.
- It is rare for one public organization to possess all the means to achieve its mission, goals and objectives. Cooperation amongst a constellation of bodies is often required to enable strategic plans to be fulfilled. Public managers are therefore increasingly being called upon to perform a reticulist role, as the boundaries between the public and private domains blur.

There is also the 'public service ethic'. This is associated with the notion of public officials serving the needs of the community, protecting the public interest and acting as buffers between government and the governed: they are not just managers of markets and controllers of resources.

In summary, then, public officials are becoming increasingly managerialized, whilst private managers are becoming more aware of the social responsibilities of their businesses. Further, with voluntary and community bodies playing more prominent roles in delivering a mixed economy of welfare provision, they too are being managerialized. This is resulting in the professionalization of management and a synthesis between management in the public and private domains. However, public managers can never be totally divorced from the political missions and constitutional accountabilities of the organizations they manage and work in. For public managers, it is the legacy of politics which ultimately underpins their role, not the market place.

References

Bacon, R. and Eltis, W. (1976) *Too Few Producers?* London: Macmillan.

Bamber, G. and Lansbury, R. (eds) (1983) *International and Comparative Industrial Relations*, London: Unwin Hyman.

Bamber, G. and Lansbury, R. (eds) (1993) *International and Comparative Industrial Relations*, London: Routledge.

Beaumont, P. (1992) *Public Sector Industrial Relations*, London: Routledge.

Bercusson, B. (1986) 'Workers, corporate enterprise and the law' in R. Lewis (ed.) *Labour and the Law*, Oxford: Blackwell.

Cawson, A. (ed.) (1985) *Organized Interests and the State*, London: Sage.

Coase, R. (1988) *The Firm, the Market and the Law*, Chicago: University of Chicago Press.

Cyert, R. and March, J. (1992) *A Behavioral Theory of the Firm*, London: Sage/Open University.

Deming, W. (1986) *Out of Crisis*, Cambridge, Mass.: Cambridge University Press.

Drennan, D. (1992) *Transforming Company Culture*, Maidenhead: McGraw-Hill.

Drucker, P. (1954) *Principles of Management*, London: Heinemann.

Drucker, P. (1974) *Management: Tasks, Responsibilities, Practices*, London: Heinemann.

Drucker, P. (1989) *The Practice of Management*, Oxford: Heinemann.

Drucker, P. (1990) *Managing the Non-Profit Organization*, Oxford: Butterworth Heinemann.

Elcock, H. (1993) 'Strategic management' in D. Farnham and S. Horton (eds) *Managing the New Public Services*, Basingstoke: Macmillan.

Farnham, D. (1992) 'Citizen's Charter', *Talking Politics*, Winter 1991/92.

Farnham, D. and Horton, S. (1993) *Managing the New Public Services*, Basingstoke: Macmillan.

Fayol, H. (1949) *General and Industrial Management*, London: Pitman.

Fredman, S. and Morris, G. (1989) *The State as Employer*, London: Mansell.

Friedman, M. (1962) *Capitalism and Freedom*, Chicago: University of Chicago Press.

Gray, A. and Jenkins, B. (1985) *Administrative Politics in British Government*, Brighton: Wheatsheaf.

Gunn, L. (1987) 'Perspectives on public management' in J. Kooiman and K. Eliassen (eds) *Managing Public Organizations*, London: Sage.

Handy, C. (1988) *Understanding Voluntary Organizations*, London: Penguin.

Hayek, F.A. (1944) *The Road to Serfdom*, London: Routledge.

Hayek, F.A. (1976) *Law, Legislation and Liberty*, London: Routledge Kegan Paul.

Heclo, H. and Wildavsky, A. (1974) *The Private Government of Public Money*, London: Macmillan.

Herzberg, F., Mausner, B. and Snydermann, G. (1959) *The Motivation to Work*, New York: Wiley.

Hogwood, B. and Gunn, L. (1984) *Policy Analysis for the Real World*, Oxford: Oxford University Press.

Hood, C. and Schuppert, G. (1987) *Delivering Public Services in Western Europe*, London: Sage.

Juran, J. (1989) *Juran on Leadership and Quality*, New York: Free Press.

Keeling, D. (1972) *Managing in Government*, London: Allen & Unwin.

Kooiman, J. and Eliassen, K. (eds) (1987) *Managing Public Organizations*, London: Sage.

Kotter, J. (1990) 'What managers really do', *Harvard Business Review*, May–June.

Lane, J-E. (1993) *The Public Sector: Concepts, Models and Approaches*, London: Sage.

Lawrence, P.R. and Lorsch, J.W. (1969) *Organization and Environment*, London: Irwin-Dorsey.

Lehmbruch, G. and Schmitter, P.C. (eds) (1982) *Patterns of Corporatist Policy-Making*, London: Sage.

Lindblom, C. (1977) *Markets and Politics*, New York: Basic.

McGregor, D. (1960) *Human Side of Enterprise*, New York: McGraw-Hill.

Mintzberg, H. (1973) *The Nature of Managerial Work*, New York: Harper & Row.

Mintzberg, H. (1979) *The Structuring of Organizations*, New York: Prentice Hall.

Mintzberg, H. (1983) *Structures in Fives*, Englewood Cliffs, New Jersey: Prentice Hall.

Moss Kanter, R. (1983) *The Change Masters*, New York: Simon & Schuster.

Moss Kanter, R. (1989) *When Giants Learn to Dance*, New York: Simon & Schuster.

Ohmae, K. (1982) *The Mind of the Strategist*, New York: McGraw-Hill.

Ohmae, K. (1985) *Triad Power: The Coming Shape of Global Competition*, New York: Free Press.

Ohmae, K. (1990) *The Borderless World*, New York: Harper.

Page, E. (1992) *Political Authority and Bureaucratic Power*, Hemel Hempstead: Harvester Wheatsheaf.

Pattakos, A.N. (1992) 'Growth in activist groups: how can business cope?' in D. Mercer (ed.) *Managing the External Environment: A Strategic Perspective*, London: Sage/Open University.

Peacock, A. (ed.) (1984) *The Regulation Game*, Oxford: Blackwell.

Perry, J. and Kraemer, K.L. (1983) *Public Management: Private and Public Perspectives*, California: Mayfield.

Peters, T. (1987) *Thriving on Chaos*, New York: Macmillan.

Peters, T. and Austin, N. (1985) *A Passion for Excellence*, London: Collins.

Peters, T. and Waterman, R. (1982) *In Search of Excellence*, New York: Harper & Row.

Pollitt, C. (1990) *Managerialism and the Public Services*, Oxford: Blackwell.

Pollitt, C. (1993) *Managerialism and the Public Services: The Anglo-American Experience*, Oxford: Blackwell.

Porter, M.E. (1980) *Competitive Strategy*, New York: Free Press.

Porter, M.E. (1985) *Competitive Advantage*, New York: Free Press.

Porter, M.E. (ed) (1986) *Competition in Global Industries*, Cambridge, Mass: Harvard University Press.

Porter, M.E. (1990) *The Competitive Advantage of Nations*, London: Macmillan.

Prime Minister's Office (1991) *The Citizen's Charter*, London: HMSO.

Reed, M. (1989) *The Sociology of Management*, Hemel Hempstead: Wheatsheaf.

Rice, A.K. (1963) *The Enterprise and the Environment: A Systems Theory of Managing Organisations*, London: Tavistock.

Richards, S. (1992) 'Changing patterns of legitimation in public management', *Public Policy and Administration*, 7 (3), Winter.

Schmitter, P.C. and Lehmbruch, G. (eds) (1978) *Trends Towards Corporatist Intermediation*, London: Sage.

Seldon, A. (1990) *Capitalism*, Oxford: Blackwell.

Self, P. (1971) 'Tests of efficiency: public and business administration', *Public Administration Committee Bulletin*, 11.

Simon, H.A. (1957) *Models of Man*, New York: Wiley.

Stewart, R. (1967) *Managers and Their Jobs*, London: Macmillan.

Stewart, R. (1988) *Managers and Their Jobs*, London: Macmillan.

Taylor, F. (1911) *Principles of Scientific Management*, New York: Harper & Row.

Thurley, K. and Wirdenius, H. (1989) *Towards European Management*, London: Pitman.

Tomkins, C.R. (1987) *Achieving Economy, Efficiency and Effectiveness in the Public Sector*, London: Kegan Paul.

Urwick, L. (1944) *The Elements of Administration*, London: Pitman.

Velianovski, C. (1991) *Regulators and the Market*, Guildford: Institute of Economic Affairs.

Whitehill, A. (1991) *Japanese Management: Tradition and Transition*, London: Routledge.

Wickens, P. (1987) *The Road to Nissan*, London: Macmillan.

Wildavsky, A. (1979) *Implementation*, London: University of California Press.

3 The Competencies of New Public Managers

Turo Virtanen

In a recent collection of essays, Ott, Hyde and Shafritz (1991, p. ix) provide a working definition of public management:

> The term *public management* refers to a branch of the larger field of *public administration* or *public affairs*. It is the part of public administration that overviews the art and science of applied methodologies for public administration program design and organizational restructuring, policy and management planning, resource allocations through budgeting systems, financial management, human resources management, and program evaluation and audit.

The editors specify that public management 'focuses on public administration as a profession and on the public manager as a practitioner of that profession' and 'on the managerial tools, techniques, knowledge, and skills that can be used to turn ideas and policy into programs of action'. Whilst the boundaries between public administration and public management are blurred and subject to disagreement, public administration includes 'most of the activities involved in the establishment as well as the implementation of public policy', whereas public management connotes 'the more limited set of within-agency functions and skills that once had defined public administration' (Ott *et al.*, 1991, p. 2). Overman (1984) states that the distinguishing characteristics of public management compared with public administration are: the inclusion of general management functions; an instrumental orientation favouring the criteria of economy and efficiency in lieu of equity, responsiveness, and political salience; a pragmatic focus on mid-level managers in lieu of the perspective of political or policy elites; a tendency to consider management as generic; a singular focus on the organization; and a strong philosophical link with the scientific management tradition in lieu of close ties to political science or sociology.

The term public management has been used since the 1950s. The 'new public management' (NPM), however, refers to a doctrine that has emerged over the past fifteen years and is considered 'one of the most striking international trends in public administration' (Hood, 1991, p. 3). Although the NPM is often seen as a uniquely British development, various forms of it have entered public organizations in virtually all western countries (Ministry of Finance, 1993; Pollitt, 1993). The adoption of the NPM is linked with the rise of neo-liberalism and its political variants such as 'Reaganism' and 'Thatcherism'. Hood (1991) sees its origin as a marriage of two different streams of ideas: the 'new institutional economics' and a business-type 'managerialism'. The former is built on public choice theory, transactions cost theory and principal-agent theory. The latter is built on the scientific management movement with the idea that professional management expertise is portable. Hood's summary of the doctrinal contents of the NPM is represented in Table 3.1 in a slightly modified form.

The NPM can also be seen as a rightist version of the radical new public administration outlined in the Minnowbrook Conference in 1968 (Marini, 1971). Social equity, like the enhancement of the political power and economic well-being of minorities, is pushed into the background and the world of competition and markets is introduced instead. In both doctrines, public managers are seen as active agents in the policy process, not only as implementers of given policies. Moreover, decentralization, devolution, projects, contracts, sensitivity training, organization development, responsibility expansion, confrontation and client involvement are nearly all tenets of the NPM too. Whilst the Minnowbrook approach sees customers of public services as citizens with the right to direct participation, the NPM approach sees customers as rational consumers whose basic influence comes from the exit-option when they make rational choices between public and private producers competing with each other. As Dunsire (1994) points out, in a democratic society citizens have the right to define public services (the voice-option), not only the right to make the choice of whether they use them or not (the exit-option). One solution to this type of problem of the NPM is 'the direct participation of the public in the design, delivery and assessment of public services' (Pollitt, 1993, p. 195) to get politicians more committed to the reform of public services.

The purpose of this chapter is to systematize the competencies of the new public manager that this doctrine assumes. The framework provided is a fourfold taxonomy: (1) task competence; (2) professional competence, both in core administration functions such as budgeting and staffing and in substantive administration such as health-care and agriculture; (3) political competence; and (4) ethical competence (Virtanen, 1991). Competencies are often implicit or not mentioned at all in the literature on the

Table 3.1 *Doctrinal components of new public management*

No.	Doctrine	Meaning	Typical justification
1	'Hands-on professional management'	Active, visible, discretionary control of organizations from named persons at the top, 'free to manage'.	Accountability requires clear assignment of responsibility for action, not diffusion of power.
2	Explicit standards and measures of performance	Definition of goals, targets, indicators of success, preferably expressed in quantitative terms, especially for professional services.	Accountability requires clear statement of goals; efficiency requires 'hard look' at objectives.
3	Output controls	Resource allocation and rewards linked to measured performance; break-up of centralized personnel management.	Need to stress results rather than procedures.
4	Disaggregation of units in the public sector	Break-up of formerly 'monolithic' units, un-bundling of U-form management systems into corporatized units around products, operating on decentralized 'one-line' budgets and dealing with one another on an 'arms-length' basis.	Need to create 'manageable' units, separate provision and production interests, gain efficiency advantages of use of contract or franchise arrangements inside as well as outside the public sector.
5	Competition	Term contracts and public tendering procedures.	Rivalry as the key to lower costs and better standards.
6	Private-sector styles of management practice	Move away from military-style 'public service ethic', greater flexibility in hiring and rewards; greater use of PR techniques.	Need to use 'proven' private sector management tools.
7	Greater discipline and parsimony in resource use	Cutting direct costs, raising labour discipline, resisting union demands, limiting 'compliance costs' to business.	Need to check resource demands of public sector and 'do more with less'.

SOURCE: Adapted from C. Hood, 'A public management for all seasons?', *Public Administration*, 69, 3–19.

descriptions and evaluations of administrative reforms or the needs and instruments of them. This makes it necessary to speak of the determinants of competencies rather than of competencies *per se*. There is no comprehensive description of the whole NPM doctrine, and tracing it involves 'reading between the lines'. Its operation varies from organization to organization and nation to nation, although they share a family resemblance. The empirical focus of this study is the British experience, as reflected in three books: Metcalfe and Richards (1990); Flynn (1990); and Pollitt (1993).

A FRAMEWORK OF THE GENERAL COMPETENCIES OF PUBLIC MANAGERS

A competency means a criterion which an agent must satisfy in order to succeed in an action in terms of its value or instrumental content. In this study, we proceed from the more obvious elements of the competence of public servants to those of a more complex nature. In each competence area, we also distinguish between value competence and instrumental competence. Value competence relates to the goals of action and instrumental competence relates to the means of action.

A public manager is a public servant who operates through subordinates in a public organization. Public managers can be both subordinates and superiors within a managerial hierarchy. In the NPM approach, a public manager has responsibility for a programme which involves the production of a good or service. He or she also has a job description setting down the role of the job and a budget for which s/he is responsible and accountable. The framework of this study is, however, more general and provides a basic structure for analysing the competencies of the new public managers.

Task Competence

Task competence is the most concrete competence. This is the level of performance required to accomplish a specific task. At the level of a task, goals and means are given. The achievement of the goals requires the use of instruments which are social and physical materializations of the means. A task is an action that is not yet undertaken. There must be *motivation* (value competence) and *abilities* (instrumental competence) before any task is fulfilled. Knowledge of goals and means and the existence of instruments is not enough. There must be commitment to fulfil the task and personal ability to use the instruments. Abilities are skills, capacities and talents, rather than knowledge. The task competence of a public manager involves the motivation and abilities to deal with other people:

subordinates, other managers and elected or appointed political executives.

Performance, as capacity to achieve desired results, sets the basic criteria for the sufficiency of motivation and abilities. It is at the level of performance that personal output is created. Performance here is the basic concept of efficiency: it means the ability to finish the task, produce the output and make it real. Other concepts of efficiency – productivity, economy and effectiveness – are only useful if the output can be realized. The performance of a public manager is normally the same as the performance of his/her unit.

Professional Competence

The professional competence of a public servant embraces both the subject of administration and the administration itself. The professional competence in a *subject* refers either to a specific task field in the support staff, or in the technostructure of a public organization, or to the substantive field of the line organization. In the former case, the competence may be a professional competence in personnel management, information technology or the law. In the latter case, professional competence refers to the service such as housing, defence or education. The value element of the professional competence in the subject area is *control of the policy object* of professional work (e.g. agriculture). The instrumental competence is the *know-how of the policy object* of the particular field.

The central professional competency is the autonomous creation of new instruments for one's own professional work, using one's own professional know-how. Professional standards delimit the criteria of the acceptable performance in the control of the substantive object. It is the demand of professional pride to improve the work in order to be able to improve the object by more effective treatment and manipulation. This is why the *development of the policy object* is the main criterion of the good control of the object and good mastery of subject know-how.

Professional competence in *administration* refers to administration as an independent area of professional value and instrumental competence. The core of administration is classically distinguished from both policy and politics (Wilson, 1887; Goodnow, 1900). Administration is defined here as the execution of a policy given by politicians. Politicians may be representatives of the parliament or government or even managers who should be 'mere administrators'. The anti-institutionalism of the definition makes it different from the ordinary definition of administration, as the executive machinery of government. The crucial assumption is that policy is given and no longer questioned. The value competence of an administrative public servant is, therefore, *control of the policy programme*. This requires specifying the goals and means of the given policy in order that a programme can be formulated. The instrumental competence of an administrative public servant is the *know-how of co-operation*, because administration is acting through other people. It also requires a detailed allocation of resources to implement the policy. The know-how of co-operation includes the know-how of politics, power and conflict. This does not indicate the actual possession of power – only knowledge about power and the skills to use it. The power of an administrator in the analytical model is always the power of someone else, that of politicians whoever they are.

As a modern agent, an administrator attempts to improve his/her work. The work is the execution of the given public policy. This is independent of the substantive value content of public policies. A professional administrator will even seek to improve the execution of policies intended to lower the standards established by the professional community such as decreasing unemployment services or public schooling, easing pollution norms or lowering safety standards. There is often an ethical dilemma faced by public officials who are torn between their commitment to serve the politicians well and to maintain high professional standards within their public service. However, the *development of policy execution* is the main criterion of good administrative work.

When administration is defined as execution, a public administrator or public manager is expected to execute the values reflected by those in power. If the constitution is democratic, a public manager should appreciate and implement democratic values. This means that one of the permanent obligations of public managers is the maintenance of 'law and order'. Even though some values are related to professional competence, there are values that are outside professions too. When these values are contested, they are related to politics and ethics.

Political Competence

The political competence of a public servant has to do with values and power. The value competence consists of the *ideology and interests* of a public servant. These have an effect on the creation and authorization of the goals and means of a public policy. Every public servant has ideological beliefs and a conception of their own interests, even if they do not consciously support any politically intensive world view.

The instrumental content of the political competence is *possession of power*. With power, it is possible for public servants to create the resources needed for both the preparation and implementation of a public policy that they consider relevant according to their ideology and interest. This means, by the use of power, that resources are detached from the formulation and execution of other policies. The political power of a public servant is derived from the power of office and official authority. Other sources may be membership of a party and membership of other public and private organizations relevant to the policy field. In this sense, political power is not necessarily party-political power. The ethical justification of this may constitute a problem but the concept of political competence also covers the competence that is unjustified in ethical terms.

The political competence of a public servant aims at the *legitimacy* of one's own action, and normally that of one's organizational unit, perhaps the organization as a whole or even the whole government. Legitimacy means the acceptance by the masses or by those ranked among the best, according to the criteria characteristic of the particular political culture. It is the legitimacy that sets the limits for the effectiveness of public policies, because it is through the lenses of legitimate ideologies and interests that the outputs and their effects are interpreted. These ideologies and interests constitute the value system according to which the output is 'measured' and is given political acceptance.

From the point of view of a public manager, political competence may be threatened not only by other public managers but also by subordinates. Delegating to competent subordinates may result in loss of power where public managers cannot control what they are formally responsible for. This highlights the importance of the control of subordinates and the need to adapt the formal authority to the changes in redivisions of the power.

Ethical Competence

The ethical competence of a public servant refers to conforming to the moral values and moral norms that prevail in a culture or a group. The value competence of a public servant is *morality*. As the 'right' morality, the ethical competence of an administrator fulfils the requirements of the ethics proper, where the criterion of justification is not the general acceptance of some particular means of action but whether the action itself is right or wrong.

Morality, as the prevailing conception of what is right and what is wrong, does not include moral problems but only moral answers. An administrative morality takes for granted the constitution and laws determining the general rights and obligations of public servants.

Otherwise, the ethics of an administrator are not part of the identity of administration. But an administrator has an obligation to review the ethical acceptability of the goals and means of public policies. Administrative ethics does not mean that a public servant is not allowed to make propositions for reformulating administrative and substantial norms regulating public policies or the goals of the given policy. This means that the public servant has to implement the decisions of elected representatives or resign, if the propositions are rejected.

The instrumental competence in ethics is competence in *argumentation,* a process of reasoning in terms of ethics. Argumentation is needed for the ethical review and justification of policy goals. In argumentation, the ethical acceptance of the resources and their instrumentalization is also at stake. Argumentation aims at the ethical *justification* of the goals and means of a proposed or given public policy. Argumentation is aimed at solving moral problems. When the right answer is known, there is no longer a moral problem. Instead, there may be problems in that people do not follow the moral norms they consider acceptable. These are political and administrative problems, not moral ones. To some extent, a public manager is responsible for the morality of others, as well as for the competence of the argumentation of others.

All the elements of the competence of a public servant and, to some extent, that of the special case of a public manager have now been defined. The elements are presented in Table 3.2. The efficiency of the actions of public servants can be evaluated by ethical argumentation, possession of power, know-how of co-operation, know-how of the policy object, and abilities. This group of criteria covers only the most instrumental efficiency. The more value-laden, normative, content of the competence of public servants can be evaluated by morality, ideologies and interests, professional control of policy programmes, professional control of the policy object and motivation. Both the normative and instrumental content of the actions of public servants can be evaluated by ethical justification, political legitimacy, development of execution, development of the policy object and performance.

The core competence is ethical competence. What is ethically possible may not be politically possible. What is politically possible may not be professionally possible. What is professionally possible may not be possible at the level of task. What is acceptable in principle may not be possible in practice because of lack of resources. What is possible in practice may eventually become acceptable on the level of principles. This idea is illustrated in Table 3.2. These two-way interactions have also created the practice and doctrine of the NPM.

Table 3.2 *The competence areas of public managers*

Competence area Criterion of competence	Contingencies of public service	Value competence	Instrumental competence
Task competence	Given goals and means	Motivation	Abilities
Performance	Use of instruments		
Professional competence			
In subject area	Known selection of means, implicit goals	Control of the policy object	Know-how of the policy object
Development of the policy object	Formation of instruments out of resources		
In administration	Specification of the policy goal	Control of the policy programme	Know-how of co-operation
Development of policy execution	Allocation of the resources		
Political competence	Creation and authorization of the goal	Ideology, interests	Possession of power
Legitimacy	Creation and detachment of resources for the goal		
Ethical competence Justification	Acceptability of the goal Acceptability of the resources and their instrumentalization	Morality	Argumentation

DETERMINANTS OF THE NEW MANAGERIAL COMPETENCIES OF PUBLIC SERVANTS

The competence of the new public manager refers to new task competencies, new professional competencies in substantive policy fields, new professional competencies in administration, new political competencies and new ethical competencies – or a combination of all these. The neo-liberal

social and political background of the NPM suggests that the new competencies include not only new instrumental qualifications but new value
qualifications as well. We begin with the ethical competence and end with
the task competence, because it is more informative to proceed from
general to particular features of competence. Two relationships of a public
manager are specifically focused upon. These are how the public manager
deals with his/her subordinates and with both political and other superiors.

Determinants of Ethical Competence: From Egalitarianism and Public Interest to Prudentiality and Private Interests?

Is there a new morality in the NPM? Following the tenets of the NPM outlined by Hood (Table 3.1), the emphasis placed on competition and
private-sector management styles (Flynn, 1990; Metcalfe and Richards,
1990; Pollitt, 1993) seems to refer to concepts where the morality of self-
interest is directly outspoken. You cannot compete without self-interest;
self-interest is the prime motor of private-sector management styles; and
self-interest is also the co-ordinating mechanism of markets and the basis
of freedom to make choices. Consumer choice is the freedom that the
NPM largely strives for, with privatization as one of the instruments for
creating competition, and the conditions for consumer choice.

From the point of view of ethics, self-interest is rooted in egoism and
prudentialism (Gauthier, 1986). It is both rational and acceptable to pursue
one's own welfare, if one does not take advantage of other people and if the
welfare is distributed according to one's contribution to its creation, applying the same rules for everyone. In this sophisticated version, moral action is
not always in accordance with the maximization of self-interest. It is rational
to follow the contracts that set the limits for the articulation of self-interest.
This is, however, quite hypothetical, because normally contracts are
not made between rational and equal people. In the down-to-earth
promulgations of the NPM doctrine, self-interest is often implicit and the
conditions for the acceptability of the maximization of self-interest are not
specified. In the current literature on the NPM, ethics is rarely mentioned
(Flynn, 1990) and, where it is, it is not located in terms of moral philosophy.

From the subordinate's perspective, the ethics of the NPM is said to
include the public managers' 'right to manage' (Flynn, 1990; Metcalfe and
Richards, 1990). This means that they should be in control of the organizations which they run and that they should be proactive. If we take this seriously, the right to manage is a right that imposes obligations on other
people, in particular subordinates, and restrictions on their rights. The
right to manage is seen, however, as a political rather than an ethical right.

The lack of ethical specification is perhaps a reflection on the value poverty of the NPM doctrine. This has to do with beliefs about the motivation of the people. The NPM relies on merit pay, performance-related pay (OECD, 1993) and perceives that people are money-driven, not value-driven. The same idea is reflected in the criticism of professionals who monopolize the provision of particular services and oppose many reforms (Pollitt, 1993; Flynn, 1990). The professional ethos is lost along with the reductions of professionals and the imposition of more managerialistic control systems.

Professional co-operation based on egalitarian principles is displaced by the competition of individuals for appointments and 'zero-sum game' bonuses under the system of performance pay. Self-respect and identity are not supported by loyalty to colleagues but by loyalty to superiors. Solidarity is not felt for the profession and the administrative branch in question, but for one's own unit in a single organization. Adoption of the models of flexible personnel management (OECD, 1990), with their short-term appointments and local conditions of service, emphasizes the need for ethical justification where it is right to regard a subordinate 'as an instrumental value for me and my unit' rather than 'as a human being with inherent value'.

Looking at the relationship between public managers and their superiors, the ethics of the NPM is related to the competition between different units that operate decentralized 'one-line' budgets. When success is measured by output and outcome, the ethics of management is related to the adequacy of output indicators. These indicators may be formed in a manner that makes success easier, although quality of service may become inferior. The ethics of output measurement includes the public managers in the debate on the results as well as justifying performance pay. Under the conditions of self-interested agents, the public interest may be replaced by the private interests of public managers and their individual organizations, or their relatively autonomous sub-units, in the fight for survival with their rivals. An extreme conclusion is that those who win the favour of customers and survive are morally more valuable than those who lose. In any case, the public interest is only considered possible as a consequence of striving for the realization of private interests.

Determinants of Political Competence: From Ideological Tyrannies to Markets of Disillusioned Power?

The conception of politics, implicit in the NPM doctrine, is that of rational egoists fighting to maximize their share of public resources. Co-operation is the product of rational egoists who compete for power resources to gain their own objectives through other people. The neo-liberal or New Right ideology is one of self-interest and self-reliance, in contrast to etatist principles of public service within a welfare state. This NPM ideology does not concentrate on the specifications of good public services but on 'rolling back the state'.

When this ideology relies on self-interest, it leaves the specification of services to individual customers who 'know best'. This is why there is no need for a well-defined, comprehensive ideology of public services and the objective needs of citizens. Each individual, it is assumed, has a perception of his/her needs and there is no single self-interest. Comprehensive ideologies, it is claimed, lead to ideological tyrannies when their supporters are in power, so it is best to leave choice to markets. The provision of public services should be decentralized to local organizations, competing with each other, leaving citizens the opportunity to move to another community where their preferences are better satisfied.

The relationship between the public manager and their subordinates is based on distrust. In the collective action of rational egoists there is only confidence if there are sanctions. This is why the NPM makes use of the idea of hierarchy in management. Managers on different levels control each other by their outputs. Resource allocation and rewards are linked to the performance of lower levels, measured by the upper level. Public managers use their power, not as impersonal representatives of the system, but as individual key players. Decentralization of power is giving power, not to organizational units or professionals, but to managers who have the right to delegate (Flynn, 1990). Top-down procedures define and assess the results, whilst bottom-up procedures may be used to activate the efforts of subordinates.

A public manager's relationship with a superior is also based on distrust, because a manager cannot be certain about the superior's relationship to other managers. When public managers are competing with each other, it is the sectional interests of their units that matter, not organizational, national or professional interests. Consumer interests are taken into consideration if they can be measured by the behaviour of individual customers and if superiors can get the information. Strategic management, including SWOT analysis, is a power game that involves lobbying amongst superiors, not rational planning or striving for consensus with formal representatives of stakeholders. Public managers are openly accountable to individual customers and superiors above their own level (Flynn, 1990; Metcalfe and Richards, 1990) but not to the secret élites of interest groups of citizens or to layers of anonymous politicians. Only top managers are accountable to ministers.

Determinants of Professional Competence: From Administration to Management?

The only profession that the NPM doctrine accepts without reservations is, not surprisingly, that of management. Management is considered generic in the sense that there is no difference between 'running a factory and running a hospital, or between a company and health authority' (Flynn, 1990). This genericism or universalism of management is a direct return to the ideas of Taylor (1911) and Fayol (1955 [1916]), the founding fathers of administrative and management science. Within the NPM, administration is associated with routine, bureaucratic work as distinct from the work of the public manager which is controlling and managing resources. Metcalfe and Richards (1990) have systematized the roles of the public manager into the administrator role, the integrator role, the innovator role and the producer role concerned with improved results and stability. The authors contend that it is the producer role that is 'the most widely articulated view at present of the meaning of public management'. This, together with the principles of 'hands-on commitment to product or service', lean staff and few middle managers, is sufficient evidence to draw the conclusion that the emphasis of the competence of a public manager is in the transition from the distant spheres of administration closer to management activities in the subject area itself.

The Subject Area: From Public Welfarism to the Residual State?
Professional competence in a substantive area of government activity is related to ideas about the role of the state in a society, because this determines the substantive fields where state intervention and public policies are regarded as acceptable. The widespread transformation from a welfare state to a lean state, with a minimum of public services, has its origin both in the need to curb public expenditures and in the ideological transition from etatism to citizen activism and market ideologies.

This is reflected in the measures taken by governments, such as privatization, contracting out and cutbacks in staff (Dunsire and Hood, 1989). Public choice theory, which underpins 'rolling back the state' ideologies, argues that the state should only intervene where private enterprises, associations and other agents of the market are not able to produce and distribute services needed by citizens. In other words, only where the market fails should the state step in (Buchanan and Tullock, 1962; Nozick, 1974).

Law and order, defence and foreign affairs are the core activities of the state, because they are pure public goods. But market mechanisms can be used in education, health, trade, industry, agriculture, social services and the environment. This means that public managers should concentrate primarily on following up market failures. The interaction between public managers and the civil society should take the form of direct interaction with individual customers.

All in all, a public manager is more like a night-watchman seeking to maintain public order and intervene to cope with market failure. This brings with it a new type of orientation. Instead of being active in the design of common forms of action to bring about good services, public managers are encouraged, not to intervene in organizations of civil society to prevent problems, but to react to problems that have become so serious that they cannot be solved without the help of the state. Instead of being 'in and together', a public manager is 'out and alone'. A competent public manager has to be passive in the right way.

In Administration: From Detailed Regulation to Back-Seat Driving by the Measurement of Efficiency Failures?

In the NPM, the control of policy programmes is not based on the detailed regulation of actions of the subordinates and stakeholders in the implementation process. Formal norms are still used but they are only meant to regulate the definition, goal-setting, performance measurement and appraisal, performance pay and similar result-oriented actions, not the actual production process itself. This requires a new kind of system for managing resources. Ott *et al.* (1991) state that the emerging sub-fields of public management are budgeting and financial management, human resources management (HRM) and information technology (IT). The NPM emphasizes all of these but also time management, because time is an essential factor in efficiency appraisal. The NPM emphasizes resources management, because increased autonomy in the production process makes it necessary to measure not only inputs, but outputs and their connection to inputs. Public managers must be able to follow up resource allocation efficiency, goal achievement efficiency and be able to make decisions based on efficiency information about every type of resource.

In HRM, the NPM emphasizes performance-related pay and the active modification of organizational culture to make it more innovative and results-oriented. Performance-related pay has been widely used but has encountered problems which have made it necessary to enlarge the incentive structures of public organization (OECD, 1993; Pollitt, 1993). Wholey (1983) identifies a range of possible incentives available to public managers, including not only financial incentives but also intangible incentives such as recognition, honours, interesting assignments, increased responsibility, removal of constraints, delegation of authority and perks such as training, educational leave, flexible working hours and additional leave. The 'right to manage' of the NPM assumes decentralization of personnel management and flexible practices in pay agreements, which contradict the traditional centralization of personnel policy and national pay agreements. Decentralization effectively empowers managers and individual decision-making. Collegial decision-making is discredited as it means degeneration from the pursuit of organizational goals and personal responsibility. In HRM, the NPM seems to have encountered many problems stemming from too narrow an approach to human motivation in public service. This approach is labelled neo-Taylorian due to its emphasis on measurement, merit-pay and hierarchical management (Pollitt, 1993). The deprofessionalization of many occupations, in order to create more room for the managers to manage by performance measurement, has offended those whose motivation has been based on professional value systems and standards of quality.

In financial management, the NPM has created more initiatives than in any other area of resources management (Flynn, 1990; Metcalfe and Richards, 1990; Henley *et al*, 1987; Chan, 1991 [1981]). The major reform has been the transfer of budgetary responsibilities to line managers, causing changes in accounting and auditing practices. Performance management involves relating performance to budget, through calculating unit costs of services. The principle of cost-consciousness means that the monetary value of all measures must be calculated where possible.

Privatization, contracting out, public tendering, pricing, marketing and other economic instruments, favoured by the NPM, can only be used if financial information is continually provided. With good financial infomation, managers can manage from the 'back-seat' without controlling the details of the production processes. However, when money is considered a key motivator in orthodox NPM, financial management increases its value outstripping the softer instruments of HRM. Financial management has become the key instrument in productivity improvement (Flynn, 1990) and the price mechanism is now the key instrument in the control and co-ordination of operational and administrative practices, not regulation and central planning.

Information management is also important in the NPM. For many decades, computerized information systems have been used for rationalizing information needs as part of the modernization of administration (Virtanen, 1992 and 1993; Kraemer and King, 1991 [1986]). But high-quality management information systems that support policy-making in public organizations are still a new phenomenon. In the NPM, new information needs of the public manager embrace information about costs, output, contracts, results of performance appraisal, prices, supply and demand, market share, environment changes and so on. Following the principles of the NPM, managers should not be interested in detailed information about production but measures of economy, productivity, effectiveness and other efficiency-related matters.

A great part of the information is about the efficiency of subordinates, because public managers are accountable for their results to their own superiors. To make control of performance possible at the top of the hierarchy, there must be quantitative information about inputs, outputs and outcomes. This information replaces traditional patterns of management information where inputs were specified quantitatively but outputs, and perhaps outcomes, were specified qualitatively and where information was mediated, reinterpreted and manipulated by administrators. When decision-making is largely based on a few indicators, these become instruments of political power-play where the adequacy of the indicators becomes of central importance. If the indicators do not cover the essential operationalization of policy goals, the implementation of policy becomes distorted. The know-how of the measurement of organizational goals and interpretation of political and administrative communication about results become an important competence of managers. In the literature of the NPM, information management has rarely been examined compared with financial management.

Time management has not emerged as a separate aspect of resources management, but it is present in productivity measurement and the rationalization of work-flows, as well as in the improvement of client-service by making public services more easily available through the extension of working hours (Flynn, 1990). Probably due to the idea of the process autonomy of the NPM, the rational allocation of time has concentrated more on the formal procedures of the management of results than on the daily activities of managers, or on the development of 'just in time' solutions in the provision of services.

In the NPM, non-profit management is perhaps a more emerging than well-known theme, because articulation of the NPM has evolved largely from the principles of private-sector management (Flynn, 1990). The difficulties met in the quantitative measurement of non-profit goals and provision of non-profit services by competition are bringing to light the need for a more sophisticated approach, like that of the 'public service orientation' in the UK, that emphasizes citizen participation (Pollitt, 1993). Also international management is still a missing theme in the NPM.

These issues highlight the relevant professional know-how that public managers should possess. Along with the NPM, there is a transition in the body of knowledge drawn from the theories of politics, justice, law, sociology and social policy to those of economics, accounting, management and information science. The professional commitment to the value system of modernism is exemplified by statements like 'the new ethic that all managers and professionals at all levels should accept a need to do better' and 'managers should improve *on a continuing basis* what they have agreed to administer' (Brown, 1991, pp. 399–400). It is also said that there should be a transition 'from standards based on static, business-as-usual performance levels to expectations of year-on-year improvements in performance' (Metcalfe and Richards, 1990). And there is a 'constant rhetorical emphasis on the need to improve service "quality"' (Pollitt, 1993, p. 180). This indicates how the professionalization of public managers is adopting the principle of the development of the policy object.

Determinants of Task Competence: From Value-Driven Motivation and Group Dynamics to Money-Driven Motivation and Game Strategies?

The tasks of the new public managers are the articulation of professional competence. The classical list of the main functions of a manager – POSDCORB – presented by Gulick (Gulick and Urwick, 1973 [1937]) has been transformed to PAFHRIER by Garson and Overman, in 1983, with the purpose of updating the former. This means a change from planning, organizing, staffing, directing, coordinating, reporting, and budgeting to policy analysis, financial management, human resources management, information management and external relations (Graham and Hays, 1991 [1986]). Both these are general lists of the functions of a manager. The same applies to the roles of a manager developed by Mintzberg (1973). The interpersonal roles of a figurehead, leader and a liaisor; the informational roles of a monitor, disseminator and spokesman; and the decision-making roles of an entrepreneur, disturbance handler, resource allocator and negotiator identify the general subgroups of roles. The roles are functions that can be fulfilled by tasks. The new tasks relevant to the NPM can be inferred from the new contents of resources management.

In the HRM aspects of the NPM, the conception of motivation of both subordinates and superiors is instrumental and money-centred (Pollitt, 1993). People are considered more money-driven than value-driven. Not only subordinates but also managers must have performance-related incentives. Rewards are based on performance, not on personal feedback about rule-following. An orthodox new public manager should also encourage the self-interested action of subordinates. This is likely to cause problems in controlling the behaviour of free-riding subordinates but, at the same time, it may add to their willingness to compete and increase productivity. The interaction of self-interested managers on the same hierarchical level is negotiation amongst competitors, not problem-solving amongst partners. When the publicity of more autonomous public organizations increases through competition and PR functions, skilful media-behaviour in accordance with organizational image design becomes important, not only impressive meeting-behaviour. The international environment demands knowledge of foreign languages and cultures as well as skills of small-talk, not only knowledge of professional terminology.

One of the most important competencies needed by new public managers is tolerance of uncertainty, including willingness to take risks. This is necessitated by both the games of rational egoists presupposed by the NPM and the dynamics of the rapidly changing post-industrial environment of public organizations. Limited tenure is one factor that increases uncertainty and instrumental motivation, because the main objectives come from above.

Financial management makes it necessary to be able to think and act through the terminology of accounting and auditing. The interpretation of local norms and rules that make up traditional professional culture is secondary. Qualified measurement techniques are seen as more effective in performance improvement than the mastering of taken-for-granted ways people tend to act. Wide experience in the use of computers is an asset that makes communication more effective. In many cases, networked information systems surmount reading paper documents. In time management, the time horizon of the NPM is the present and the on-going period of performance appraisal, rather than yesterday or tomorrow.

CONCLUSION: COMPETENCIES IN TRANSITION

The competencies of the new public manager identified here are based on an interpretation of the general philosophy of the NPM doctrine. It is a doctrine which emphasizes the instrumental competencies of public managers rather than their value competencies. Value competencies can be inferred, however, from the tenets of the NPM. The instrumental competencies are easier to infer, because the preferred new structures and processes of public organizations are openly described. The instrumental competencies of the new public managers are grounded in the new functions that public managers are responsible for. The functions are the determinants of competencies, which are summarized in Table 3.3. These

Table 3.3   *Doctrinal transition in the determinants of the competencies of public managers*

Competence area	Determinants of the 'old' competencies	Determinants of the 'new' competencies
Ethical competence	Public interest, redistributive justice	Private interest, freedom
	Egalitarian principles in co-operation	Fair play in competition
	Solidarity to administrative branch and profession	Solidarity to organizational sub-unit
	Loyalty to colleagues	Loyalty to superiors
Political competence	Egalitarian and étatist ideologies	Individualist and neo-liberalist ideologies
	National, professional and sectional interests of interest groups	Sectional interests of one's organizational unit and consumers
	Impersonalization of power	Personalization of power
	Decentralization to interest groups, professional autonomy	Decentralization to local organizations, managerial hierarchy and delegation
	Strategic management as planning together with the stakeholders	Strategic management as power-play with competitors and lobbying among the superiors
	Accountability to the interest groups of citizens and politicians	Accountability to individual clients and to one's superior
Professional competence		
(a) In subject area	Extension of the control of the object	Decline and specification in the control of the object
	Expansion in the objects controlled, state interventionism	Reduction of the objects controlled, anti-interventionism
(b) In administration	Input consciousness in productivity improvement	Output-consciousness in productivity improvement

Table 3.3   *Continued*

Competence area	Determinants of the 'old' competencies	Determinants of the 'new' competencies
In administration (continued)	Efficiency increase by rule-consciousness and human resources management	Efficiency increase by cost-consciousness and financial management
	Centralization and flexibility in personnel management	Decentralization and flexibility in personnel management
	Professionalization of everyone	Professionalization of managers, deprofessionalisation of workers
	Quantitative information about inputs, qualitative information about outputs and outcomes	Quantitative information about inputs, outputs and outcomes
	Information on request to everyone	Automated information provision for superiors
	Time management for the co-ordination of routines	Time management to speed up the processes
	Political measurement of non-profit goals	Quantitative measurement of non-profit goals
	Predictability of the actions of superiors	Unpredictability of the actions of superiors
	Control by regulations, co-ordination by planning	Control by pricing, co-ordination by competition
	Collegial decision-making, log-rolling with interest groups	One-boss principle, personal risk
	Theories of politics, law, sociology, social policy, justice	Theories of economics, accounting, management, information systems
Task competence	Value-driven motivation Group dynamics	Money-driven motivation Game strategies
	Problem-solving amongst partners	Negotiation between competitors
	Inclination to add certainty and predictability	Willingness to take risks and make changes

Table 3.3 *Continued*

Competence area	Determinants of the 'old' competencies	Determinants of the 'new' competencies
	Rewarding by personal feedback about rule-following	Rewarding by performance
	Punctuality in following the rules of the process, innovativeness in the generation of more complete rules	Innovativeness in process, punctuality in following the result-oriented norms
	Meeting-behaviour	Media-behaviour
	Professional terminology	Small-talk in foreign languages and cultures
	Interpretation of professional norms and local rules	Measurement techniques, accounting and auditing
	Paper documents	Attendance at networked information systems
	Time horizon: yesterday, tomorrow	Time horizon: today, now!

determinants refer either to value competencies, instrumental competencies or both. The competencies are in transition, to the extent that the NPM is articulated in the practice of public management. Only empirical studies, however, can illuminate what kinds of value and instrumental competencies have become part of organizational reality. The frameworks of these competencies provided in this paper may be useful for this research.

In the British context, a competencies approach has been developed along the lines of the Management Charter Initiative, which dates from 1987 (Cabinet Office, 1993). The system of nine criteria – leadership, strategic thinking and planning, delivery of results, management of people, communication, management of financial and other resources, personal effectiveness, intellect and creativity and expertise – covers the instrumental rather than the value competencies in task and professional competence. Political and ethical competence is neglected to a great extent. Why? Perhaps they refer too clearly to dissensual ingredients of political culture that cannot be part of training programmes.

The qualifications of public servants are related to what has been called by Lane and Wolf (1990), in the US context, a 'human resource crisis in the public sector'. The authors connect this crisis to changes in the structure of the workforce, poor leadership, lack of competitiveness in the labour market and demotivating working conditions. They argue for an effective, responsible, energetic, and committed workforce to contribute to a stronger and more effective public service in the long run. What does this mean in terms of the competencies of public managers? The authors speak about technical competence, programme/agency competence, and governance competence but, in my view, a more multidimensional framework is needed.

References

Brown, David S. (1991) 'The managerial ethic and productivity improvement,' in J. Steven Ott *et al.* (eds), *Public Management: The Essential Reading*, Chicago: Lyceum Books/Nelson-Hall, pp. 388–401.

Buchanan, James and Tullock, Gordon (1962) *The Calculus of Consent*, Ann Arbor: University of Michigan Press.

Cabinet Office (1993) *Career Management and Succession Planning Study*, Efficiency Unit, London: HMSO.

Chan, James L. (1991) 'Standards and issues in governmental accounting and financial reporting (1981)' in J. Steven Ott *et al.* (eds) *Public Management: The Essential Readings*, Chicago: Lyceum Books/Nelson-Hall, pp. 358–367.

Dunsire, Andrew (1994) 'John Major's Citizens' Charter', *Hallinnon Tutkimus* (*Administrative Studies*), 13, 91–6.

Dunsire, Andrew, Hood, Christopher and Huby, Meg (1989) *Cutback Management in Public Bureaucracies: Popular Theories and Observed Outcomes in Whitehall*, Cambridge: Cambridge University Press.

Fayol, Henri (1955) *General and Industrial Management* (in French 1916), London: Sir Isaac Pitman.

Flynn, Norman (1990) *Public Sector Management*, New York: Harvester Wheatsheaf.

Gauthier, David (1986) *Morals by Agreement*, Oxford: Oxford University Press.

Garson, G. and Overman, E. (1983) *Public Management Research in the United States*, New York: Praeger.

Goodnow, F. (1900) *Politics and Administration*, New York: Macmillan.

Graham, Jr, B.C. and Hays, Steven W. (1991) 'Management functions and public administration – POSDCORB revisited (1986)' in J. Steven Ott *et al.* (eds) *Public Management: The Essential Reading*, Chicago: Lyceum Books/Nelson-Hall, pp. 10–27.

Gulick, L. and Urwick, L. (1973) *Papers on the Science of Administration*, New York: Institute of Public Administration.

Henley, Douglas, Holtham, Clive, Likierman, Andrew and Perrin, John (1987) *Public Sector Accounting and Financial Control*, 2nd edn, Wokingham: Van Nostrand Reinhold.

Hood, Christopher (1991) 'A public management for all seasons?,' *Public Administration*, 69, 3–19.

Kraemer, Kenneth L. and King, John Leslie (1991) 'Computing and public organizations (1986)' in J. Steven Ott *et al.*, (eds) *Public Management: The Essential Readings*, Chicago: Lyceum Books/Nelson-Hall, pp. 62–77.

Lane, Larry M. and Wolf, James F. (1990) *The Human Resource Crisis in the Public Sector: Rebuilding the Capacity to Govern*. New York: Quorum.

Marini, Frank (ed.) (1971) *Toward a New Public Administration: The Minnowbrook Perspective*, New York: Chandler.

Metcalfe, Les and Richards, Sue (1990) *Improving Public Management*, 2nd Enlarged edn, London: European Institute.

Ministry of Finance (1993) *The World's Best Public Sector?* Helsinki: International Public Management Comparison Project.

Mintzberg, Henry (1973) *The Nature of Managerial Work*, New York: Harper & Row.

Nozick, Robert (1974) *Anarchy, State and Utopia*, Oxford: Basil Blackwell.

OECD (1990) *Flexible Personnel Management in the Public Service: Public Management Studies*, 1st edn, Paris: Organization for Economic Co-operation and Development.

OECD (1993) *Private Pay for Public Work: Performance-Related Pay for Public Sector Managers. Public Management Studies*, Paris: Organization for Economic Co-operation and Development.

Ott, J. Steven, Hyde, Albert C. and Shafritz, Jay M. (eds) (1991) *Public Management: The Essential Readings*, Chicago: Lyceum Books/Nelson-Hall.

Overman, E. Sam (1984) 'Public management: what's new and different?', Book Reviews, *Public Administration Review*, 44, 275–8.

Pollitt, Christopher (1993) *Managerialism and the Public Services: The Anglo-American Experience*, 2nd edn, Oxford: Basil Blackwell.

Taylor, F.W. (1911) *The Principles of Scientific Management*, New York: Norton.

Virtanen, Turo (1991) *Välineellinen virkamiespätevyys ja virkamiesten koulutus (Instrumental Competence and the Education of Civil Servants)*. Tampere: University of Tampere, Department of Public Administration, Publication Series A, no. 1.

Virtanen, Turo (1992) 'Informatization and administrative modernization in Finland' in *European Public Administration and Informatization*, P.H.A. Frissen *et al.*, (eds), Amsterdam: IOS Press, pp. 505–35.

Virtanen, Turo (1993) 'Co-ordinating public policy making by interorganizational information systems: the case of the Cadastral Information System in Finland', a paper presented at the Conference of International Institute of Administrative Sciences, Toluca, Mexico, 27–30 July.

Wholey, Joseph S. (1983) *Evaluation and Effective Public Management: Foundations of Public Management*, Boston: Little, Brown.

Wilson, Woodrow (1887) 'The study of administration', *Political Science Quarterly*, 2, 197–222.

Part II
National Studies

4 Belgium

Roger Depré and Annie Hondeghem

As in other European countries, the public sector in Belgium is undergoing rapid change. For some years, there has been pressure upon government to adapt and modernize. There are several reasons for this. First, Belgium has an enormous public debt: almost 10 000 billion Belgium francs or 140 per cent of its gross national product (GNP). This debt is the result of unorthodox public spending in the past. In order to maintain the equilibria in Belgian society amongst linguistic, ideological and religious groups, a policy of compensation was carried out. If one group obtained something, other groups received an equivalent. In this way conflicts were avoided but at enormous economic cost. Pressure is now coming from the European Union and the Treaty of Maastricht to curb public expenditure and reduce the national debt.

Second, the legitimacy of government in Belgium has decreased. There is an anti-government movement challenging any further growth in state activity and demanding privatization. In particular, government monopolies are attacked because, it is claimed, they are seriously dysfunctional. Furthermore, new European regulations require changes to their organization. As a result, public organizations now have to face competition and they are increasingly being evaluated on the same criteria as private organizations, namely client orientation, effectiveness and efficiency.

Third, the position of the citizen is evolving from that of a passive subject to a critical consumer. Citizens now expect not only justice and legality from government but also answers to the problems of society and quality services. The relationship between government and citizens is moving from an hierarchical to a relational one of supplier and consumer.

Modernization of government in Belgium has been slowed down by the federal structure. The demands for privatization, deregulation, increased responsibility and accountability only entered the political agenda after a constitutional change in 1988. This transferred important areas, such as education and public works, from national to state level. After that the modernization process began. The Flemish government has been a pioneer in this matter and has inspired governments at other levels.

79

The emergence of the new public manager in Belgium must be situated in this context. In several public organizations, there has been an evolution from a bureaucratic model (static and rule-oriented) towards a managerial model (dynamic, client and result-oriented). In the managerial model, public officials or public managers have a totally different role from classical public administrators. The transition to the new public manager is not complete, however, and is having to contend with the legacy of a traditional system, unique to Belgium. Compared with other countries, top civil servants in Belgium have, in the past, been less involved in policy-making and have had less freedom of action concerning their own organization. This is due to the presence of ministerial cabinets, which have reduced the administration to a purely executive function. Although membership of ministerial cabinets has fallen, and top civil servants are more involved in the policy process, the situation of the past cannot be rectified at once. As a result not all top civil servants in Belgium can be described as public managers, especially when the strict definition of the European Group of Public Administration (EGPA) Study Group on Personnel Policy is used.

In this chapter, public managers are identified as the top managers of those public organizations which have made most progress towards new public management. These organizations include four autonomous public enterprises (APEs) at federal level and two Flemish public enterprises. These organizations have management contracts with responsible ministers, and their top officials meet the seven EGPA criteria. Top civil servants do not meet all the EGPA criteria and are excluded, although it is clear that throughout the public service there is a trend towards new public management.

Research on public managers in Belgium, involving a series of interviews with members of both the personnel and public relations services of the relevant organizations and in-depth interviews with top managers, mostly the general managers, was carried out in 1995. Some journalists who follow the public enterprises under investigation were also consulted. The collection of the empirical data was undertaken by Stefan Ghijsen for his dissertation on new public managers in Belgium (1995).

THE PUBLIC SECTOR

The public sector in Belgium employs about 900 000 people. The distribution of staff among different public organizations is shown in Table 4.1. Federal government has declined in size and now accounts for 24 per cent of public employees. In contrast, total state employment has

Table 4.1   *Public sector employment in Belgium, 1994*

		Number	%
1.	**Federal government**	**214 223**	**24**
	ministries	57 130	6
	institutions		
	● scientific	3 096	–
	● regies and public corporations	21 918	2
	● financial institutions	11 807	1
	● autonomous public enterprises	120 272	14
2.	**State government**	**353 187**	**40**
	ministries	24 244	3
	institutions		
	● scientific	198	
	● public corporations	48 737	6
	education	280 008	32
3.	**Particular bodies**	**77 276**	**9**
	(courts, army, federal police)		
4.	**Local authorities**	**237 368**	**27**
	Municipalities	119 406	14
	Public centres for social welfare	79 406	9
	Intercommunales	22 391	3
	Provinces	16 165	2
5.	**Legislature**	**2 264**	**–**
	Total personnel strength	**884 318**	**100**

grown to 40 per cent. This is the result of successive reforms in 1970, 1980, 1988 and 1993, which have transferred functions from national government to the state level.

Federal and state governments are organized into ministries and institutions. Belgium has a long tradition of creating new organizational units outside the classical administration. The reasons for this differentiation process include the search for more appropriate organizational structures, financial systems other than the strict cameralistic budget system, and more flexible personnel policies. Table 4.1 shows that more personnel are now employed in institutions than in ministries.

The degree of autonomy of the institutions varies according to whether they are regies, public corporations, public financial institutions or autonomous public enterprises (APEs). Regies are public organizations with a technical independence. They have an appropriate budgetary system but they function under the close hierarchical supervision of a minister or, in the case of municipalities, the city mayor. Their financial system is designed to accommodate price setting and tariffs. Most of the regies provide public utilities, such as water, gas and telephone, which are sold on the market. They are the least autonomous of the organizations. Until 1991, three of the four APEs were regies.

Public corporations are separate legal bodies authorized to act in their own name. They are established by separate laws which define their precise functions and organizational structure. They are capable of entering contracts and acquiring property, and their finances are separate from the state budget. They are run by executive boards, invested with wide powers. As functional, decentralized institutions, they have formal autonomy *vis-à-vis* the minister, although in practice this autonomy is restricted by tutelary rules. Examples of public corporations are the institutions responsible for executing social security legislation.

The public financial institutions have more autonomy than the public corporations and the current trend is to privatize them. This has already happened with the General Savings and Pension Bank (ASLK).

A further category is the APE. This new type of institution was created by the law of 1991. APEs are found particularly in the transport and communication sector and include the Post, Belgacom (the former Telephone and Telegraph Company), the National Railways Company, and the National Company for Air Traffic. The APE was seen as an alternative to privatization, where government wanted to keep control over enterprises because of their public-interest role. APE status provides enterprises with considerable autonomy and enables them to function more effectively and efficiently in a competitive market. The instrument created to facilitate this is the management contract (see below). The experience of the APE has not been altogether positive, however, and at the end of 1994 the law of 1991 was adapted to allow the privatization of Belgacom.

The penultimate group in the public sector is the 'particular body'. This is a heterogeneous category of public organizations including the courts, army, and federal police force which account for 9 per cent of public employees.

Finally, there is local government. Local administrations, municipalities and provinces have always occupied an important position in the public sector. Their existence is guaranteed by the constitution and they have a general authority on all matters of local interest. In order to perform on an optimal scale, municipalities have the right to create intercommunal associations. In many intercommunales, private enterprises are involved in the association, for example in the provision of gas, electricity and economic expansion. As a consequence, intercommunales often have a more business-oriented management style and have been in advance in introducing management techniques from the private sector.

In the overview in Table 4.1, some sectors where government is, or has been, active are not included such as the airline company (SABENA) and public holdings. Although government intervention in the economy has never been as large in Belgium as in France and the UK, public holdings were created to support employment in some strategic economic sectors, such as steel and coalmining. When the state became owner of more than 50 per cent of the shares of a company, it assumed responsibility for its management. It inherited or appointed managers with industrial or commercial experience as in the steel sector (Gandois) and the coal mines (Ghyselink). These managers were often crisis managers in charge of the restructuring and the closing-down of industries. In the Belgian Airline Company, an external manager was also brought in (Godfroid). These managers were the precursors of public managers in other public sectors.

In interpreting the figures in Table 4.1, it is important to note that government has always allowed private organizations to provide some public services. These include: social housing, by social housing societies; unemployment benefits by trade unions; and health insurance administration by mutual aid societies. These organizations are funded or subsidized by the state but they are the providers of the services. The welfare state in Belgium, therefore, has traditionally been financed by government but not totally delivered by public organizations, as in the UK. This delegation of public tasks to the private sector is part of a philosophy of the state which accepts that government does not have to do everything by itself and should call upon private initiative. It also respects and accommodates the disparate political, ideological and religious interests in society. The main concern of the welfare state in Belgium today is not privatization but controlling public expenditure.

TRENDS IN THE PUBLIC SECTOR

At macro level, government is gradually withdrawing from some sectors. Privatization is being used to transfer activities from the state to the private sector. First, a minority of shares are sold to a private partner such as SABENA and Belgacom. Second, the rest of the shares are gradually transferred to the private partner until it gets complete control over the organization, for example the public financial institutions.

At micro level, there are clear trends towards more efficiency, effectiveness and client orientation. In several sectors new financial management systems have been introduced. These include programme budgeting at federal level, new accounting systems in local government and experiments with result-oriented budgeting in the Flemish admininstration. Personnel policy has been modernized in the direction of human resources management. Important changes here include less hierarchical control, the introduction of some elements of performance-related pay, job descriptions, new staff evaluation systems and more attention to training. In order to enhance the client orientation of administration, new initiatives include legislation to increase the transparency of public organizations and the introduction of ombudsmen.

A major innovation at organizational level is the management contract. A management contract is made between a responsible minister and an organization. The contract is designed to balance 'intervention' and 'autonomy'. The responsible minister sets down the objectives of the organization and the means of achieving them but the organization then has freedom of action concerning its internal management and deployment of resources, including personnel.

At federal level, the formula of the management contract has been applied to the four APEs and management contracts are currently being prepared for the 18 institutions responsible for the execution of social security legislation. In the Flemish state, there are management contracts with the Flemish Transport Company, the Flemish Institute for Technological Research and the Flemish Employment Service (VDAB). A contract is also being prepared with the Radio and Television Company.

THE NEW PUBLIC MANAGERS

In identifying public managers in Belgium, we have started from the definition of the EGPA Study Group on Personnel Policy (see Introduction). Using this strict definition, only a few top civil servants in Belgium can at this moment be considered public managers. In particular, the criterion of being appointed for a fixed time is an important obstacle, since security of employment is still one of the key features of public employment in Belgium. Nevertheless, a few public managers do meet the EGPA definition. These are found mainly in the transport and communication sectors, which are more exposed to competition than other sectors. This is in part a result of decisions taken at the European level to abolish government monopolies by 1998.

We have studied the top managers of six public organizations: four APEs at federal level – the Post, the National Railway Company, Belgacom and the National Company for Air Traffic – and two Flemish enterprises, the Flemish Transport Company and Flemish Institute for Technological Research. Within these organizations, we located 32 managers who meet the EGPA criteria.

The six public organizations collectively employ about 125 000 people or 13 per cent of total public employment. Their top management consists of 32 senior officials who form the core of this study. The Post originated as a direction of the Ministry of Transport, became a regie in 1971, and is now an APE. With over 49 000 employees, it is the biggest employer in Belgium. The National Railways Company (NMBS) started as a direction of a ministry, became a public corporation in 1926, and is now an APE. The company employs 43 500 people. Belgacom started as a direction of a ministry, became a regie in 1930 (the regie of telephone and telegraph), and an APE in 1991. It employs a workforce of over 26 000. As a result of conflicts between the executive board and the board of directors and the growing competition in the telecommunication sector, the statute of Belgacom was changed at the end of 1994 into a limited liability company of public law. Both the executive board and the board of directors were renewed. At this time the state is still owner of the shares of the company but the government plans to sell shares to a private company and ultimately to privatize Belgacom. Because the collection of the empirical data for this study took place in 1994, the analysis of Belgacom relates to the former six members of the board of directors. Where important differences with the current top managers arise these will be mentioned.

The National Company for Air Traffic (NMLW) is the successor of the former regie (1970) which had to be transformed into an APE in conformity with the law of 1991. Four years later, however, the management contract has not yet been approved. As a result the organization cannot fully function as an APE. The company has over 1500 employees. The Flemish Transport Company (VVM) was created by the Flemish government in 1990 out of existing companies for regional and city transport. The company has almost 5000 employees. The Flemish Institute for Technological Research (VITO) was created by the Flemish government in 1991. Its purpose is to undertake research concerning energy, environment and raw materials. VITO employs 347 highly qualified people.

As stated above, this study of new public managers in Belgium is restricted to the 32 top managers of six public organizations who constitute the boards of directors. Each of the organizations has an executive board and a board of directors whose members are appointed for a limited period of six years. Table 4.2 below shows the size of each board. Appointees to the executive boards are part-time appointments. Because of this part-time status and their largely supervisory role we have excluded them from our category of public managers. It is evident from our study, however, that the relation between the board of directors and the executive board is a close one and that their roles can overlap, for example in Belgacom.

Biographical Details

The 32 NPMs are all Belgian men (no women) between 39 and 64 years of age. The average age is 51 years. A relatively large number of the NPMs are former top civil servants, although the younger members come from the private sector or from a ministerial cabinet. Only three of the 32 NPMs are non-graduates and most have engineering or economics degrees. This can be explained by the technological nature of the enterprises under investigation.

In conformity with the rule that posts within the Belgian administration are equally distributed between the two language groups, there is an equal number of Flemish- and French-speaking NPMs in the APEs. Three out of the four federal general managers, however, are Flemish, whilst in the Flemish enterprises all directors are Flemish.

Legal Status

The NPMs in the APEs have a renewable mandate or contract with the organization for six years. Civil servants are seconded to the organization and at the end of the mandate can resume their former function. The general manager, or chair of the board of directors, is appointed by the King by Royal decree. He can only be dismissed with the approval of two thirds of the appointed members of the executive board. The other members of the board of directors are appointed by the executive board, on the proposal of the general manager, and with the approval of the responsible minister. They can only be dismissed if two-thirds of the executive board agree and with the approval of the responsible minister.

In practice, the former rules are not uniformly applied. In the National Company for Air Traffic, the appointments are still a political responsibility as the company does not function yet as an APE. In the other enterprises, the autonomy of the general manager to propose the members of the board of directors is limited by the political agreements which are made on a higher level. This explains why the rules have been changed in

Belgacom: the general manager has now the authority to appoint and dismiss the other directors by himself.

In the Flemish enterprises, the legal status of the new public managers is very similar. The general manager, and his assistant in the Flemish Transport Company, has a renewable mandate of six years. He is appointed by the Flemish government. The other directors have a long-term contract and are appointed by the executive board, on the proposal of the general manager.

Recruitment and Selection

The different laws establishing the APEs specify the number of directors but not the selection criteria. The government is responsible for the recruitment and selection of the general manager. First, it is decided which political party can choose the general manager. This party then looks for a suitable candidate. The candidate can come from the organization itself, from a ministerial cabinet, or from the private sector. If the political party cannot find a candidate a head-hunting agency can be called in. The former general manager of Belgacom (Kok), who was recruited with the help of head-hunters, came from a private company specializing in telecommunications (SWIFT).

The selection of other directors is the responsibility of the general manager, who makes a proposition to the executive board. The most important selection criteria are expertise and acceptability to government. Most of the time, the general manager looks for suitable candidates among the staff members of the organization. As one of the general managers said when interviewed, 'The enterprises are big enough to find good candidates for every political party'. It is also possible to select a candidate from outside the organization either for political reasons or because of a lack of expertise within the organization.

In the Flemish enterprises the recruitment and selection of NPMs is based on the same principles. In both the Flemish Transport Company and the Flemish Institute for Technological Research, most directors are recruited from within the organization.

Career Backgrounds

Two of the six general managers come from the private sector, one from a ministerial cabinet, and three from their respective organizations (one with additional experience in a ministerial cabinet). Almost two-thirds of the 32 NPMs have developed their careers within their current organization.

Thirteen had been within the organization for less than 10 years, five between 10 and 20 years, and fourteen for more than 20 years. This demonstrates that, in conformity with the closed career system in Belgium, seniority is still an important factor in becoming a member of the board of directors.

In the public organizations under investigation, the first mandate of six years has not yet finished and it is difficult to predict whether the mandates of the NPMs will be renewed. The expectation is that not all NPMs will be offered new contracts and that mobility at the top will increase. The experiences of the members of the board of directors of Belgacom may offer a guide. Due to a conflict between the executive board and the board of directors, the general manager of Belgacom (Kok) was dismissed and replaced by John Goossens, a former top manager of Alcatell Bell, a private enterprise specializing in telecommunication. The other five members of the board, however, had their contracts renewed for a further six years.

Staff Evaluation

It is the responsibility of the executive board to evaluate the board of directors and its individual members. A negative evaluation can lead to the dismissal of a NPM. This is quite revolutionary since security of tenure is one of the key features of the public service in Belgium. As the executive board generally has little knowledge of the performance of individual members of the board of directors, they rely on the opinion of the general manager. It is the general manager, therefore, who assesses the performance of board members and has influence over their tenure as well as their rewards.

Remuneration

In the APEs, the remuneration of the general manager is fixed in his contract for the period of his mandate. Other members of the board have a salary based on grade and seniority. As long as they are a member of the board they also get an extra premium. This premium is cancelled when the mandate expires. In general, the salaries of the NPMs in the APEs are lower than those of their colleagues in the private sector. At present, civil servants among the NPMs are compensated by the pension system which is more favourable in the public sector than in the private sector.

In the Flemish Transport Company, the remuneration of the general manager and his assistant is fixed by the Flemish government. An external consultant recently audited the organization's remuneration system and recommended that salaries should be raised to the level of those in comparable positions in the private sector. To date this has only partly been executed. In the Flemish Institute for Technological Research, a new remuneration system is also to be introduced. In addition to a fixed salary, NPMs will receive a premium which is dependent on their individual performance as well as the performance of the organization. This new system still has to be approved by the Flemish government.

Summary

At the time of writing there is no human resources management policy for the NPMs in Belgium. The most revolutionary change is that the NPMs no longer have security of tenure, but limited contracts. Also in contrast with the former tradition of the closed career system, NPMs can be recruited from outside the organization. They are evaluated on their results according to the objectives which have been defined in the management contract and their rewards are partly performance-related.

AUTHORITY, RESPONSIBILITY AND ACCOUNTABILITY

One of the main features of new public management is the shift in responsibility between politicians, public servants and citizens. Politicians steer on strategy, top civil servants have a greater responsibility for performance and citizens have more direct contact with public servants. This involves changes in the mechanisms of accountability. This shift in responsibility and accountability is formalized in the six organizations investigated. One of the most important innovations is the management contract. A management contract is a contract between the responsible minister and the public organization which defines the rules and the purpose of the organization as a public service.

In conformity with the law of 1991, the contract stipulates:

- the mission of the enterprise;
- a description in detail of the quantity and quality of the tasks of public service;
- the basic rules for price setting and tariffs;
- the line of conduct for the relations with the public;
- the amount of subventions from the state (if this is the case) as a compensation for the tasks of public service which are executed by the company;

- sanctions in case of non-fulfilment of the contract;
- the way profits are to be distributed;
- the monopoly status of the organization.

The contract extends for a minimum of three and a maximum of five years, with the opportunity for annual adjustments. The management contract is negotiated between the minister and the board of directors. In this way, the NPMs can influence the policy of the organization to a large extent. The contract has to be approved by the executive board with a majority of two-thirds and by the government. It is important to note that the management contract only relates to the tasks of public service. The organization is allowed to execute other tasks not covered in the contract.

The management contract is an instrument which enables ministers to control the policy and the goal attainment of the organizations. It also defines the financial involvement of the state and sets down financial parameters. The management of the organization is responsible, in turn, for fulfilling the contract and reaching the objectives within the financial restrictions. In the Flemish enterprises, the content and the procedure of the management contract is slightly different but the general principles remain the same.

The NPMs are generally positive about management contracts. They see them as enlarging the freedom of action of managers, and most welcome an extension of their use. Only the time period is seen as a problem, as three to five years is too short for long-term strategic management.

The management of each organization is accountable for its performance to a variety of bodies. Table 4.2 shows who the NPMs of the six public organizations have to account to.

Accountability to the *general assembly* only exists in those public organizations which have the status of a partnership or a company. The general assembly represents the shareholders. It has to approve the accounts and has ultimate control over the executive board.

The *executive board* has a maximum of 18 members in APEs and 11 members in the Flemish enterprises. In the APEs members of the board of directors are also part of the executive board. In Belgacom and the Flemish enterprises only the general manager is a member of the executive board. Members of the executive board, or a part of the members in the case of Belgacom II, are appointed by the government. They have a renewable mandate of six years and political criteria are dominant in their selection. The authority of the executive board is extensive including the power to carry out any act which is necessary to obtain the objectives of

Table 4.2 *Responsibility and accountability of the six public organizations under investigation*

	Post	NMBS	NMLW	Belgacom I	Belgacom II	VVM	VITO
General assembly	no	no	no	no	yes	yes	yes
Executive board: number	18	18	18	18	18	11	11
General manager responsible for day to day management	no	no	no	no	yes	yes	no
Board of directors: number	6	6	4	6	max. 10	5	5
Number of directors on executive board	6	6	4	6	1	2	1
Administrative supervision	gov. com. (1)	gov. com. (1)	gov. com. (1)	gov. com. (1)	gov. com. (1)	gov. com. (2)	gov. com. (2)
Financial control	fin. com. (4)	fin. com. (4)	fin. com. (4)	fin. com. (4)	fin. com. (4)	fin. com. (4)	fin. com. (1)
Ombudsman	yes	yes	yes	yes	yes	no	no

the organization. The executive board also controls the board of directors. but may delegate functions to it.

The *board of directors* is responsible for the day-to-day management in the APEs and in the Flemish Institute for Technological Research. In Belgacom II and in the Flemish Transport Company, however, day-to-day management rests with the general manager (and his assistant). In the APEs the board of directors functions as a college which means that, although responsibilities can be distributed, decisions are taken jointly.

The administrative supervision of the six public organizations is executed by *government commissioners*. A commissioner represents the responsible minister on the executive board and watches over the legality of the decisions and the execution of the management contract. The government commissioner enables the minister to control the public organization indirectly and at a distance. The minister is obliged to present a yearly report to parliament and may be questioned on the management and the policy of the organization at any time.

The financial control of the six organizations is executed by *financial commissioners*. In the APEs, they also have a mandate for six years.

Finally there is an *ombudsman* in every APE. These were created in conformity with the law of 1991. The ombudsman receives the complaints of the clients-citizens, and tries to solve them. The members of this service have an independent position and are appointed for a renewable mandate of five years.

The creation of this plethora of controlling bodies indicates the increase in accountablity of these organizations but this is counterbalanced by an increase in the delegation of important responsibilities from ministers to both the executive boards and the boards of directors. Executive boards in the APEs, for example, are now responsible for important aspects of personnel policy, including the personnel statute and personnel planning. Compared with other top civil servants, the NPMs have far more freedom of action, and most importantly they can negotiate the content of the management contract. Citizens have also increased their impact on the public organizations by means of the ombudsman.

This distribution of authority among so many different actors does give rise to problems. First the authority distribution between the executive board and the board of directors is not well defined. The authority of the executive board is large, and this conflicts with one of the basic principles of new public management, namely the 'right of managers to manage'. Moreover, as the composition of the executive board is politically determined, the members are not always experts concerning either the public enterprise or public management.

The wide authority of the executive board and its intervention in the day-to-day management of the organization is part of the Belgian tradition and has been part of the public corporation's experience. In Belgacom, the ambiguity in the roles of the executive board and the board of directors led to a major conflict. The president of the executive board saw his job as a full-time occupation and he involved himself with daily management of the organization. The policy of the board of directors was criticized in the press, the government had to intervene, the executive board was dismissed and the general manager (Kok) was replaced. According to the actual statute of Belgacom, the day-to-day management is the responsibility of the general manager and the responsibilities of the president of the executive board are limited.

A second problem concerning the APEs arises from the fact that members of the board of directors are also part of the executive board.

This restricts control by the executive board of the NPMs. This has changed now in Belgacom II as only the general manager is a member of the executive board.

A third problem in the APEs is the functioning of the board of directors as a college. This restricts the authority of the general manager. In Belgacom II this has also changed with the general manager exercising more power. He can appoint and dismiss the other members of the board of directors and he alone is responsible for the daily management of the organization.

PUBLIC MANAGERS AND POLITICS

The top positions in the Belgian administration have always been politicized, and the trend towards new public management has not changed that fundamentally. There is an attempt to maintain the traditional Belgian equilibria in both the executive boards and the boards of directors. It is important to note that not only the political or ideological equilibrium is looked for, but also the equilibrium between the two language groups. Moreover, the last equilibrium is rooted in legislation. The law of 1991 on APEs requires that both the executive board and the board of directors be composed of equal numbers of Flemish- and French-speaking members, with the exception of the president and the general manager. Moreover, the president of the executive board and the general manager must belong to different language groups. These rules actually disadvantage the Flemish people as they represent 60 per cent of the Belgian population.

When the APEs were created in 1991, there was, on the federal level, a coalition of three Flemish political parties (the Christian Democrats (CVP), the Socialists (SP), the Volksunie (VU) and two Walloon parties (the Christian Democrats (PSC) and Socialists (PS)). In the Flemish government, there was a coalition of the same three Flemish parties: CVP–SP–VU. As a result, the NPMs are proportionally divided among the political parties which were in government. In the executive board, there is also some representation of the opposition parties including the Flemish Liberal Party (VLD) and the Walloon Liberal Party (PRL). If some of the members of the board of directors or the executive board do not belong to a political party they are assigned to one so that the equilibrium can be maintained.

The example of Belgacom in Table 4.3 shows an equal representation of both political and language groups. The ordinary members of the executive board are drawn from industry, the trade unions, and the universities.

Table 4.3 *Party composition of the executive board and board of directors of Belgacom*

Ordinary members of the executive board
Flemish: CVP (2) + SP (2) + VU (1) + VLD (1) = 6
French: PSC (2) + PS (3) + PRL (1) = 6

Members of the board of directors
Flemish: CVP (2) + SP (1) = 3
French: PSC (1) + PS (2) = 3

SOURCE: derived from P. Berkenbaum, *De Belgacomedie*, Antwerpen-Baarn: Hadewijch, 1995.

They have often had experience in a ministerial cabinet. This was the case with the president of the executive board of Belgacom (Remiche) who was formerly a member of the ministerial cabinet of a vice prime minister (PSC). The attempt to maintain the traditional Belgian equilibria is often to the detriment of the management capacities of the board members. Although the general manager has a formal authority to select members of the board of directors, political factors often override his choice. The former general manager of Belgacom (Kok) had no choice at all since the members of the board of directors were selected beforehand.

Since the reorganization of Belgacom some things have changed. The statute now requires that members of the executive board be selected because of their juridical, economic, financial or social experience or because of their expertise in telecommunications. It is difficult to judge whether this rule has been applied for the new executive board. The new president comes from a private company and belongs to the PSC, just like the former one. The other members of the executive board all have relations with the political world and few with the world of telecommunications. However, the position of the general manager has been strengthened, and appointments of NPMs in the future are likely to be less influenced by political criteria although the equilibrium between the language groups will remain.

The relation between the NPMs and politics in the other five public organizations remain the same. In all organizations, the executive board is politicized. The executive board is the political component of the organization, where the different political parties of the coalition and their allied pressure groups like the trade unions are present. In this way politics directs the policy of the public enterprise. One view is that the loss of political control of the minister, in creating more APEs, is partly compensated by the political control of the executive boards. The ordinary members of the executive boards are often drawn, as stated above, from staff members of political parties and ministerial cabinets. The political appointees on the executive boards also often accumulate a number of different mandates, and this leads to a concentration of power amongst a small political élite. The NPMs, when interviewed, said they would prefer to see more experts and entrepreneurs on the executive boards.

The degree of politicization varies amongst public organizations. The organizations in this study can be divided into three groups. Politicization is very high in the National Company for Air Traffic, which compares with the regies and public corporations. This is due to the fact that the company does not function as an APE because the management contract is not yet approved. The general manager (Kirch) has worked on several ministerial cabinets and was engaged in the preparation of the law of 1991 on the APEs. Other members of the board of directors have strong political ties and political criteria were decisive in their nomination. It was necessary to be politically active and to belong to an appropriate network to become a member of the board.

In the National Railways Company (NMBS), the Post, and the Flemish Transport Company (VVM) politicization is a reality, but expertise is more important. Technocrats and business-oriented managers are preferred. As one general manager, stated, 'Expertise has priority, taken for granted that the proposed managers are politically acceptable'. This is not a problem as in these organizations there are enough public servants, at a higher level, who can be selected for a management position. Amongst this group, every political party can find suitable representatives. This means, however, that the NPMs in the Railways Company, the Post, and the Flemish Transport Company must have a political profile, although it is not necessary for them to be politically active or to belong to the same network as the minister.

The general manager of the Flemish Institute for Technological Research has been recruited from the private sector and other members of the board of directors come from another federal scientific institution. The NPMs in this public organization do not have relations with politics and are not politically active. The Institute is thus an example of a public organization where appointments are based on merit. This can probably be explained by the technological and scientific character of the organization, which calls for specific expertise.

TRENDS IN OTHER SECTORS

The study of NPMs in Belgium has been limited to those public organizations which have made most progress towards new public management. However, there is an evolution towards new public management in other sectors of federal, state and local government.

Flemish Administration

The Flemish administration has been a pioneer in modernization of the public service, starting in 1988 after the third reform of the constitution. First a new mission for the Flemish administration was defined and a political project was drawn up for the next 15 years. Second, a new organizational structure for departments was designed with less hierarchy and fewer divisions. Third, a new personnel statute and new personnel instruments were developed. Fourth, a new organizational culture was introduced.

All this had important consequences for the role and position of top civil servants. From the beginning, efforts were made to create a team spirit through the use of management seminars. Top civil servants were given more influence in political decision-making. A good example of this is that the government declarations in 1991 and 1995 were inspired by documents prepared by secretaries general. Top civil servants were also given more autonomy over the use of resources. Under new personnel statutes, the secretaries general have authority to appoint personnel in the lower levels. This represents a small revolution because of the Belgian tradition of political interference in all personnel matters.

Management by objectives has also been introduced in each part of the administration. Top civil servants will be evaluated, at the beginning of 1996, against the objectives set for their administrations. They can receive a premium of up to 20 per cent of their salary if the objectives have been reached. Clearly the top civil servants of the Flemish administration are evolving in the direction of NPMs. As they still have lifetime employment, however, they do not meet all the criteria of the EGPA Study Group. Only when limited-term appointments are introduced will they be held ultimately accountable, with the threat of removal, for poor results.

Local Government

The innovations in the Flemish administration have had an influence on other sectors of the public service especially local government. In 1993,

Minister Kelchtermans approved the principles for a new personnel statute. In addition to a financial revaluation, these principles include the obligation to introduce a personnel planning system, personnel evaluation, and more attention for training. An important innovation is that from now on external recruitment to the top grades is possible, but only of civil servants who have worked in other public organizations. It is also possible to use the mandate system for top posts. These two innovations weaken the closed career system, but whether local administrations will use these options remains to be seen.

As a result of the new personnel statute, middle and top management now have greater responsibility for personnel matters. Their personnel evaluation will in future determine the financial rewards of their subordinates. Again it is too early to consider top civil servants in local government as NPMs, as a lot of the conditions for result-oriented management are not fullfilled. In particular, local politicians are still heavily involved in daily policy-making and implementation instead of steering the organization. It will be some time before this reality has changed in local government.

Federal Government

There is also evidence of a trend towards new public management at the federal level. Again, one of the most important ideas is the introduction of a mandate system for top civil servants. Top civil servants will be temporarily appointed to a position which may be higher or equivalent to their actual grade. At the beginning of the mandate, clear management objectives will be set down. At the end of the mandate performance will be evaluated and only if the goals have been achieved will the mandate be renewed. The mandate system must be situated in the trend to make top civil servants more responsible and accountable. They will have more autonomy concerning the means of their administration (personnel and finance) but they will be held accountable for the results.

In 1994, the federal government decided that the mandate system would be introduced for all top civil servants in federal ministries, the public corporations, and the scientific institutions, covering 250 to 300 posts. Only civil servants who have proved their management competencies by obtaining a certificate in management could be selected for a mandate. The mandate would be for five years, with a possibility of renewal. This means top positions may be occupied for a maximum of 10 years. This would enhance the mobility at the top of the administration.

The government intended to implement the mandate system at the end of 1994 but the policy is blocked at the moment. It is uncertain whether it will now be implemented as the new government elected in 1995 did not include it in its manifesto.

CONCLUSION

The Belgian case is a good example of a public sector in transition. There is evidence of a trend towards new public management in the Belgian administration, although at the moment the numbers of NPMs who meet all the EGPA criteria is limited. They can be found in some public enterprises which are situated on the border between the public and the private sectors. It is expected that some of these organizations will be privatized in the near future and the NPMs will transfer to the private sector.

There is evidence, however, of a trend towards an expansion of the number of NPMs in other parts of the public sector including the Flemish administration, local government and some parts of the federal government. The major constraint upon the introduction of new public management in the Belgian context is the interference of the political system in the administration. There is still no acceptance that politicians set down political goals and objectives and leave matters of internal management to the administration. In those public organizations where the direct political control of the minister has been diminished by the management contract, control is still indirectly executed by the executive boards in which the political parties and their allied pressure groups are represented. In practice those executive boards also continue to play an important role in the daily management of the organization.

In order to understand the Belgian case, it is important to bear in mind that there is a long tradition of delegating public tasks to private organizations (trade unions, mutual aid companies, private hospitals). This reflects the idea of subsidiarity, namely that the state does not have to do everything by itself but can rely upon private initiative. This philosophy is not the same as managerialism, which rests upon the assumption that public tasks are best performed by private organizations because these are more efficient and effective. Subsidiarity is rooted in collectivism and neo-corporatism and a belief in the distribution of power between interests within society. The result is that the state is occupied by pressure groups which are dependent on state subsidies for their survival.

New public management in Belgium is associated with a more business-oriented style of management, cutting back on public spending and privatization. The tradition of neo-corporatism, however, is still firmly in place. In the new structures of the APEs, traditional political and interest groups are settling down in the executive boards with a view to controlling the policy of the public organizations. In these circumstances, the freedom of action of the NPMs is likely to continue to be limited.

References

Berkenbaum, P. (1995) *De Belgacomedie*, Antwerpen-Baarn: Hadewijch.

Bouckaert, G., Hondeghem, A. and Maes, R. (eds) (1994) *De overheidsmanager, nieuwe ontwikkelingen in het overheidsmanagement*, Leuven: VCOB.

Depré, R. and Hondeghem, A. (1987) 'Recruitment, career and training of higher civil servants in Belgium', in *The Higher Civil Service in Belgium and in the Industrialised Countries: Recruitment, Career, and Training*, Brussels: IIAS.

Depre, R. Hondeghem, A. (1991) 'Rapport sur la représentativité de l'administration belge', in V. Wright (ed.) *La représentativité de l'administration publique*, Brussels: IIAS.

Ghijsen, S. (1995) *Studie van de nieuwe overheidsmanagers in België*, Eindverhandeling aangeboden tot het verkrijgen van de graad van Licentiaat in de Politieke en Sociale Wetenschappen, K.U. Leuven.

Hondeghem, A. (1994) 'De politisering van de ambtenarij', in *Strategie en beleid in de publieke sector*, Samsom.

5 Britain

John Barlow, David Farnham and Sylvia Horton

The boundaries of the public sector in Britain have changed radically since 1979. The seeds of some of the changes were sown earlier, as governments responded to socio-economic forces within the environment. However, a significant factor in explaining the direction and the extent of the changes lies in the political control by Conservative Governments for over a decade and a half. Influenced by the political ideology of the New Right with its faith in markets, free enterprise, competition, a minimal state, low taxation and low public expenditure, successive Governments have rolled back the frontiers of the state. They have transformed public bureaucracies into public businesses, reduced the powers of the professions and managerialized the public services, with the introduction of pseudo-markets and competition as means of increasing efficiency. Public-sector organizational cultures have been changed to embrace 'business' values together with private-sector managerial practices. Using a range of strategies, including privatization, compulsory competitive tendering (CCT), contractorization, market testing and restructuring, Governments have redrawn the boundaries between the public and private domains.

One of the major consequences of the reforms permeating the British public sector since 1979 has been the emergence and growth of the 'new managerialism' or the 'new public management'. 'Public administrators' have also metamorphosed into 'public managers' (Pollitt, 1993; Hood, 1991; Hughes, 1994) whom we describe as budget holders with responsibility for executing a programme, which may involve the provision of a service or the production of a good. They are appointed to a specific post with a job description setting out their responsibilities and areas of discretion. They are responsible for staff and are located within an organizational hierarchy. They have a degree of autonomy and freedom in the way they use and control resources and are normally assessed in terms of preset financial and performance criteria. They are accountable directly or indirectly to a public body for the actions they take and for the overall outcome of their work. The model presented here is one against which we can assess the extent to which public managers have become a major feature of contemporary British public organizations.

THE CHANGING CONTOURS OF THE PUBLIC SECTOR

Constitutionally, Britain is a unitary state with power concentrated in central government and the national Parliament. Sovereignty rests with Parliament, which is the supreme law-making body, but the executive dominates Parliament and is the source of policy which Parliament formally approves. All government organizations, including local authorities, are created by and derive their powers from central government. Local authorities claim some political authority because local councils are democratically elected bodies but, in the absence of a written constitution, British local government does not enjoy a legal right of existence, and neither do local authorities have general powers to provide for their communities. Local authorities are the creation of Parliament and must operate within specific legislation. Central government can exert considerable influence and control over local authorities through the use of legal and financial instruments approved by Parliament. In the past, the political relationship between the two has been one of partnership (Rhodes, 1981; 1988). Since 1979, however, central government has asserted its control and has used its powers to subordinate, reduce and transform the role of local government, within both the political and the administrative spheres (Gray, 1994; Stoker, 1988). Local government, along with central government, has embraced the new managerialism and many new public managers are located within it.

The British public sector has been radically reshaped and restructured since 1979. A mixed economy, involving public, private-for-profit and voluntary bodies, now exists in most areas of state activity, where once the state had a monopoly (Johnson, 1990; Starks, 1991; Le Grand and Bartlett, 1993). Public organizations can, however, be distinguished from private organizations in terms of their ownership, goals, stakeholders and accountabilities (Farnham and Horton, 1993). Technically, they constitute bodies created by government to carry out state functions and achieve political goals. They are financed wholly or in part out of taxation and are accountable to political and legal institutions. They are staffed by public officials but may be led by politicians, appointed boards or career executives. We define the machinery of government as all those bodies for which a Minister of the Crown is accountable to Parliament. These can be classified into government departments, non-departmental public bodies (NDPBs), public corporations, National Health Service (NHS) the armed services and local government.

Government Departments

There are 21 major government departments headed by Ministers of the Crown and some 30 satellite departments not headed by ministers but under the umbrella of one. Within departments, programmes of work are normally located in divisions headed by responsible officials with their own budgets. Since 1988 most executive activities have been hived off into agencies. There were 108 agencies in April 1995 and another 65 agency candidates were under review. Agencies are headed by chief executives, appointed on fixed-term contracts. They operate within 'framework documents' setting down their objectives and performance indicators. Chief executives have more autonomy than managers within departments and fit the public manager model.

Non-Departmental Public Bodies (NDPBs)

In 1994, there were over 1300 NDPBs but their variety makes classification difficult. Pliatzky (1980) identified three groups: executive, advisory and adjudicatory. In 1994, there were 325 executive NDPBs, headed either by executives or boards; 814 advisory bodies; 71 tribunals; and 135 miscellaneous ones. Public managers are identifiable in the executive NDPBs, employing over 110 000 public officials.

Public Corporations

Public corporations are public trading bodies with substantial degrees of financial independence from government. They are self-financing or rely upon government subsidies. They are, however, publicly controlled by ministers who appoint their boards and are answerable to the House of Commons in exercising their statutory responsibilities. Many previous public corporations were nationalized industries and managed by public managers in similar ways to private industries. Since 1979 most nationalized industries have been privatized, and some 24 corporations dissolved. The remaining ones are managed by boards, consisting of executives on fixed-term contracts, with salaries and 'performance bonuses' comparable with those in the private sector. Since 1991 a series of 'new' public corporations have been set up, including NHS 'trusts', university corporations and further education corporations.

The NHS

The NHS is the largest employer in the public sector, employing over one million people in 1995. In 1984 a system of general management was introduced, replacing the consensus professional administration characterizing the service since its creation in 1948. A further radical change occurred in 1990 when the NHS was divided into 'purchasers' and 'providers', operating competitively within an internal market. This was accompanied by the creation of independent trusts and general practitioner units, each of which requires managers to negotiate contracts and ensure that the units are competitive.

It was estimated that by 1995 there were more than 17 000 general managers in health authorities and trusts. This figure does not include nurse managers and managers within clinical directorates or community units. Probably some 20 per cent of NHS employees are now in managerial posts, whilst spending on general manager salaries increased tenfold between 1987 and 1991 alone (Department of Health, 1992).

The Armed Services

A major contraction of the British armed forces took place after 1961, with decolonization and the final demise of the British Empire. This slowed during the 1970s and 1980s but increased again after 1989, due in part to the end of the Cold War. Important changes have occurred in the ways in which the services are managed under the New Management System introduced in 1991. Senior officers are now trained in management skills and techniques, manage budgets and have to meet performance criteria. The Bett Report (1995), if implemented, will introduce further changes in personnel policies and practices.

Local Government

There are 514 principal local authorities in Britain, 404 in England, 65 in Scotland and 45 in Wales. These are multi-purpose organizations responsible for environmental and other services, ranging from land-use planning, roads, transport and environmental health to education, housing and personal social services. Many services and responsibilities have been transferred from local government to central government, or to the private sector, since 1979 (Horton, 1990). CCT and market testing have also meant that local authorities now contract both internally and externally for many of their activities (Walsh, 1990; 1991), resulting in changes in the ways in which they are managed.

Public Servants

In Britain, there are distinctions in the status of public officials depending upon level of government, type of body and nature of their employment contract. Civil servants are civilian employees of the Crown found in central government departments, agencies and some NDPBs. Local government officials are employed by local authorities. All other groups are designated as employees of the organization within which they work, such as NHS employees, Post Office employees and members of the armed forces. These statuses confer different employment rights and duties and provide different terms and conditions of employment for staff (Fredman and Morris, 1989).

Changes in the public sector, since 1979, have resulted in a contraction of public employment. In 1981 there were over seven million public employees. By 1994 this had fallen to 5.2 million, with the major reductions in central government. Between 1983 and 1994 the public-sector share of employment fell from almost 30 to 20 per cent. This largely reflected the impact of privatization programmes and reclassifications of public-sector bodies. Over this period, employment in central government fell from some 10 per cent of total public employment to 6.4 per cent, local government from 12.3 to 11 per cent and public corporations from 7 to 5 per cent. This contraction was matched by increased productivity, falling unit costs and greater efficiency (Audit Commission, 1987).

THE CIVIL SERVICE

Civil servants make up 2 per cent of the working population and 10 per cent of public employees, in central, regional and local offices of government departments, agencies and some NDPBs. They provide services to the public, advice to decision-makers and service-wide support functions. Civil servants are classed as either industrial or non-industrial. They are divided vertically according to the type of work they do and their qualifications, and horizontally according to levels of responsibility. The largest groups are the administration, scientific and professional groups.

There is mobility within each group but only at the top of the civil service is there an open structure, where jobs can be filled by either an administrator or a specialist, and there is no formal classification of posts by occupational group, though some posts require professional qualifications. In part, this reflects the generally high management responsibilities demanded, making specialist qualifications less important than skills, ability and experience relevant to the job. This open structure has seven grades, the top five constitute the Senior Civil Service (SCS).

Managerialism and Change

Significant changes have occurred in the civil service since 1979 and these reflect the transition from an administrative to a managerial culture. First, these have resulted in a reduction of staff from 732 000 to 533 000 between 1979 and 1994, reflecting 'transfers out of the Civil Service to the private sector and to other public sector organisations such as NDPBs, productivity improvements and the benefits of information technology' (Cm 2627, 1994).

The second major change has been the introduction of new managerial structures and processes. A series of internal managerial scrutinies on efficiency introduced by Sir Derek Rayner in 1980 (Collins, 1987) began a process of changing the attitudes and behaviour of civil servants. These led to new management and financial information systems, such as the Financial Management Initiative (FMI), which resulted in the devolution of budgeting and resource management to operational units and middle managers. The policy was reviewed in 1987 by Sir Robin Ibbs who concluded that although much had been achieved in increasing efficiency and reducing costs, there was a long way to go. The major barriers were the size and complexity of the service and the reluctance of central departments to relinquish control. He recommended the creation of separate agencies to manage the executive functions within departments and the appointment of chief executives to run them (Ibbs Report, 1988).

This was the third major change generally referred to as 'Next Steps'. A federal structure is emerging, with smaller core departments and semi-autonomous agencies headed by the new public managers on fixed-term contracts and operating within framework documents. They have considerable managerial freedoms over staffing, terms and conditions of employment and pay. They are accountable to ministers but are also required to submit an annual report to Parliament and give evidence to select committees of the House of Commons. Several agencies have trading accounts and are self-funding. It is intended that all executive activities will either be provided by agencies or privatized by 1996–97. This will leave a small core of civil servants in the departments providing policy advice to Ministers and monitoring the activities of agencies.

In 1991, during the first Major Government, the thrust of the new managerialism changed from reducing input costs and increasing economic efficiency to outputs and improving quality of service delivery. The Government published *The Citizen's Charter* (Prime Minister's Office, 1991) which set down aims to respond to the needs of public 'customers' and to find more effective ways of delivering services. Its principles are standards, information and openness, choice and consultation, courtesy and help, putting things right and value for money. The Government believes that 'one way to deliver increased choice and efficiency in the provision of public services is to bring private sector disciplines to bear on the way they are run' (Cabinet Office, 1994).

In line with its belief that competition is the best guarantee of quality, the Government issued a White Paper in 1991, requiring departments and agencies to market test their activities and, where justified, to contract out to the private sector. Combined with the process of privatizing those government functions that can be provided by private organizations, this is resulting in a shrinking state and smaller civil service. Where activities remain within the public sector they have to be managed in an efficient way in order to retain the competitive advantage.

The New Civil Service Managers

The refrain being sung by most civil servants is: 'we are all managers now'. According to the Treasury (H.M. Treasury, 1991), 'if you are responsible for staff and budgets you are first and foremost a manager no matter what your area of work'. By this criterion, most civil servants above the basic level are 'managers'. A distinction can be made, however, between different management levels. Executive Officers operate at a supervisory level; Higher Executive Officers at first managerial grade; and those in the Open Structure, Grade 7 and above constitute the middle management/senior management levels.

There were 21 000 in the Open Structure in 1995 and about 14 per cent were women. The civil service reflects the general pattern of vertical gender segregation found in most organizations, although there has been a significant increase in the number of women in higher management since 1990 (Horton, 1996). An arbitrary distinction can be made between higher civil servants working in agencies, whose primary function is the management of an executive activity, and those working in the 'core' departments who combine policy, management and other functions. More than 60 per cent were in agencies in 1995, with the rest in core departments. However, amongst the 775 top managers in the top three grades, operating at strategic level, only 99 were in agencies. The composition of senior grades is connected to the processes by which they are appointed. Chief executives in agencies are appointed on fixed contracts and are normally recruited by open competition to ensure that the best qualified person is appointed. Responsibility for selecting chief executives rests with the civil service Commission. Other posts in the SOS are not externally advertised and appointments are made on the advice of a Senior Appointments Selection Committee, and appointments have to be approved by the Head of the Home Civil Service and the Prime Minister. The civil service intends to extend time-limited contracts and open competition to all members of the top five grades in the SOS in 1996 (Cm 2627, 1994).

Human Resources Aspects

The single most important point of entry into the Open Structure, particularly for posts in the SCS, has traditionally been the junior generalist fast stream. Young graduates, generally with arts degrees, recruited to a career in the civil service, have been promoted into the highest grades. Between 1988 and 1993, nearly 60 per cent of the SCS entered by that route. Promotion prospects have slowed down with the contraction of the SCS and the trend towards external recruitment, which is likely to affect the attractiveness of the civil service as a career.

A further trend has been for the fast-stream entrants to leave the service. In 1993 the loss rate was approaching half by the age of 40. This 'pantouflage', similar to that in the French civil service, involves experienced civil servants moving out into other parts of the public sector and the private sector. There is now a much greater readiness to contemplate career change and not the same commitment to a lifelong career. In 1994, 46 per cent of the SCS stated they would leave for a better-paid job, if other terms and conditions were similar (Review Body on Senior Salaries, 1994).

The civil service is no longer a job for life. Less than half of the SCS now complete a 'full career', and the appointment of agency chief executives on limited-term contracts is likely to accelerate that trend. Of the first 100 chief executives appointed, 10 were military appointments, 90 were civilians and two-thirds were recruited by open competition. Of the 44 chief executives appointed at SCS level, 34 were filled by open competition and 10 went to external candidates (OPSS, 1994). Chief executives have a wide variety of backgrounds, including the civil service, the armed forces, local government, NHS and private sector, but only eight to date have been women. Although most appointees are still 'insiders' the number of 'outsiders' is rising.

The salaries and rewards of top public officials are determined by the Review Body on Senior Salaries (RBSS). The traditional system consisted of grades and incremental scales and automatic progression within a grade. Salaries were linked to external payments for comparable positions within the private sector but fixed at the top of the third quartile, on the grounds that civil servants were compensated by security of tenure and other benefits. Since 1988 changes in policy on top salaries have been linked to the creation of executive agencies, appointment of chief executives on short-term contracts, use of open competition to recruit to top jobs and introduction of performance-related pay (Horton, 1996). Salaries offered to external recruits to the top three grades have been 10 to 18 per cent higher than the equivalent civil service range. Additionally, chief executives have been paid performance bonuses of between 10 and 15 per cent of annual salary and generous terminating bonuses. The outcome was a differential of up to 25 per cent in the salaries of internally and externally appointed public managers.

These differences fostered discontent and led to substantial increases in the pay of all top civil servants in 1995. A new performance-based system has been installed and these developments are likely to lead to a growing convergence between the salaries of top public managers in the civil service, other public and private organizations. It is also likely to result in wider variations in top salaries and those of other managers.

Many of these changes in rewards reflect new criteria for appointment to posts. Most departments now have clear job and person specifications for managerial posts and well-developed career development strategies. Officials earmarked as 'high fliers' are now given experience in an agency. Identification of potential for promotion results from individual appraisals undertaken by line managers, although about one-third of departments now use assessment centres and panel interviews. Departments also have their own management development programmes. In the past, experience of policy and planning was given precedence. Today more emphasis is placed on managerial skills and competencies. The Oughton Report (1993) stated that the core values of probity, impartiality, intellectual rigour, frankness, independence, adaptability, energy and political awareness, combined with good oral and written communication skills, negotiating abilities and a thorough knowledge of governmental and parliamentary practices, were still required. However, policy advisers also need to have an in-depth expertise and understanding of the effects of government policies on clients and customers and their implications within the European Union. Additionally, top managers need finance and management skills, including budgeting, contracting, leadership and motivation skills. The Office of Public Service and Science (OPSS), with the help of the private consultants Price Waterhouse, identified a range of core competencies for those entering middle and strategic management posts (Oughton Report, 1993).

Responsibility for training civil servants rests with individual departments and agencies. They are free to provide internal training or use outside bodies, including the Civil Service College. The College is now self-financing and provides a full range of training programmes, open to public-sector organizations and companies. Set up in 1970, to emulate *L'Ecole Nationale d'Administration* in France, it never developed into a staff college, as it catered for both the élite administrative corps and specialists. Today it provides about 3 per cent of civil service training, with a throughput of over 8000 Open Structure civil servants a year.

Authority, Responsibility and Accountability

The civil service has no constitutional personality of its own; it is an embodiment of the Crown. There is no Civil Service Act or written constitution setting down the powers and status of the service. It is governed by the Royal Prerogative. The principles on which the civil service rest were established in the nineteenth century. They stated that civil servants were there to serve Ministers of the Crown, and their main functions were to advise on policy, prepare legislation and policy documentation and take responsibility, on behalf of ministers, for implementing, administering and controlling the work of departments. It was considered that this was best done by a politically neutral body of people, selected on merit through open competition to a career structure. Civil servants were accountable to a minister who was accountable to Parliament. The civil servant was anonymous and could not be 'named or blamed'. Decisions taken within departments were officially the decisions of the minister, who had to accept final responsibility.

With the growth of government, the principle of ministerial responsibility was partly undermined. By the 1960s it was widely accepted that at most the minister should be accountable to Parliament for the actions of officials, but only resign on grounds of moral culpability and not for the mistakes of officials. More open government in the 1970s and 1980s removed much of the anonymity of civil servants, who were increasingly named, spoke before the committees of the House of Commons and addressed public meetings. During the 1980s a number of incidents led to an open debate about the status of civil servants and their relationship to the government, Parliament and the public (Hennessey, 1990).

The management reforms of the 1980s led to further examination of the responsibility and accountability of civil servants, which are becoming increasingly unclear. Government and the Head of the Civil Service have argued that the Next Steps programme has left the traditional doctrine of ministerial accountability unaffected and there is now a clearer distinction between 'responsibility, which can be delegated, and accountability, which remains firmly with the Minister' (House of Commons, 1993, p ix). Others have argued that the creation of the new agencies with their quasi-contractual relationship with government departments has blurred responsibility and accountability and that the situation requires a formal contractual relationship identifying who is responsible and accountable for what (Massey, 1994).

For civil servants in policy advisory roles, the position is even less clear. There is the possibility of conflicts of interest between a civil servant's loyalty to an individual minister, government and Parliament. In the absence of a formal code of ethics, a civil servant's political neutrality can be compromised. If she or he disagrees with the actions of a minister on moral grounds, s/he has no recourse to an independent body and is considered bound to loyalty to the Government of the day. The First Division Association, the trade union of senior civil servants, has argued the case for a code of ethics and for an independent appeals procedure for civil servants. In 1995, on the recommendation of a select committee of the House of Commons, the Government produced a code summarizing the constitutional framework within which civil servants work and the values they are expected to uphold.

At present, the developments taking place in civil service management raise major issues for accountability and responsibility, in particular for the new managers in the agencies. Although they are still accountable to a minister, who in turn is responsible for their activities, in reality they are becoming directly answerable to the House of Commons and its select committees. As the accounting officers for their agencies, chief executives may be called to account before the Public Accounts Committee. They are required to submit an annual report and annual accounts to the House, on which they may be called to answer questions. And they are increasingly involved in replying to letters from MPs concerning the running of their organizations. Whilst this creates greater transparency and extends public accountability, it also politicizes the role of the new public manager and threatens the principles of political neutrality and independence.

Civil Service Managers and Politics

The British civil service is politically neutral. Although some political appointments are made to advisory positions, there is no ministerial 'cabinet' as in France. Further, civil servants, particularly those in higher echelons, are expected to refrain from political activity, including membership of political parties. Unlike their European counterparts, they are not able to participate in national and local politics as elected representatives and there are no civil servants in Parliament. The principle of appointment on merit, combined with a career service, has meant that senior public administrators in the past have not been political affiliates. Nevertheless, the fact that appointments to the top two levels of the SCS are subject to prime ministerial approval has laid them open to political influence.

During the 1980s, when almost all top posts changed hands and Prime Minister Margaret Thatcher took an active interest in appointments, there was talk of a politicization of the civil service. This was fuelled by the significant increases in the number of people brought in from industry. There was also some evidence that those sympathetic to the Government's drive for greater efficiency were considered 'one of us' by the Prime Minister (Richards, 1993). Although there is no evidence to support the claim that the civil service is moving towards the American 'spoils system', it is likely that people prepared to pursue enthusiastically the aims and objectives set for the new agencies are likely to be appointed. Although the majority of appointments are made by the Civil Service Commission, and still come from the service, the trend towards delegation of personnel responsibilities to agencies, and the move towards breaking up the national pay and grading system, opens up appointments to more political influence. This, however, is likely to be tempered by the parallel trend towards competency-based criteria for selection. The introduction of the new SCS in 1996, and the opening of these posts to competition and time-limited contracts, will be a radical change and will lay those public managers more open to political influence than in the past. At present, it is not possible to say whether the new public managers in the civil service are more or less politically neutral than their predecessors. Their role as the agents of change in the new public management, however, means there is a political identification with the policies of government and the new managerialism.

LOCAL GOVERNMENT

Each local authority is an independent legal entity employing its own staff. Although there are many common characteristics between public managers in both central and local government, there are sufficient differences between them to make a comparative study of both sectors worthwhile.

Local Government Managers

The traditional model of local government management has been dominated by professionalism and departmentalism. Local authorities are multi-purpose organizations, with each function having an appropriate department. Senior management positions are open to staff with appropriate qualifications. The execution of the local authorities' policies requires professional expertise from engineers, architects, surveyors, social workers, teachers and so on. These professions enjoyed considerable autonomy within each local authority.

In addition to the service-providing departments such as education or social services, two professions have had a particularly important role, namely law and accountancy. Lawyers have provided a range of legal and administrative support to the other departments in the office of the town clerk, who was designated as the senior official, with a variety of roles. Accountants played the key role in planning and controlling the finances of the authority, in a separate finance or treasurer's department.

The chief officer in each of these departments had a degree of discretion to manage his/her department, subject to the limitations placed on him/her by political accountability. The professionalism of these chief officers has been a source of power and influence, enabling them to shape policy as well as implementing it. Appointments are made to specific posts with both internal and external competition. Chief officers will probably have worked in three or more different local authorities during their careers. Jobs are not guaranteed for life, though in practice there has been a very high degree of job security.

The shift away from the traditional model towards that of the new public management has been taking place over 20 years, though the pace of change has accelerated since the Local Government Act 1988 which firmly established CCT for local services. The prevailing theme in the emergence of new public managers is the reduction of the power of the professional in the delivery of services. Professionals have been constrained by a growing emphasis on general management, the development of a customer orientation, external competition and the need for a more business-like approach.

In the 1970s, departmental autonomy of the professional chief officer was challenged by the ideas of corporate planning, which emphasized inter-departmental co-ordination. The Bains Report (1972) redefined the role of the town clerk, calling for the creation of a chief executive who would be a general manager responsible for overall policy and resource allocation. These posts were not to be the preserve of lawyers but opened up to all the professions and managers outside local government. Although lawyers continued to occupy approximately 50 per cent of these positions, there has been a noticeable increase in the number of accountants appointed as chief executives (Mills and Norton, 1990). This reflects the resource constraints placed on local authorities from the late 1970s.

The ideas of the New Right, with the promotion of the market as the most efficient allocator of resources, has produced profound changes in local government management. Local services have been privatized or opened up to CCT. Initially only manual occupations were affected but legislation in 1992 has brought a wide range of professional, technical and administrative work into this framework of competition, and in the view of some commentators may prove to be the lasting legacy of Thatcherism on local government (Williams, 1993). The jobs of public managers will therefore become increasingly open to competition from outside. The growing concern to develop a customer orientation, along with schemes of decentralization, are also widening the net of officials who might be considered as public managers.

The Conservative Government's belief in the inefficiency of the public sector and the desire to curb the corporate power of the professionals have driven some of these reforms. Conservative-controlled councils such as Wandsworth and Westminster were instrumental in influencing that thinking in the early 1980s (Ascher, 1987). Privatization and contractorization have been enthusiastically embraced on the right of the political spectrum, while innovatory approaches to the management of services can be found irrespective of party politics, ranging through neighbourhood decentralization schemes (Burns *et al.*, 1994) in urban authorities to organizational decentralization in rural ones (Holliday, 1991a and b). It is now becoming accepted that the role of the local authority as a provider of services is shifting to that of an 'enabling' role, in which the local authority co-ordinates and regulates the provision of services by other agencies. Local government monopoly provision is being replaced by a 'mixed economy of welfare', as social services are provided by a range of public, private and voluntary agencies.

All these developments are having a profound impact on the management of local government. A managerial revolution is taking place, albeit at a different pace in different authorities. The key features of Hood's model of the NPM are increasingly found in local government, with the emphasis on performance measures, output controls, competition and the break-up of traditional structures (Hood, 1991). Although it is difficult to estimate precisely the extent of the change across 500 local authorities, the authors of one survey conclude (Isaac-Henry and Painter, 1991, p. 86): 'What is now almost universally accepted are the arguments for a managerial ethos and culture, and therefore recognition of the importance of basing organisational practice on sound management principles.' The question of who constitutes a 'public manager' is not immediately obvious and, with current changes, contentious. However the focus of this chapter is on top managers, which embraces some 6500 chief officers (heads of department) and an additional 14 000 second- and third-tier officers, who are their deputies and major section leaders.

Human Resources Aspects

Top management posts are occupied by professionals. The extent to which they can be identified as public managers, rather than as public administrators or professional bureaucrats, depends on whether the nature of their jobs has changed, their own perceptions and whether there has been a change in personnel occupying these positions.

To understand the shifts taking place, it needs to be recognized that traditionally departments have been fiercely independent of one another, based on a distinct body of expertise and staffed by professionals. Chief officers are the senior line managers and members of the appropriate professional body. Typically, a surveyor's department is run by highway engineers and a planning department by town planners.

A distinction can be made between those departments delivering services to the public, like education, and those providing central support services to 'service delivery departments'. The main central support services are legal, personnel and finance services, as well as administrating the committee system. Typically, they were provided by the town clerk's and the treasurer's departments. From the 1970s, the power of the independent professional manager became constrained by that of the general manager. There was much opposition from the professionals (Haynes, 1980; Jennings, 1984) but some changes occurred, notably with the adoption of chief executives.

Chief executives, today, play a much more interventionist role in the management of the authority as a whole. They chair the management team of departmental chief officers, have responsibility for developing the strategic vision of the organization as well as having a role in resource allocation (Bains Report, 1972). Although chief executives have certain tasks which must be performed by law, there is no statutory requirement for a local authority to have such a post. In fact, the vast majority have chief executives who have been given significant scope to define their role. Survey evidence by Mills and Norton (1990) demonstrates that they perceive their role to be very different from that of the town clerk. The core of the job is to appoint other chief officers, lead the management team and appraise the performance of senior officers. They are responsible for giving policy advice to local politicians, developing strategic plans and translating political requirements into managerial action. Over 90 per cent see these tasks as 'essential', in contrast with the traditional tasks of the town clerk. Only 3.8 per cent thought secretarial work and 1.5 per cent that legal work was 'essential'.

Occupants of this senior management role are still more likely to be lawyers than any other profession, although the number of accountants is increasing. A small number have been recruited from outside local government, particularly from the higher civil service. Appointment to posts is by open competition, and local politicians play a dominant role in hiring and firing.

The chief officers of service delivery departments have also been experiencing considerable changes in their roles. The shift from direct service provision to the enabling role has required managers to develop skills in network co-ordination. Competition in the provision of services also requires ability to manage contracts and to develop a 'business orientation'. In those services already subject to CCT, departments have been split into purchasers and providers. In the first round of tendering in 1989, most of the 'provider' organizations were successful with their in-house bids. In the process they have had to transform their management structures and processes. Many new posts have been designated as 'business managers', at the head of 'business units', a development which fits in with current managerial orthodoxy in local government. Some authorities have split up large departments based on a single profession, by simultaneously breaking up their work into discrete units and creating broader directorates responsible for corporate strategy and policy, such as Cheshire County Council (Leach, Stewart and Walsh, 1994; Barlow and Harkin, 1996). Devolution of budgets and creation of cost centres have meant that many senior officers have taken on the characteristics of public managers.

The impact of these developments is profound. A clear split is emerging in a number of authorities between a core of strategic managers responsible for purchasing services in line with the values of the mission of the council, with a second cadre of managerially inclined, or entrepreneurial officers (Cochrane, 1994), competing to provide services. The creation of a commercial culture amongst the latter has been well documented in earlier work on the introduction of CCT (Walsh, 1991). The extension of CCT to white-collar services is likely to hasten the fragmentation of hierarchical professional bureaucracies even further, as internal markets develop. The use of 'service level agreements' is becoming more commonplace, as devolved budget holders strive to cost the services they provide.

Recruitment into senior posts is still very largely from local government, due to the nature of the professions in local government and the relative financial rewards offered in the public and private sectors. Teaching and social work, for example, are professions in which 90 per cent of all jobs are in local authorities. Similarly, clear distinctions have been made in the training of accountants for the public sector, as opposed to the private sector, so the two sectors have remained largely separate. In contrast, other professions, such as architecture and surveying, are more interchangeable and recruitment from the private sector is more likely, depending on the state of the labour market and recruitment opportunities in local government.

Although the Bains Report advocated recruitment to chief executive jobs from non-traditional, non-legal, non-local-government backgrounds, only a small minority have been recruited in this way. The language of advertisements is very exclusive and the pattern of rewards does not encourage applicants from the private sector. However, CCT is having an impact on the language of public-manager posts, with jobs being advertised as business managers, and this may attract more external applicants in the future. There is evidence that even if the financial rewards are satisfactory, there is a cultural gap with which many managers from the private sector cannot cope (Barlow and Harkin, 1996).

Grading and pay structures have traditionally been determined by national collective bargaining, so there is comparability across all local authorities. The pay of chief executives and chief officers is linked to the size of the authority, measured in terms of population. The pay of all other staff is fixed by the point on the grading structure to which they were appointed. An incremental scale point is awarded each year until the top of the grade is reached and a bar is placed on further increases, unless the employee is promoted. Increments for seniority can be withheld if performance is unsatisfactory, but in the majority of cases it is automatic. Thus pay has not been directly related to current performance. A small number of authorities have formally abandoned national pay bargaining, in favour of local deals (Joyce and McNulty, 1994), whilst others recognize that, in activities subject to competition, erosion of conditions of service may be necessary to survive.

Performance-related pay [PRP] is now being introduced in some authorities, as are short-term contracts for chief officers. Such arrangements are still the exception rather than the rule. A survey in 1990 estimated that 30 000 non-manual workers were on performance-related schemes, which represented 4 per cent of such workers. A more recent estimate is that over 25 per cent of local authorities now have PRP (LGMB, 1994). Areas of work which have been subjected to CCT provide the greatest scope for adopting a PRP element.

It follows from patterns of recruitment that career development is driven by the availability of promotional opportunities. There is no equivalent of the civil service promotions board which judges suitability for promotion. However, opportunities for public managers to develop their careers in a single authority are limited. There is a high degree of mobility from one authority to another, as ambitious managers seek promotion.

Training is the responsibility of each authority, and there are significant variations in the level and type of support for staff training. For the most part, the main thrust of training has been professional development, emphasizing 'on-the-job' training. Professional training has traditionally been at the expense of management training. That has changed over the last twenty years, as the number of graduates recruited with professional qualifications has increased. Such prospective managers are being increasingly supported to study for management qualifications at their local universities. The Master of Business Administration degree (MBA) is now growing in importance as an acceptable qualification for senior management. The possession of professional qualifications, however, is still very much the passport to senior positions in local government.

Evaluation of public managers is becoming more systematic and staff appraisal more common. A survey in 1987 reported that 27 per cent of local authorities had schemes, 34 per cent were considering them, but 39 per cent had neither schemes nor plans to introduce one. For 76 per cent of those with schemes, the main purpose was staff development, whilst 81 per cent quoted improved performance as a major reason (Fowler, 1988).

The public service orientation in local government is still very strong and remains largely underpinned by professional training and values

(Stewart, 1986). A public service ethos still dominates (Pratchett and Wingfield, 1994), though it is increasingly confronted with the challenge of a commercial ethos. Nevertheless, many District Service Organization (DSO) managers still support the traditional values of local government, whilst also arguing for sharper management (Barlow and Harkin, 1996). However, there has been a shift away from the requirements for specialist skills to those of the generalist manager. That shift has not been accompanied by a major influx of managers from the private sector.

Authority, Responsibility and Accountability

Any assessment of the roles, responsibilities and competencies of local government managers requires an understanding of the formal legal position of officers, and conventions governing their behaviour. The formal position is clear: officers carry out the policies of the council and the instructions of the council as directed. At the same time, specific areas of discretion are delegated to officers. Elected representatives are ultimately politically accountable for the decisions taken by the council. But local politicians operate on a part-time basis and cannot exercise the same supervision expected of a salaried minister.

As a consequence, senior public officials exercise considerable influence over policy formulation and implementation. There is an ambiguity surrounding their roles and a number of tensions in the way they perform their duties. A specific tension lies in the interface with politicians wishing to intervene in detailed implementation issues. This question has been raised by successive reports on local government management from Maud (1967) through to Widdicombe (1986). Paradoxically, most councillors are more interested in pursuing individual, constituency cases than in setting policy objectives, whilst senior officers prefer to get involved with broad policy and devolve detailed decisions to junior officers. The emphasis on political accountability has often precluded such delegation, thus inhibiting the development of managerial accountability.

As local politicians take on a strategic role, public managers are being given more responsibility to manage their department or function. The 'street level bureaucrat' thus becomes a central figure in the management of the local authority. Public managers are also being required to be more open and accessible to their customers. Many will be close to the local community they serve, where their offices are moved out into the neighbourhood or housing estate. Their performance will come increasingly under the microscope through, for example, the use of performance indicators required by the *Citizen's Charter*.

The requirement to set up purchaser and provider roles within departments has resulted in a clearer focus on cost, the need to develop business plans and make profits. Providers (contractors) have to ensure that they are competitive. Accountability for these groups of managers is defined in terms of the contract they are operating to. Purchasers (or clients) are responsible for setting the goals or purpose of a service and hence defining what needs to be delivered. Managing the contract by regulating the performance of the contractor requires a different mix of professional and managerial skills than was required when delivery of the service was central to the role of the senior manager. The purchaser must still remain accountable to local politicians. Relationships with local councillors on the provider side become more complex where the department's staff successfully compete for service provision. Ethically, there must be a clear division between provider and purchaser at both councillor and officer levels. Where the providers are the in-house DSOs, they will report to a board of councillors whose main concern is to monitor the performance of the DSO against the agreed business plan. Typically, they will not interfere in the day-to-day running of the DSO.

Emphasis on customers and competition has thrown into question traditional models of accountability. There are now a variety of stakeholders to whom the provider of the service is accountable. In education, for example, accountability to parents as consumers has been stressed, as well as accountability to government through the national curriculum and OFSTED (Office of Standards in Education). Local citizens are also stakeholders, though accountability to them has diminished as the role of the local education authority has been reduced.

It is certainly the case that the ethos in which local government managers operate has changed. The language used is very different, as business plans and mission statements have been grafted on to more traditional processes of budgeting and decision-making. However, there has not yet been a major sea-change in its personnel and the values held by them. When CCT begins to have an impact on white-collar professionals, the pace of change will certainly quicken.

Local Government Managers and Politics

Local government officers serve their council as a whole and are career bureaucrats who are politically neutral. They implement the policies of their council. Although senior managers are appointed by politicians, they are not seen as 'political appointments'. Appointments are made on the basis of professional qualifications and experience, not political affiliation or loyalties. In addition, local government officers have always been excluded from being elected to the council of their employing authority. However, developments in the organization of political parties have raised questions about the political neutrality of senior officers. Those concerns have been raised largely by the political right and have been directed at Labour-controlled authorities.

There was evidence in the 1980s of an increasing number of local officers becoming councillors in neighbouring authorities, notably in the London and Metropolitan Boroughs. Such 'twin-tracking' was thought to give rise to conflicts of interest and to destroy the notion of political neutrality. Since 1989 senior managers have been prevented by the Local Government and Housing Act from becoming councillors in other authorities.

In authorities where there is overall control by one political party, public managers work with the members of the majority party, acting as advisers to committee chairs and the party leadership. They may even attend the informal party group meetings prior to the formal council meetings to fulfil their advisory role effectively. In those authorities that are developing a clear emphasis on strategic management, leading politicians work closely with the chief executive, director of finance and other members of the management team.

The Conservative Government set up a review of the internal management of local authorities in 1991 (Department of the Environment, 1991), with a view to finding a more efficient alternative to the committee system as a means of decision-making. One option is the creation of a small group of paid politicians running the authority with the permanent officers. This Whitehall model, with a clear political executive and a council of back-benchers, would change the relationship between officers and councillors. The future is uncertain but is destined to change.

CONCLUSION

There is a general consensus that the old 'public administration' has given way to a 'new public management', throughout the down-sized public sector. A new culture, reflecting many of the values and attitudes associated with private-sector businesses, is replacing the administrative and professional cultures of the old bureaucracies and is being injected into public organizations. Public officials throughout central and local government now see themselves as managers, rather than as administrators. They have accepted and implemented the changes externally imposed upon them and in some instances have been prime movers of the changes. Dunleavy's (1994) bureau-shaping theory provides one explanation for this apparent collusion by senior civil servants with the deconstruction of state organizations. Others identify the vested interests of a new profession of management in the restructuring taking place (Clark, 1993). It is difficult to assess how far the new managers have internalized the new managerialist culture, but they have been the main agents of change, as well as one of the main beneficiaries. There is evidence that many of the chief executives of Next Steps agencies and NDPBs are enthusistic about their new status and would support further managerial autonomy, if not privatization (Massey, 1994 and 1995). There is also evidence that top managers in local government are responding positively to their new 'business' role (Barlow and Harkin, 1996).

A new cadre of new public managers is emerging but currently there are no biographic studies of them. Impressionistic observations suggest that there are differences between various segments of the public sector and between the private and the public sectors. There are, however, similarities. They are still predominantly white, male and middle-aged. Although most have emerged from traditional career structures in the civil service, NHS and local government, an increasing number are mobile across the public sector and between the public and the private sectors. As differences between managing public and private organizations are reduced, generic management education and training increases, rewards converge and barriers to mobility are fading. With the generic MBA becoming common currency for professional management, and core competencies and skills continuing to fashion job descriptions, the best person for the job could come from inside or outside the organization. To ensure that top posts can be filled internally a new public-sector MBA programme, aimed specifically, although not exclusively, at civil servants, was launched by the Civil Service College in 1995.

The movement of public-sector managers into the private sector will be a consequence of further privatization and contractorization. Although a change of government could slow down the contraction of the state and the residualization of its role, there is little evidence that there will be a strong backlash. Existing moves to reduce the state to its core activities, and to use the market as the main mechanism of social exchange, seem to have caught hold amongst public managers as well as politicians. The ideas of 'reinventing government' which have taken root in the USA, and are reflected in President Clinton's National Performance Review in 1993, have not found support amongst Conservative politicians or, it would appear, amongst their permanent advisers. Neither is there any indication that a Labour Government would seek to overturn the managerial revolution.

Although there are national variations in the forms that the new public management is taking, it is clearly an international trend. Combined with the proliferation of contractorization and the overlapping of public and private markets, it is likely that public managers of the future will be drawn from a wider labour market. The internationalization of the new public management and the globalization of public services production could, as Dunleavy (1994) suggests, lead to the dominance of an international management cadre located in monopolistic organizations servicing the state or providing public services directly to consumers

References

Ascher, K. (1987) *The Politics of Privatization: Contracting out Public Services*, London: Macmillan.

Audit Commission (1987) *Competitiveness and Contracting out of Local Authorities Services*, London: HMSO.

Bains Report (1972) *The New Local Authorities: Management and Structure*, London: HMSO.

Barlow, J. and Harkin, G. (1996) *Competition and Local Government*, Luton: Local Government Management Board.

Bennington, J. (1975) *Local Government Becomes Big Business*, Coventry Community Development Project Working Paper no. 7.

Brooke, R. (1989) *Managing The Enabling Local Authority*, Essex: Longman.

Burns, D., Hambleton, R. and Hoggett, P. (1994) *The Politics of Decentralization*, Basingstoke: Macmillan.

Cabinet Office (1994) *The Citizen's Charter: Second Report 1994*, London: HMSO.

Cochrane, A. (1994). 'Managing change in local government' in J. Clarke and A. Cochrane (eds) *Managing Social Policy*. London: Sage.

Clarke, M. and Stewart, J. (1988) *The Enabling Authority*, Luton: Local Government Training Board.

Clark, J. (1993) *A Crisis in Care?* London: Sage.

Cm 2627 (1994) *The Civil Service: Continuity and Change* (London: HMSO).

Collins, B. (1987) 'The Rayner scrutinies' in A. Harrison and J. Gretton (eds) *Reshaping Central Government*. Bristol: Policy Journals.

Department of the Environment (1991) *The Internal Management of Local Authorities in England: A Consultation Paper*, London: HMSO.

Department of Health (1992) *Health and Personal Social Services Statistics for England*, London: HMSO.

Dunleavy, P. (1989) 'The United Kingdom; paradoxes of an ungrounded statism' in F. Castles (ed.) *The Comparative History of Public Policy*, Cambridge: Polity.

Dunleavy, P. (1994) 'Globalization of public services production: can government be "best in world"?', *Public Policy and Administration*, 9 (2).

Eddison, T. (1973) *Local Government: Management and Corporate Planning*, Birmingham: INLOGOV.

Farnham, D. and Horton, S. (eds.) (1993) *Managing the New Public Services*, Basingstoke: Macmillan.

Fowler, A. (1988) *Human Resources Management in Local Government*, London: Longman and LGTB.

Fredman, S. and Morris, G. (1989) *The State as Employer*, London: Mansell.

Gray, C. (1994) *Government Beyond the Centre*, London: Macmillan.

Haynes, R. (1980) *Organization Theory and Local Government*, London: Allen & Unwin.

Hennessy, P. (1990) *Whitehall*, London: Secker & Warburg.

H. M. Treasury (1991) *A Guide for New Managers*, London: HMSO.

Holliday, I. (1991a) 'The conditions of local change: Kent County Council since re-organization, *Public Administration*, 69 (4).

Holliday, I. (1991b) 'The new surburban right in British local government – Conservative views of the local, *Local Government Studies*, 17 (6).

Hood, C. (1991) 'A public management for all seasons', *Public Administration*, 69 (1).

Horton, S. (1990). 'Local Government', in S. Savage and L. Robins (eds) *Public Policy under Thatcher*, London: Macmillan.

Horton, S. (1996) 'The Civil Service' in D. Farnham and S. Horton, *Managing People in the Public Services*, London: Macmillan.

House of Commons (1993) *Sixth Report of Treasury and Civil Service Committee. The Role of the Civil Service: Interim Report*, vol. 1, London: HMSO.

Hughes, A. (1994) 'Employment in the public and private sectors', *Economic Trends*, no. 495, January.

Ibbs Report (1988) *Improving Management in Government: The Next Steps*, London: HMSO.

Isaac-Henry, K. and Painter, C. (1991) 'The management challenge in local government: emerging themes and trends', *Local Government Studies*, May/June.

Jennings, R. (1984) *Going Corporate in Local Education Authorities*, Aldershot: Gower.

Johnson, N. (1990) *Reconstructing The Welfare State*, London: Harvester Wheatsheaf.

Joyce, P. and McNulty, T. (1994) *Local pay bargaining: a public sector response to the development of the contract state*, Paper presented at Employment Research Unit Annual Conference, Cardiff.

Laffin, M. (1986) *Professionalism and Policy: The Role of the Professions in the Central–Local Government Relationship*, Aldershot: Gower.

Leach, S., Stewart, J. and Walsh, K. (1994) *The Changing Organisation and Management of Local Government*, London: Macmillan.

Le Grand, J. and Bartlett, W. (1993) *Quasi-Markets and Social Policy*, London: Macmillan.

LGMB (1984) *Pay in Local Government*, Luton: LGMB.

Massey, A. (1994) *After Next Steps*, Report to Office of Public Service and Science, London.

Massey, A. (1995) *Public Bodies and Next Steps*, Report to HM Treasury and the Office of Public Service and Science, London.

Maud Report (1967) *The Management of Local Government*, London: HMSO.

Mills, L. and Norton, A. (1990) 'The local government executive: some new survey evidence', *Local Government Policy Making*, 17 (1).

OPSS (Office of Public Service and Science) (1994) *Next Steps Briefing Notes* (April) London: Cabinet Office.

Oughton Report (1993) *Career Management and Succession Planning Study*, London: Efficiency Unit/HMSO.

Pliatzky, L. (1980) *Report on Non-Departmental Public Bodies*, Cmnd 7797, London: HMSO.

Pollitt, C. (1993) *Managerialism and the Public Services*, Oxford: Blackwell.

Poole, K. (1978) *The Local Government Service*, London: Allen & Unwin.

Pratchett, L. and Wingfield, M. (1994) *The Public Service Ethos in Local Government*, London: ISCA.

Prime Minister's Office (1991) *The Citizen's Charter* London: HMSO.

Review Body on Senior Salaries (1994) *Report No.34: 16th Report on Senior Salaries*, Cm 2464, London: HMSO.

Rhodes, R. (1981) *Control and Power in Central–Local Relations*, Aldershot: Gower.

Rhodes, R. (1988) *Beyond Westminster and Whitehall: The Sub Central Governments of Britain*, London: Unwin Hyman.

Richards, D. (1993) *Appointments in the Higher Civil Service*. Papers on Government and Politics, University of Strathclyde.

Ridley, N. (1988) *The Local Right*, London: Centre for Policy Studies.

Rosenberg, D. (1989) *Accounting for Public Policy*, Manchester: Manchester University Press.

Starks, M. (1991) *Not for Profit Not for Sale*, Newbury: Policy Journals.

Stewart, J. (1971) *Management of Local Government: A Viewpoint*, London: Charles Knight.

Stewart, J. (1986) *The New Management of Local Government*, London: Allen & Unwin.

Stewart, J. (1988) *Understanding the Management of Local Government*, Essex: Longman.

Stoker, G. (1988) *The Politics of Local Government*, London: Macmillan.

Walsh, K. (1990) *Competition for Local Government Services*, London: HMSO.

Walsh, K. (1991) *Competitive Tendering for Local Authority Services: Initial Experiences*, London: HMSO.

Widdicombe Report (1986) *The Conduct of Local Authority Business*, Cmnd 9797, London: HMSO.

Williams, T. (1993) 'Local government role reversal in the new contract culture' in Bennett, R. (ed.), *Local Government in the New Europe*, London: Bellhaven.

6 Finland

Manzoor Alam and Markku Kiviniemi

Most governments in western Europe are transforming their societal roles in a substantial way. The prevailing concept of the basic state functions, the relationship between state and society and the overall steering and planning role of the state are changing. The function of public administration is also changing as a result of new political strategies by governments. Perry and Kraemer (1983), representatives of a 'generic school of management', introduced the term 'public management', which they defined as a new approach that has grown naturally from weaknesses in other prevailing educational philosophies. They describe 'public management' as a merger of the normative orientation of traditional public administration and the instrumental orientation of generic management. By 'normative orientation' Perry and Kraemer mean a concern with issues of democracy and accountability and values such as equity, consistency and equality. By the 'instrumental orientation' of generic management, they evidently mean that the public sector shares with business enterprises the aim of achieving its goals effectively and efficiently by developing coherent strategies, well-defined tactics, appropriate structures, motivated personnel and mastery of relevant managerial techniques for deploying and controlling the use of limited organizational resources (Gunn, 1987).

The environment of governmental actions is changing due to changes in the content of political issues and the extensive competition amongst societal groups and institutions for specific outputs of governmental actions. Thus, public management is a dynamic and strategic process of interpreting the environment, struggling over the political agenda and handling public bureaucracy in accordance with intended outcomes. In the field of public administration, the rise of NPM and new public managers is one of the most noticeable trends. It is linked with several other trends: slower growth; shifting services away from core government institutions to the private sector; contracting for in-service provision; promoting automation, particularly information technology, in the production and distribution of public services; and increasing focus on general issues of public management, policy design, decision styles and inter-governmental co-operation. (Dunsire and Hood, 1989; Dunleavy, 1985; Hood, 1991).

Recent tendencies point to new orientations in public management. It is becoming commonplace for public organizations to limit their activities and in many cases to leave traditional activities to private organizations (Alam, 1994). Public managers are expected to be more concerned about optimizing existing resources instead of securing growth, adjusting client expectations downwards, and breaking down vested interests which act as barriers to reprioritizing and reorganizing public services. These trends represent a general change in management orientations towards more concern about internal organizational issues combined with emphasizing clientele characteristics (Jorgensen, 1987).

To sum up, new trends in public management are taking place within a much tighter financial framework, with more emphasis being put on a critical review of the activities of government and the services provided. The questions arising include: What do services cost? Could they be provided more efficiently? Is it necessary to carry them out by public agencies? How is it possible to maximize results out of reduced resource investment?

THE PUBLIC SECTOR IN FINLAND

The Finnish public sector consists of ministries, central agencies, universities, regional and local agencies, services and public enterprises. Municipalities take care of the main part of local government and service provision including school education, social and health services. For historical reasons, central government agencies have been established within the state administration. These are relatively independent of ministries and each is responsible for a specific branch of administration nationwide. Each central government agency is subordinate to a ministry but the powers of the ministry are limited. Thus, for example, the Minister cannot override decisions by a central agency and individual matters cannot be transferred from a central agency to the general meeting of the Council of State.

From 1950 to 1990, the Finnish public sector expanded rapidly. The duties and powers of local government were extended and central government was strengthened by structural reforms (Kiviniemi, 1994). The growth of the public sector was accompanied by a growth in public expenditure as shown in Table 6.1. The Finnish economy experienced a severe recession in 1991, with more than a 6 per cent drop in GDP. Unemployment rose rapidly, whilst inflation slowed significantly, reflecting increased slack in both the labour and product markets.

Table 6.1 *Public expenditure as a percentage of Finnish GDP, 1970–94*

Year	Percentage of gross domestic product	
	(1)	(2)
1970	30.5	31.3
1980	36.6	39.0
1985	41.6	45.2
1990	41.2	46.8
1991	48.7	55.5
1992	52.0*	60.8
1993	50.0*	62.4*
1994	N/A	60.0*

SOURCE: The Budget Proposal of 1995, Ministry of Finance, Finland, 1994.
(1) According to the old National Accounting system in which the public sector excludes the legal security contributions of the employee pensions.
(2) According to the new National Accounting system in which the public sector includes the legal security contributions of the employee pensions.
* estimates.

Slower economic growth, increasing unemployment and financial problems in the public part of the economy led Finland to reassess the role of the public sector. Growing public expenditure, lower tax revenue and large budget deficits were considered to be distorting the allocation of national resources and restricting economic growth. Cutting back public expenditure and raising the efficiency of the public services were considered crucial. In comparison with other Nordic countries, the share of the public sector in the Finnish national economy has been low but it is higher than in many other European countries, Japan and the USA. The share was growing rapidly in the 1980s but, due to economic recession, a trend downwards has accelerated since 1990.

The Public Sector and its Recent Changes

Economic pressure linked with new demands on the state compelled the Finnish Government, like other European governments, to modernize its various institutions to increase their competitiveness and responsiveness to social and economic change. Two general approaches are evident: changes in organizational arrangements and changes in the internal and external functioning of the public sector. To achieve these, several operational programmes have been initiated to improve managerial performance. These include relaxing internal controls; sharing information among various branches of government organization; enhancing personnel competencies; improving client access to the administration; increasing the involvement of clients in the administrative process; greater use of contracting out and user charging; and creating market pressures by establishing new public enterprises.

From 1987, a special ministerial committee has had responsibility for administrative development and modernization. The operational execution of the reforms rests mainly with the Ministry of Finance and an Administrative Development Agency, acting under the Ministry of Finance. Major reforms have been implemented throughout the central ministries. In 1988, the Cabinet joined all major public sector organizations in a Service Declaration intended to change the bureaucratic culture into a modern service culture. It also adopted a blueprint for administrative reform which included 24 enumerated declarations of intent. This framework for administrative development was enlarged a year later when the Cabinet issued 33 enumerated declarations of intent (Ståhlberg, 1989). In 1992, the Cabinet decided on a public management reform programme, linked with a new project set up by the Government to investigate the tasks and structures of the central administration. In 1992, the report of the project proposed several major reforms including the decentralization of decision-making, the introduction of evaluative mechanisms for governmental administration and the abolition of central administrative boards.

The proposed reform programme for the central administration involved a single level central administration and a reduction in the number of central units subordinate to the ministries. The tasks of the ministries were to: (1) prepare regulations and budgets for the Parliament and the Cabinet; (2) be responsible for international co-operation; (3) be responsible for administrative decision-making in their respective fields; and (4) be responsible for management by results in their own branches. All remaining tasks should be delegated to other levels of administration. The implementation of these reform proposals has already started.

The reform project for the state regional administration, proposed in November 1992, involves a reduction of the regional administration by merging different sectoral units, and reducing the organizational networks at the regional level. The present government has decided upon a new division of the country into functional-economic provinces having powers of decision in regional planning and development.

All the reforms of the organizational structure and distribution of governmental authority are to be based on the 'front line policy' principle.

That is, decisions are to be made at the front line where services are provided and customers encountered. Service units should have the authority to determine the use of their resources including personnel, and to control their own operative methods. Government has taken several measures designed to reduce the costs of the public sector. Thus, proposals have been made to cut pension benefits within the public sector and to raise the general pension age. Several state agencies have been reorganized into public enterprises and some public enterprises have been transformed into joint-stock companies. One of the most important reforms of the present Government is the adoption of a new central government subsidy system to the municipalities. The new system cuts the links between local expenditure and central government grants and recognizes the independence and economic responsibility of the municipalities. Within the public sector, the introduction of 'frame' budgeting is changing the role of the Ministry of Finance from controlling the expenditure details of individual ministries and agencies to focusing more on overall spending levels and setting targets.

The number of people employed in the state sector is also falling. Excluding staff paid under various special employment programmes, the budgeted personnel figure declined by 2200, or 1.6 per cent, in 1991–92. The staff of the new public enterprises decreased by 4700 or 7.2 per cent over the same period. Also 9100 state employees were in jobs subsidized out of special employment funds in 1992, i.e. 3400 more than in 1989.

Reforms: Objectives, Principles and Priorities

Public sector management reform is considered to be one factor which may enable and support the process of readjusting the public sector to changing circumstances. It is believed that this can be facilitated by managerial innovations, focusing on performance, monitoring results, developing more efficient and effective organizational structures, and improving the public–private sector relationship. The main driving force behind the reforms is the need to adjust the public sector to the demands of economic development. Public sector borrowing and rising tax rates are impeding economic restructuring. Drastic measures are needed to restrain further rises in public spending. Growing unemployment, increasing pressure to support growth in the corporate sector, and the need to eliminate administrative barriers to new forms of industry, only heighten the need to achieve immediate savings in public spending. The Government's 'saving' measures are aimed primarily at internal functions of the administration, and only secondarily at services to individuals and private corporations (Ministry of Finance, 1992).

The public management reforms are designed to encourage an increase in overall productivity and social development. Cost-cutting is not the only goal of the reform process. The aim is to produce services economically and thus to offer better value for money to taxpayers and customers. Another aim is to raise the productivity of both labour and capital. Thus it is vitally important to assess the system of public subsidies and supports in terms of performance. The public management reform programme seeks to raise quality and productivity at every level of government. The structural reforms will provide the preconditions for better management in individual agencies and units. A further important reform objective is to introduce a results-oriented or performance-oriented management system into government administration. Public management-by-results is regarded as a means by which value for money can be optimized by those responsible for the results. The present reforms are being carried out by every agency and ministry. It is the responsibility of central management agencies to ensure that expert assistance is available to the ministries and agencies to carry out the reform process.

THE NEW PUBLIC MANAGERS

The Organizational Framework

In Finland, there are three main types of organization where most of the new public managers are located:

- result-budgeted agencies and net-budgeted agencies;
- institutions with business action plans and public enterprises;
- state-owned companies.

These may be subdivided again, according to their legal status, into public entities, i.e. organizations with a strong public-law status, and other statutory entities, i.e. organizations under special legislation and having a 'semi-public' status.

There are other typologies, such as that of 'independent statutory agencies', 'statutory organizations', and 'statutory companies', which are recognized not only in legal theory but also in legislation, such as the Law 598 (1982), which regulates administrative procedures. The dividing lines between these categories are not very clear. The exact boundaries between para-government organizations, central and local 'core' government administrations and the private sector are not easy to draw (Rosas and Suksi, 1988). State-owned companies also are difficult to categorize, since most of them operate under private law on a commercial basis, without any specified public function.

On the basis of our empirical findings, we have identified 134 organizations in which 'new public managers' are located. These are result-budgeted agencies, net-budgeted agencies, institutions with business action plans, public enterprises and state-owned companies. These 134 bodies listed in the Appendix are subordinate to government ministries. Most of the recently reformed organizations are in the fields of industry and trade, communications, training and public utilities. There are also areas which have experienced little reform, including education, science and culture, and defence. Table 6.2 presents the overall picture in terms of the number of agencies and bodies at the central government level.

The change process in the Finnish public sector has been comparatively rapid. There is a clear trend to reform 'basic agencies' into 'result-budgeted agencies' or 'net-budgeted agencies'; and 'result-budgeted agencies' into 'net-budgeted agencies' or 'public enterprises'. The budget-

Table 6.2   *The number of agencies and bodies at central government level in Finland, classified by budget techniques, 1989–93*

	1989	1990	1991	1992	1993
Total budgeted agencies and bodies	201	213	193	189	188
Basic agencies (not net result-budgeted)	186	199	174	129	87
Result-budgeted agencies		4	12	54	69
Net-budgeted agencies					26
Institutions with business action plans and budget financing	15	10	7	6	6
Public enterprises	3	6	7	7	5
Central government total	204	219	200	196	193
State-owned companies	26	28	27	26	28
Privatized enterprises					1

SOURCE: Personnel Department, Statistical Unit, Ministry of Finance, unpublished statistical reports, 1994.

financed institutions, with business action plans, are being transformed more and more into 'net-budgeted agencies' and 'public enterprises'. Whilst the reform process is continuing, the number of new public managers in Finland is changing all the time. The leading public managers in the result-budgeted agencies, and budget-financed institutions with business action plans clearly fulfil the criteria of the new public manager. The leading public managers in the net-budgeted agencies, public enterprises and state-owned companies are also definitely within the circle of new public managers.

Age, Sex and Educational Backgrounds of the New Public Managers

Three levels of officials in the 134 identified public organizations belong to the group of new public managers. The three levels are Director General (level I), Director (level II), and Department Head (level III). Table 6.3 shows that the new public managers at all three levels are mostly male, although the percentage of female managers increases in the lower levels, where it is over 25 per cent. In terms of academic backgrounds, the analysis shows the strong presence of law graduates at all levels although almost one third of new public managers have degrees in the social sciences. The third subgroup are managers with technical education whilst the educational background of managers at levels I and II is quite diverse. Table 6.3 indicates that future public managers will probably be dominated by graduates in law and the social sciences.

Figure 6.1 elaborates on the distribution of public managers according to age, compared with the total number of personnel in the central government in 1993. The largest group of new public managers are in the 45–49 age range.

Table 6.3   *Age, sex and educational background of three levels of new public managers in Finland, 1993*

Level of position	Average age (years)	Sex		Education			
		Male (%)	Female (%)	Law (%)	Soc. sci. (%)	Tech. (%)	Others (%)
Level I	53	95.7	4.3	25	23.3	23.3	28.3
Level II	53	88.1	11.9	combined analysis with level I			
Level III	47	72.2	27.8	50.5	32.6	9.5	7.4

SOURCE: Personnel Department, Statistical Unit, Ministry of Finance.

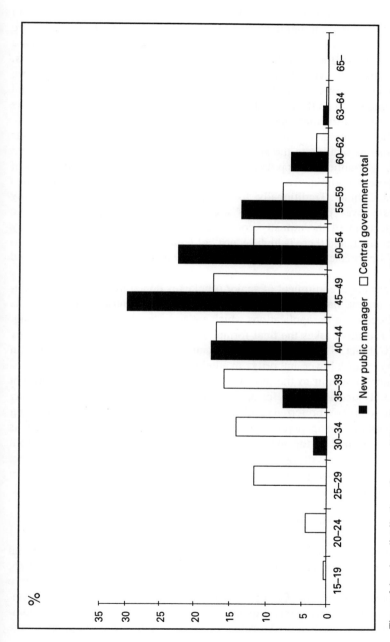

Figure 6.1 Age distribution of new public managers in Finland compared with total personnel in central government, 1993

The legal status of the new public manager is changing as the reform process gains momentum. Traditionally, public administrators were recruited for life-time employment. Most of the new public managers are drawn from these earlier recruits, and enjoy the traditional status. Recently, however, the contract-basis of recruitment is becoming more general for new recruits. Contracts are for fixed terms of appointment and are renewable on the basis of the requirements of the organization and the efficiency of the manager concerned.

The particular features of the Finnish constitution are reflected in its provisions relating to the appointments of top officials. It is the President of the Republic who appoints most senior public servants. The majority of these senior administrative officials are appointed on the recommendations of the Cabinet. Traditionally, following the rules of the constitution, many middle-level public managers are appointed by the Cabinet on the suggestions of the ministry concerned. Appointment to office is usually permanent, and there is high security of tenure. Today, however, the traditional permanent job system is moving towards the fixed-term contracted job.

Formally, recruitment of senior officials is done through open competition on the basis of merit and qualifications. Generally, a position is declared open for applications which are considered by a Cabinet meeting. The President takes the final formal decision, after a recommendation by the Cabinet. There are some important exceptions to this procedure. In many cases a lower authority, an administrative agency, selects three candidates to submit to the ministry. In some other cases, positions are not formally declared open for application and the appointing authority may try to identify a preferred candidate for the position. Today, the appointing authority in the agencies, with the exception of the top public managers, is mostly vested in top management; which is authorized to recruit from inside or outside of the organization according to the demands of the job. In effect the new public managers are as free as private managers are in recruiting their staff.

Careers and Mobility

All public managers in Finnish agencies of the state are bound by a special body of law and regulations including the State Civil Servants Act (1986, partially changed in 1992 and reformed in 1994) and the Collective Agreements for State Civil Servants Act (1970). Article 86 of the constitution states that the general qualifications for promotion are 'ability, competence and verified civil virtue'. The judicial interpretation, given by the

Attorney General in 1971, stated that the appointing authority has discretionary powers to deliberate how general qualifications are weighted against each other in making appointments (Volanen, 1983). There is no automatic promotion system in Finland. In principle, every vacant post should be advertised and applications should be invited. However, under special provisions issued by Act or decree, a public office may be filled without inviting applications. This is generally the case in public enterprises and companies. Traditionally, individual institutions provided career patterns for officials. There was a lifelong career system, typically within one administrative branch. An internal and closed labour market existed and there was little exchange of personnel with the private sector.

Since the mid-1980s, the closed mobility system has been exposed to pressure from the market as the demand for special groups of professionals has increased. The gap between wages in the state and the private sector has widened and the closed internal labour market has gradually become more open. This was legitimized by the governmental reform programmes for the public sector, where demands for deregulation and market-oriented ideas contributed to reducing the differences between the public and private sectors.

In Finland, the numbers of relocations and job changes have increased during the 1990s, due to downsizing and decentralization of administrative units, mergers of public agencies, the establishment of new companies and public enterprises, rationalization and the use of new technologies. However, the internal and external mobility of public managers in Finland is still low, compared with many other European countries. In the 1990s, the mobility issue has become one of the priorities of the present reform process. Senior public officials are now encouraged to participate in different forms of mobility (Ministry of Finance, 1991). Every ministry has its own mobility policy. In principle, an official seeking to move has several possibilities:

- Secondment allows officials to be released from their original corps, whilst maintaining the rights enjoyed in that public office. Their salaries are paid by the new offices to which they are seconded. Secondment allows officials to move to other central government units, public bodies, state agencies and international organizations.
- Leave of absence allows officials to take posts outside their original organization whilst retaining the right to return to their original post.
- Temporary transfers are a means of providing temporary assistance to a unit which needs specialists, but officials continue to draw their normal salary.

Training and Development

In order to support the reform process, the Ministry of Finance has initiated two top-level strategic management training programmes for 500 top managers from ministries, agencies and other public and private institutions. The first programme is called The 'National Development Strategy'. Its target group is 150 executives. The main topics are strategic and corporate management, management of human resources and management of change. One week of the programme takes place in Central Europe and deals with internationalization. The second new training programme, called the 'Strategic Management Programme', is planned for top- and second-level public managers from the ministries, national boards and public agencies, about 400 managers in total. Participants from the private sector are also invited. The special focus of the programme is to develop strategic and corporate management in the context of a functional ministry and between the ministries, national boards and agencies. European integration and experiences in public sector reform are the main topics of the overseas one-week course. This programme started in 1992.

Two other new programmes have also been initiated. The first is for personnel managers with strategic responsibilities. Its aim is to support the growing independence and power of ministries and agencies to decide upon their own personnel policies and resource allocation. The second is designed to support the development of new budgeting, accounting and financial steering procedures. The Diploma Programme in Management Studies is a new type of postgraduate diploma launched in 1991. It was designed by the public sector training institutions, three universities and the main trade unions. It comprises 40 weeks of studies on different topics including professional studies, management studies, skills development, cultural studies, and a development assignment. The Administrative Development Agency, which was reorganized into the Finnish Institute of Public Management in 1995 and which offers these programmes, is the central training institute for the new public managers, although public agencies are free to buy training services from other suppliers.

Remuneration

According to the traditional State Civil Service Act (1986, and before), a public office had to be established by decree. The decree should state the name of the office and the salary category or other basis of the determination of salary. From 1992, public offices are established by decisions of agencies within the limits of annual budgets. A public office may be established with a fixed salary or a contractual one. Placement on salary grades and pay scales is reviewed generally in collective agreements between the negotiating authorities and the associations of public officials. However, salaries, for the majority of new public managers, are determined by the Ministry of Finance.

Research indicates that the average salaries of senior managers in the private sector are about 36 per cent higher than the average salaries of the top-level management in the public sector. The average salary of a senior public manager is about 33 000 FIM or £4800 per month (1995), whereas the corresponding salary in the private sector is about 45 000 FIM or £6600. On the other hand, holiday benefits and pension benefits are generally better for public managers than for private managers.

The cost-of-living bonus is approximately 4 to 5 per cent of the basic salary of public managers. There is also a maximum of six seniority bonuses and their total effect is to provide about 25 per cent in addition to basic salaries and local bonuses. Traditionally, incentive wages or bonuses are not offered in Finland. Recently, however, systems of 'result bonuses' or performance bonuses have been introduced in some agencies and public enterprises. Office working hours are 36.25 hours per week in the state administration. Vacations are determined according to general principles that state officials receive between 36 and 45 weekdays per year. The distribution of the earnings of new public managers, in the top three managerial levels in 1993, is outlined in Figure 6.2.

Retirement age and pensionable age are decided according to the same principles for all state officials, i.e. at 65 or 63 years. A full pension is 66 per cent of the average salary of the five latest years in service, which is the basis of the pension, and presupposes 30 years in service. Furthermore, there is pension security based on the State Pension Act (280/1966) and the Supervisor's Pension Act for the State (774/1968) and rules and regulations in connection with these.

Personnel Policy

The personnel policy and management of public officials is undergoing reform too, to adapt to changing conditions. The new policy is allowing the authorities more independence and flexibility as employers. It is transferring authority for personnel management and responsibility for labour costs to the agencies and institutions, including the authority to create, abolish and change posts. The public personnel system in Finland is a mixture of centralized and decentralized elements. Traditionally, wage and salary policy has been quite centralized, although demands for greater

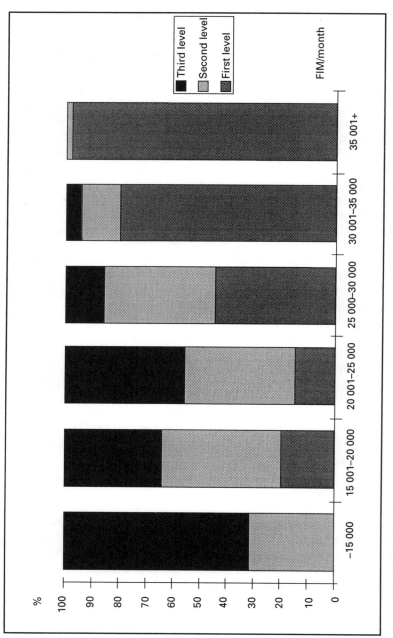

Figure 6.2   Distribution of earnings of new public managers in Finland in the top three management levels, 1993

flexibility and differentiation in wages and salaries are gaining ground. Individual ministries and agencies are now exercising more autonomy in recruitment and non-pay personnel issues. Today, personnel policy is seen as a means towards efficient, executive management. The trend is towards devolution and freedom from central authority. The career system, wages and salary system, co-determination policy and recruitment policy are being used as the basic instruments of personnel policy to create the new public management.

The Ministry of Finance still determines general personnel policy and oversees personnel management of state employees. It has set up different projects for reforming personnel policy, including the Management Development Project, the Personnel Development Project, the Good Working Community and Working Environment Project, the employment relationship system reform, and the reform of the state employer's salary and wage policy. Projects are based on the policy decisions of the central government. The 1991 White Paper on personnel policy development included the following commitments:

- introduction of a new pay-system based on staff qualifications, duties, personal factors and achieved results;
- decentralization of the bargaining system;
- better management development and management structure;
- better in-service training;
- improvement of recruitment;
- better quality of working life;
- continued decentralization of personnel management;
- development of the role and functions of personnel departments.

Personnel participation in the activities of the administrative and executive bodies of agencies and institutions is codified by the law requiring personnel representation in the management of companies (725/1990) and the co-operation law for companies (1195/1990) whilst observing the specific functional needs and the model of management of the administrative body in question.

Systematic evaluation criteria for new public managers are still to be developed in Finland. However, the financial accountability of the new public managers and performance appraisal through the result-budget and net-budget mechanisms are indicators of performance evaluation for managers. Each public manager has to submit an annual report of agency performance to the respective ministry. The ministry may evaluate the functioning of the public managers on the basis of agency performance.

AUTHORITY, RESPONSIBILITIES AND ACCOUNTABILITY

Each agency's branch of operation is defined in law. There are specific laws for each public enterprise which define the general framework of its operation, such as why it exists and what its main tasks are. Recent changes in the budget and budgetary system form the basic framework which defines financial autonomy. These changes have included the introduction of result agreements between ministries and agencies. These 'contracts' are more flexible than the traditional documents which defined the limits of autonomy of public managers. The core of result agreements is oriented towards the concrete output of agencies, i.e. what results should be achieved.

In practice, each ministry and agency makes a contract about the results to be achieved. Then there are control processes and follow-up discussions between ministry and agency. The exact method of interaction is not determined, and it is up to each ministry and agency to agree how they do it. When the agreement is made, the leading public manager starts a similar results-oriented process with different units within the agency. Each unit manager is then responsible for achieving his/her specified results. In general:

- Agreement documents between ministries and agencies are not very formal in nature. The working document is generally made at the beginning of the year and is mainly limited to the coming year.
- Accountability is often a problem. To improve things there is a development programme of the accounting system. The aim of the programme is to develop operating accounting systems in each agency, similar to private-sector accounting systems.
- According to these new accounting requirements, each agency has to produce an annual results report. Ministries are supposed to evaluate the result reports very carefully and draw conclusions on which to base measures for the next year. These reports are public documents.
- The board of an agency and the ministry are interconnected, as the chairman of the board often has responsibilities in the ministry, thus playing a linking role.
- The annual budget gives the limits of the resources available to public managers. Their target is defined within the budget framework. The ministry is expected to give guidelines of a strategic nature.

In the matter of accountability, the new public manager is responsible for achieving agreed results and making oral or written reports to the board of the agency. Results are generally based on both economic and operational measures. The results report is not decided by the board but the chair and board members provide suggestions and advice to the leading public manager on the basis of mutual discussions.

New public managers have greater control over the means and instruments of their organization than traditional public administrators. They have greater possibilities for choosing between different courses of action. They enjoy freedom to decide on any matter relating to the internal functioning of the organization, for example material investment, reorganization, recruitment and delegation of power. Public managers may also choose different issues for discussion at board level. The changes in the budget and budgetary system are frameworks defining the financial autonomy of the new public managers. Budgetary reform has put all the operative funds in one lump sum, and in practice agency managers have a great deal of freedom in using the operative fund, with the exception of transfers. In 1995 quotas relating to numbers of staff were abolished.

New public managers now have a large degree of freedom and control over the information system of their agencies and they can shape and develop the internal information system according to their own requirements. In sum, the results-budget and net-budget systems provide more flexibililily to the new managers in all financial matters.

THE ROLE AND ACCOUNTABILITY OF PUBLIC MANAGERS IN POLICY-MAKING

The role of public managers in the policy-making process is quite direct. Usually an agency is divided into accountable units, which are headed by results-unit managers. During the policy-making process, all unit managers may participate actively in the overall policy-making process of the agency where unit managers are also responsible for achieving the target results of the accepted policy. New public managers can decide how much they produce, how they produce it or to whom they sell, but the basic requirements remain defined in law. In the case of public enterprises, when the ministry wants to influence it has to buy services from the enterprise. In the case of state agencies, the links to the policy process are often tight, and in practice there is much daily discussion and agency heads are frequently consulted. They are involved in working groups which plan policy changes or changes in the resource system.

Public managers are becoming more active in the national policy-making process in the form of designing target proposals. On the other hand, different ministries are becoming more reluctant to give instructions. Instead, they are encouraging agencies to achieve the proposed targets. Ministries are becoming more aware of the need to harmonize the policy-making process and to use agency capabilities in policy preparation. Generally each agency and enterprise is accountable to a ministry. However, there is a distinction between the agencies and enterprises concerning the instruments of accountability. Each agency is accountable to a ministry for defined budget results and future budget allocation depends on previous performance. On the other hand, public enterprises are not subject to budgetary control and they perform according to market principles. Their accountability is based on an economic accounting system and the budget indicates or sets the required profit they have to produce.

Public managers and their agencies are accountable to public bodies at various levels. First, they are accountable to their respective ministries and they have to submit a yearly report, which is available to the people and the press. Second, public managers are accountable to the State Revision Board and Parliamentary Revision Board. There is also a Chief Prosecutor General with the power to investigate individual complaints against the performance of any agency or public manager. Third, public managers and agencies are also accountable to the parliamentary Ombudsman whose role is to safeguard citizen rights.

THE CHANGING ROLE OF NEW PUBLIC MANAGERS

The traditional public administrator's role was determined on the basis of a formal power structure and articulated by the legal framework. On the other hand, the new public managers operate within a broad social network and often act at the informal level. The role of the new public manager differs considerably from that of the traditional public administrator. The former are expected to work in many respects like managers of private corporations. They have to monitor incomes and costs and their responsibility is to organize the unit in a cost-effective way. The new public manager has a comprehensive responsibility for the management of his/her unit.

The fundamental difference between the role of the new public manager and the private manager lies in their focus of interest. The main focus of a private enterprise is to make profits. Instead, new public managers have to consider the national interest, whilst simultaneously making the agency more economic or even profit-oriented. The means of achieving these targets do not generally contradict each other. Thus, the role of new public managers has been converging towards the role of private managers. Parliament is playing a crucial role in the reorganization and power authorization of public agencies and public companies. Correspondingly, the market situation generally determines the activity context and role of the private manager. Due to their changing role, the new public managers have to carry the ethical responsibility for economic efficiency, better performance and service orientation. They now have more managerial responsibility to run their agencies efficiently and effectively. This raises ethical requirements in:

- personal responsibilities in agency functioning;
- proper use of scarce national resources;
- risk-taking in relation to personnel and finance;
- client service;
- market orientation.

RELATIONS BETWEEN NEW PUBLIC MANAGERS AND POLITICS

The new trend of public management by results in Finland does not mean a transfer of authority over essential matters from politicians to civil servants. Rather, it is a new division of authority and responsibility between the two. The tendency is to build up an operating model based on professional management within public administration, instead of the conventional bureaucratic system. Both political decision-makers and civil servants are responsible to the customers of the system. Politicians are responsible for defining the content of public policy and civil servants for carrying it out. All the changes are taking place within the legal framework and political responsibility provided by the constitution. New public managers bear professional responsibility as experts and for taking care that public administration produces the politically required results as effectively and economically as possible.

New Public Managers and Politics

It is very difficult to assess to what extent political leadership and public management are functionally integrated, thus enabling the politico–administrative system to work effectively without personal tensions. The politics–administration dichotomy is intellectually rooted in the doctrine of separation of powers as a system of political checks and balances, in which the executive branch draws its legitimacy from parliament. Despite the professionalization of politicians, the career paths of both groups have remained quite distinct. This distinction includes a predictable career and job security in the managerial case and more 'entrepreneurial', competitive, uncertain careers and transitory maintenance of top positions in the case of politicians. In Finland, the horizontal career mobility between the realms of politics and administration allows the political recruitment of public servants as a civil right and even permits running for election while formally in office.

Today it is not only top civil servants who are involved in internal vertical communication with politicians. The frequency of external contacts among different ministries, parliamentary bodies and interest groups is also increasing. The arena of policy-making also changes in accordance with the hierarchy. Where ministerial units communicate with other departments or with subordinate authorities and exchange information, public managers are more likely to be engaged in consultation and in securing ministerial or governmental support. The mechanism for shifting controversial issues up the hierarchy also serves politically to control lower-level co-ordination and transport consensus-building to upper hierarchical levels, which are in a better political position to bargain.

The Appointment of New Public Managers

Since there are constitutional rules for recruitment and promotion within the public service, political appointments have been defined as appointments in which party political merits supersede constitutional criteria for recruitment and promotion. In an empirical assessment of political appointments, Ståhlberg (1986) argued that political appointments are relatively common within general administration and welfare administration. The share of political appointments is less than half within the economic and infrastructure sectors. Ståhlberg also concludes that political appointments are much more common within ministries than within other state agencies.

Internal recruitment in Finnish public administration has been increasing and it is somewhat higher for political than non-political appointees within general and welfare administration. For economic and infrastructure administration, non-political internal appointments are more general. Since 1965, the share of public officials among the members of different work groups within the major political parties has increased and public officials have greatly increased their influence within party organizations and, through this channel, on permanent appointments (Ståhlberg, 1986). However, during the last few years party leaders have been criticizing the increased influence of public officials within the parties, indicating that party influence has not been promoting party ideologies. It has been argued that political recruits to various senior posts eventually lose their original interest in politics and become more interested in professional specialization. Today, the new public managers are recruited mostly on the basis of their professional capabilities, not for their political affiliations.

The Culture and Networks of Politicians and Public Managers

In general, Finnish public managers and politicians belong to the same culture and social networks, but there are some dissimilarities. For example, the educational background of the new public managers is a more important social factor than their political relations. The typical education of public managers suggests that the politico-administrative culture is being modified by business culture whilst there is also a strong legal culture in the higher echelons of central government.

Typically, career patterns support the claim that Finnish public managers spend their career in a plural administrative culture. The common picture of 'administrative culture' is a mixture of political values, professional knowledge and traditional organizational procedures. Government agencies, public enterprises and public companies are characterized as a plural managerial career pattern which tends to produce a hybrid culture. Outside the organization, managers are members of different social networks. Both formal and informal structures are important for the functioning of public managers. Many, if not all, public managers are directly or indirectly linked with the political parties, and thus the network of the 'political culture'. Many public managers are the products of political recruitment in the 1960s and 1970s. Many of the new public managers have had distinguished careers in the advisory organs of the state which range from intra-administrative to 'corporatist'. In the latter case this combines participation in both social and political decision-making (Ahonen, 1989).

According to Helander (1983), the development of a unified political élite culture in the 1970s took place at three different levels: unification of party élites; unification of party élites and interest groups; and unification of these élites with the élites of the government bureaucracy. The main ingredient of unification of the élite culture, according to Helander, has been the idea of reaching consensus in the most important economic decisions. Collaboration of different élite groups, through consensus, has brought about a unified élite culture with shared beliefs, language and game rules.

The new public managers are working in very different types of organizations, dealing with different kind of phenomena. There is a strong trend for the new public managers to move from an administrative culture, or the traditional bureaucratic culture, towards an organizational culture or new business-oriented enterprise culture. At the same time, as an external factor in the societal environment of organizations, there is still the broader whole of 'national culture' (Kiviniemi, 1994).

CONCLUSION

It would be a misconception to see the development of new public management simply as a product of the reorganization process and the influence of new thinking on the efficiency of government. These forces are undoubtedly important beside the wider influence of political and managerial stimuli in precipitating change. To emphasize only the latter would neglect important internal pressures on the administrative system throughout the 1980s and 1990s. There was a change of emphasis linked closely to the growing involvement of external advisers and management consultants in departmental operations. The new views on departmental financial management were reinforced by the economic climate and attempts by the administrative centre to cope with the public expenditure crisis. It has been observed that the results-budget and net-budget systems have introduced and institutionalized a change of emphasis in public management. The primary responsibilities of managers no longer lie exclusively in the management of policy but a similar weight is now given to the management of resources. This has included a notable advance in cost awareness and procedures associated with public resource management. The change of emphasis has also enhanced the role of economic rationality in the management services. Nevertheless, there have been difficulties. Conflicts of objectives, such as financial versus holistic management, have meant that implementation has not always resulted in identifiable improvements among lower-level managers. However, the technical and organizational demands of implementing management change meet fewer obstacles than the need to change the political preconditions for managerial success. This necessitates creating a coherent politics for the new public management.

References

Ahonen, Pertti (1989) *Valtion Liiketoiminta, hallinnon teoriat ja finanssihallinto*, Helskinki: Åbo Academy Press.

Alam, Manzoor (1994) *Public Sector Performance: Perception versus Reality*, Hallinto-extra, Helsinki: Administrative Development Agency.

Dunleavy, P.J. (1985) 'Bureaucrats, budgets and the growth of the state', *British Journal of Political Science*, 15.

Dunsire, A. and Hood, C. (1989) *Cutback Management in Public Bureaucracies*, Cambridge: Cambridge University Press.

Helander, V. (1983) 'Changing patterns of political culture and changing patterns of interest articulation: Finland in the sixties and seventies' in Voitto Halender and Dag Anckar (eds) *Consultation and Political Culture: Essays on the Case of Finland*, Societas Scientiarum Fennica, Commentationes Scientiarum Socialium, 19, pp. 159–162.

Hood, C. (1991) 'A public management for all seasons?', *Public Administration*, 69.

Jorgensen, Torben Beck (1987) 'Financial management in the public sector', in J. Kooiman and K. Eliassen (eds) *Managing Public Organizations: Lessons from Contemporary European Experience*, London: Sage.

Kiviniemi, M. (1994) *Perspectives on Structure, Culture and Action: Studies in the Public Administration of the Welfare State*, Helsinki: Administrative Development Agency.

Gunn, L. (1987) 'Perspectives on public management', in J. Kooiman and K. Eliassen (eds) *Managing Public Organization*, London: Sage.

Ministry of Finance (1991) *Kiertoon, Henkilökierto-opas*, Helsinki.

Ministry of Finance (1992) *Public Sector Management Reform: Government Decision on Public Sector Management Reform*, Helsinki.

Ministry of Finance (1994) *The Budget Proposal of 1995*, Helsinki.

Perry, J.L. and Kraemer, K.L. (eds) (1983) *Public Management: Public and Private Perspectives*, Cal: Mayfield.

Rosas, A. and Suksi, M. (1988) 'PGOs in Finland' in C. Hood and G. Schuppert (eds) *Delivering Public Services in Western Europe*, London: Sage.

Ståhlberg, Krister (1986) '*The politicization of recruitment to central public administration in Finland*', *Särtryck ur Statsvetenskaplig Tidskrift*, 3: 159–67.

Ståhlberg, Krister (1989) *The Pursuit of an Administrative Policy: A Survey of Finnish Governmental Commissions on Administration*, 1975–87, Helsinki: Åbo Academy, 2.

Volanen, Risto (1983) 'Report on recruitment for the highest offices in Finland' in Tore Modeen *Recruiting for High Offices in the Central Administration*, Brussels: International Institute of Administrative Sciences.

Appendix

Result-Budgeted Agencies 1993
Ministry of Foreign Affairs
Courts of Appeal
Bailiff offices

Prison Administration
Ministry of the Interior
Population Register Centre
Register Offices
Rescue Administration
Frontier guard
Ministry of Finance
Economic Research Centre of the State
State Treasury
State Audit Office
National Board of Taxes
Provincial tax offices
Local tax offices
Customs Administration
National Board of Public Building
District Administration of Public Building
Ministry of Education
National Board of Education
Centre for International Mobility
Institute for Russian and East European Studies
The State Study Aid Centre
State colleges and schools
Matriculation Examination Board
Training Centre for Vocational Education
Government Body of Suomenlinna
Ministry of Agriculture and Forestry
The Information Centre of the Ministry of Agriculture and Forestry
District Administration for Rural Industries
The Finnish Forest Research Institute
Inspection Centre for Plant Production
Ministry of Transport and Communications
Finnish Institute of Marine Research
Finnish Meteorological Institute
Ministry of Trade and Industry
Maintenance and Supply Safety Centre
District Services for Enterprises
National Consumer Administration
The Consumer Complaint Board
Office of Free Competition
National Food Administration
Office of the Consumer-Ombudsman
National Board of Patents and Registration˙
The Consumer Research Centre
Technical Inspection Centre
Geological Survey of Finland
Technical Research Centre of Finland
Technology Development Centre
Finnish Tourist Board
Ministry of Social Affairs and Health

Unemployment Social Security Board
Inspection Board
State Accident Office
Legal Protection Centre for Health Care
National Public Health Institute
Finnish Centre for Radiation and Nuclear Safety
State reformatories
State Social Work Units for Intoxicant Abusers
State mental hospitals
Reception centres for refugees
District and Local Labour Administration
Labour College
The Labour Council
Ministry of the Environment
National Board of Waters and Environment
District Administration of Waters and Environment
National Board of Housing

Net-Budgeted Agencies, 1993 (partly or whole)
Provincial governments
Local police offices
Central Criminal Police
Security Police
Mobile Police
Police Training Units
Police Depots
Administrative Development Agency
Central Statistical Office of Finland
Course Centre of Heinola
Finnish Geodetic Institute
National Board of Survey
Survey and Information Service Bureaux
Surveying Bureaux
National Board of Forestry
Central Roads Administration
District Roads Administration
National Board of Navigation
District Administration of Navigation
Vessels of Navigation Organization
Government Body of Saimaa Canal
Telecommunications Administration Centre
National Research and Development Centre for Welfare and Health
National Medicines Administration
Ministry of Labour
District Administration of Labour Protection

State Enterprises, 1993
Map Printing Centre

Motor Vehicles Registration Centre
Aviation Administration
Posts and Telecommunications of Finland
State Railways

Institutions with Business Action, 1993 (Budget financing)
Finnish State Uniforms Factory
State Forests
Seed Centre of Jokioinen
Seed Potato Centre
The Finnish State Granary
Government Purchasing Centre

State-Owned Companies, 1993
Alko Ltd
Arsenal Ltd
Avecra Ltd
Enso-Gutzeit Ltd
Finnair Ltd
Imatran Voima Ltd
Kemijoki Ltd
Kemira Ltd
Kera Ltd
Neste Ltd
Otatech Ltd
Outokumpu Concern
Lapua Cartridge Factory Ltd
Pohjolan Liikenne Ltd
Postal Bank Ltd
The Mint of Finland Ltd
Rautaruukki Ltd
Sisu-Auto Ltd
Finnish Export Credit Ltd
Industrial Cooperation Fund
Valmet Concern
Government Printing Centre Ltd
Vammas Ltd
Vapo Ltd
Veikkaus Ltd
Veitsiluoto Ltd
The State Computer Centre Ltd
Finnish Broadcasting Company Ltd

7 France

Luc Rouban

Since the early 1980s, French public administration has been involved in a policy of modernization. As in most European countries, public administration has been subjected to systematic criticism, especially from the ranks of politicians, and notably from users and citizens, exposing the growing costs and allegedly poor results of public intervention. The influence of neo-liberal ideology, the desire of successive governments to reduce the costs of the public sector (which accounts for 40 per cent of operating costs in the national budget), the need to adapt public action to more diverse and specialized social demands, and perhaps the demagogical tendencies of politicians looking for a renewed legitimacy, have pushed forward the adoption of reforms that had appeared elsewhere in Europe. These included: privatization of public enterprises, contracting between public and private organizations and a transformation of the civil servant's professional role. Sustained attention has been dedicated to higher civil servants, considered to be the main actors in the modernization process. Since 1990 there has been a multiplicity of government reports studying the ways and means of reforming French public administration, whilst taking into account its historical and social specificity (Blanc, 1993; Picq, 1994).

The case of France is indeed special. The civil service constitutes a real political force. The French public service cannot be regarded as a tool at the disposition of government. Its force comes from a powerful social and historical anchorage in the development of the state, which has long been considered in France as the driving force of social modernization. Organized in *corps*, which benefited from their long tradition, higher civil servants played a decisive role in the transformation of the French economy in the 1960s. Their professional continuity, as well as their technical or administrative abilities, transformed them into the protectors of republican institutions in periods of political turmoil. Another factor is the quantitative importance of the public service: there are 2.5 million civil servants just at central government level (including teachers) and the public-sector workforce as a whole (including local government and public enterprises) accounts for 30 per cent of wage-earners in France. A third factor is linked to the political system of the Fifth Republic, which has allowed officials to leave public service to embark on political careers. Approximately 40 per cent of members of parliament and 55 per cent of Ministers are former civil servants including former school teachers (Quermonne, 1987). The social weight of higher civil servants is enhanced by the fact that they can use provisions in the general civil service statute to make a career in the private sector. It is noteworthy that 43 per cent of leaders of the 200 largest French business firms come from the civil service.

The introduction of a new public management within the public service therefore is not likely to be easy. Trained within specialized institutions, such as the National School of Administration (ENA) or the *Ecole Polytechnique*, higher civil servants are not used to the managerial culture that is currently taught in business schools. Their special social and legal status raises a powerful barrier to any radical transformation of mind-sets. The administrative modernization policy is founded on a compromise worked out in 1988 by the Government of Michel Rocard. The development of new managerial tools and processes, within public administration, is a necessary step in modernization, but this need not entail a drastic transformation of the public service's legal status. This is not to say that there was any definition of what the new public management was supposed to be. In a 1989 circular, the Prime Minister based the reform upon four priorities:

- a renewal of human resources management through training and professional mobility;
- a reinforcement of individual and collective accountability through the systematic use of strategic plans within each service;
- a new attention given to policy evaluation in order to access the effectiveness of administrative interventions;
- an improvement in the user's service.

The spirit of the reform was to foster a bottom-up process, without central intervention.

The new public management was not linked with any specific organizational set and civil servants were asked to find the best solutions on a case-by-case basis and to demonstrate their innovatory capacities within their own departments. Modernization has not implied institutional reforms such as the delineation of executive agencies, as in the case of Britain, nor has it resulted in a new legal status for some types of public managers, but called for a cultural transformation. The new public managers are scattered throughout French public administration and can be defined as those sharing some common features. These include: a strong interest in public management tools, willingness to implement them and professional values oriented towards user satisfaction more than towards their careers. A central question for research is precisely to define the social and political characteristics of those officials who have accepted and fostered this cultural transformation. Answers can be found in data drawn from an 85-question survey of 500 higher civil servants (lowest grade: assistant service manager) who were questioned in 1991 on the policy of modernization. The sample corresponds to 10 per cent of the total population of higher civil servants in France. It was based on sectoral, geographical and professional quotas to ensure its statistical validity (Rouban, 1994a).

NEW PUBLIC MANAGERS AND THEIR CHARACTERISTICS

In order to identify public managers (PMs) and their characteristics, a reliability scale was defined, drawn from the answers given to seven related questions, which allowed the interest of these civil servants in public management to be measured. The civil servants were rated on the following items: the overall effect of the modernization project on the functioning of their services, the usefulness of internal strategic plans (*projets de services*), programme evaluation, internal financial autonomy, personnel performance evaluation, and training in human resources management methods. The final item asked whether they had been involved in the practical management of a modernization project. The statistical test (Cronbach = 0.618) shows clearly that these items are positively correlated with each other, and that the scale in fact measures a shared behaviour. A further step in the analysis demonstrates that there are three groups of higher civil servants, which vary according to their commitment to, or their interest in, public management. Group one are those who are 'very positive', getting the best scores on the reliability scale. They constitute the population of real PMs (210 managers, 41.9 per cent of the sample). Group two are those who have 'mixed feelings' (184 managers, 36.7 per cent of the sample) and Group three are those who are clearly 'negative', opposing public management and administrative modernization (107 managers, 21.4 per cent of the sample). The PMs constitute a social group that is spread over all ministries and functions. Therefore it is impossible to identify PMs as belonging to a specific ministerial sector or to a particular legal category. Their characteristics are of a social and cultural nature and cannot be defined by reference to institutional structures as a mode of recruitment, a mode of selection or a reward system. Nevertheless, it is possible to analyse their place within French public administration.

The Location of Public Managers

Table 7.1 shows that PMs are far more frequent in field offices than in central ministries or among members of the *grands corps* (Council of State, Court of Accounts, Financial Inspectorate). This concentration of PMs is because field offices have been forced to adopt and develop managerial tools to deal with the consequences of decentralization reforms since 1982. Because they are in competition with local government administrations, central government administrations have had to reduce their regulatory activity and adopt some kind of partnership with local officials. In addition, the field offices receive the major part of users' demands.

Table 7.1   *PMs by category of service*

	Field offices (%)	Central ministries (%)	Administrative grands corps (%)
NPM	49.7	34.5	10
Mixed feelings	35.8	37.4	43.3
Negatives	16.3	28.1	46.7

Furthermore, the answers given in central ministries as well as in field offices vary according to the type of function undertaken. In central ministries, about two-thirds of department heads appear 'very positive', while deputy department heads and service managers appear to be rather 'negative' and assistant service managers have 'mixed feelings' (Table 7.2).

These behavioural differences are linked to the official's place in the administrative environment, which affects their perception of, and their will to foster, the modernization process. Service managers have often perceived modernization as a threat to their leadership within their own organizations. The effect of administrative strategic planning, especially, has been to clarify objectives and means, destroying the room for manoeuvre used by some managers to build up their organizational power. Indifference, if not hostility, within the ranks of members of the *grands corps* may be generally explained by two factors: managerial tools are not useful for institutions dedicated essentially to legal advice and expertise; and these tools are regarded as conflicting with the social values com-

Table 7.2   *PMs by category of function*

	NPM (%)	Mixed feelings (%)	Negatives (%)
Department heads	61.9	9.5	28.6
Service managers	30	26.7	43.3
Deputy department heads	25	33.3	41.7
Assistant service managers	28.1	46.9	25
General inspectors	33.3	51.3	15.4
Field office managers	48.3	35.3	16.3
Préfets	60	30	10
General accounting officers	16.7	58.3	25
State Council	10	50	40
Court of Accounts	0	40	60
Finance ministry inspectors	20	40	40

monly shared in this universe of administrative power. The institutional perception reinforces the social perception of modernization. The élitism of *grands corps*, whose social recruitment is relatively closed, conflicts with techniques which impose some kind of external control. As Table 7.3 shows, PMs are particularly common in sectors undertaking a quasi-commercial or a technical activity: the Infrastructure Ministry, the Postal Service and France Telecom are thus characterized by a strong presence of PMs. In contrast, higher civil servants are appreciably less committed to managerial reforms in ministries facing problems linked to personnel cutbacks, changing patterns of activity or new social demands. This is especially the case for the Welfare Ministry, the Agriculture Ministry and the Labour Ministry.

Another lesson drawn from the survey is that there is a strong relationship between the adoption of managerial techniques and the official's social origin (Table 7.4). As a general rule, public management is recognized and practised by members of the middle class. This social class dimension cross-correlates with all the other analyses, because it is in field offices and in quasi-commercial or technical sectors that there is the largest proportion of middle-class representatives.

Modernization and Officials' Career Paths

It might be expected that the more managers have undertaken a variety of activities during their professional life, and the more they have had experience of the private sector, ministerial *cabinets*, foreign countries (i.e. the

Table 7.3   *Distribution of PMs by sector*

	NPM (%)	Mixed feelings (%)	Negative (%)
France Télécom	68	24	8
Postal Service	63.3	26.7	10
Infrastructures	57.6	24.2	18.2
Economy	45.6	44.1	10.3
Education	45.5	29.1	25.5
Interior	41.4	34.5	24.1
Industry	40.9	31.8	27.3
Veterans	40	26.7	33.3
Culture	37.5	58.3	4.2
Agriculture	33.3	30.6	36.1
Welfare	31.1	44.4	24.4
Research	28.6	28.6	42.9
Labour	24.1	55.2	20.7

Table 7.4   *Social origins of PMs*

	Upper Class (%)	Middle Class (%)	Lower Class (%)	No answer (%)
NPM	39.5	40.5	18.6	1.4
Mixed feelings	49.5	29.9	19.6	1.1
Negatives	53.3	32.7	12.1	1.9

more managers have been open to the external environment), the more their perception of modernization would be positive. This hypothesis has nevertheless to be rejected. Neither the number of professional positions held nor administrative status has a statistical effect on the average distribution of answers. Similarly, a previous position in a field office has no significant effect. The data for civil servants who have been members of a ministerial *cabinet* contradict the hypothesis (since the proportion of 'very positive' is 39.0 per cent for this group, as opposed to 42.5 per cent for those who have not been members of a ministerial *cabinet*). The only variable having a significant effect is service abroad. This professional experience predisposes them favourably towards the administrative modernization process. Indeed, 45.5 per cent of those who have served in a foreign country are part of the 'very positive' group against 41.0 per cent of those who have not. The proportion of 'negative' is correspondingly slightly higher, 23.4 per cent, against 21.1 per cent. Finally, foreign service significantly reduces the number of those who have 'mixed feelings' (31.2 per cent against 37.9 per cent).

The type of recruitment procedure may have a significant influence. The proportion of managers giving 'very positive' answers is 48.5 per cent among those who have passed an internal competition (i.e. those coming from the civil service ranks who obtained their current position after having passed a professional exam) against 39.4 per cent among those who have passed an external competition. The proportions of the two categories being evenly distributed across all sectors (although the proportion of 'internal competitions' is about 10.9 per cent in the Postal Service and 17.8 per cent in the National Education Ministry), one can deduce that the professional path is an explanatory variable.

Managers recruited through a personal arrangement (the *'tour exterieur'*, i.e. those who have benefited from political or other recruitment without competition), are the most likely to give 'negative' answers. But their group is statistically concentrated in sectors where modernization policy is generally poorly developed (15 of these officials are in the *'grands corps'*, four in the Interior Ministry and six in the Welfare Ministry) (Table 7.5).

The Modernization Process and Personal Characteristics

Do personal characteristics explain reactions to, and perceptions of, modernization policy? The first variable to consider is 'gender' (Table 7.6). Women are characterised by a higher proportion of 'mixed feelings' but by a lower proportion of 'negative' answers. However, it is necessary to interpret these answers by taking into account the unequal distribution of

Table 7.5 *The recruitment of PMs*

	NPM (%)	Mixed feelings (%)	Negatives (%)
External competition	39.4	37.9	22.7
Internal competition	48.5	34.6	16.9
No competition, *tour extérieur*	29.7	30.5	29.7

the two genders within the various sectors. For instance, it appears that 15 women, that is 26 per cent of the female group, work within the Welfare Ministry, and that 8 of them (14 per cent of the female group) work within the Culture Ministry, where 'mixed feelings' are common. A second variable is age. PMs are not beginners nor officials close to retirement age. They are to be found within the ranks of managers in the middle of their careers, who hope their personal situation will improve. The distribution by age category shows clearly that a very positive attitude is found, especially within the ranks of managers aged between 41 and 50 (44.8 per cent). It is in this category that there is the largest proportion of managers who are sceptical about their professional future and want individual performance assessments to be introduced more widely.

Table 7.6   *PMs by gender*

	NPM (%)	*Mixed feelings (%)*	*Negatives (%)*
Men	43	35.1	21.9
Women	33.3	49.2	17.6

The type of professional institution attended plays a significant role but this variable only reinforces the effects of sector and social origin. As Table 7.7 shows, former students of ENA are less enthusiastic about the modernization process than are those managers not trained in a prestigious administrative institution and, especially, those managers trained in technical or scientific institutions.

Table 7.7   *PMs by professional school*

	NPM (%)	*Mixed feelings (%)*	*Negatives (%)*
Scientific school	55	26.7	18.3
Mines	50	50	0
Ponts et Chaussées	50	40.9	9.1
None	45.2	36.4	17.4
Ecole Normale Supérieure	42.9	42.9	14.3
Administrative school	42.6	31.1	26.2
Polytechnique	33.3	33.3	33.3
ENA	27.8	42.6	29.6

Professional training has long-term effects. As a general rule, managers trained to occupy 'generalist' positions appear less committed to the modernization process than managers who received a specialist professional training (of a technical or a scientific nature). In the same way, they are less likely to ask for more professional training during their career. Among those who give 'very positive' answers, 22.8 per cent consider they have not received appropriate training for the practical execution of their duties, against 14.9 per cent within the ranks of those who give 'negative' answers. More data are provided through the answers to an open question asking: 'Would you like to receive additional professional training?' Among the 'negative' group 41.1 per cent consider they do not need any professional training against 25.5 per cent for the 'very positive' group and 20.1 per cent for the 'mixed feelings' group.

Responsibilities and Functions of PMs

Higher civil servants participate actively in the policy-making process. One of the main characteristics of the members of the *grands corps* is participation in political decisions. The development of public management calls in contrast for a clear-cut separation of political duties and management tasks. This separation, which has been fostered in the American and British public administration systems, is difficult to implement within the French system. In France, the public service is organized in powerful *corps* which expect an important role in defining administrative policy, including those strategies aiming at reforming government machinery. A separation betwen administrative management and policy-making would lead to letting the politicians decide these matters. This prospect is resisted by representatives of the *grands corps*, whereas it is actively sought by field office managers. The question of modernization is therefore very sensitive in the French administrative world because it raises conflicting cultural and social issues.

Modernization and Professional Activities

Does an official's professional activity influence their attitudes and commitment to modernization? The answer is positive. As a general rule, it is among the population of managers thinking about their job in terms of initiative and their active relationships with their external environment where the proportion of 'very positive' answers is highest. Of course, this population is mainly composed of field office managers. If the reliability scale of PMs' attitudes is correlated with a question asking managers to explain the basic task of their office, it appears that:

- Internal administrative functions correlates with negative feelings about modernization. Managers referring to the preparation of inter-ministerial files have 'mixed feelings' (up to 39.5 per cent) or are 'negative' (up to 26.6 per cent). Those who refer to supervision tasks have 'mixed feelings' (up to 41.1 per cent).
- Management functions correlate, in contrast, with favourable attitudes to modernization. Managers referring specifically to public manage-ment activities give 'very positive' answers (47.7 per cent). This answer also applies to those referring to 'headquarters' functions (45.1 per cent of 'very positive' answers) or to relationships with profes-sional groups (46.6 per cent of 'very positive' answers).
- The most favourable answers are obtained from those managers whose answers reflect a clear idea of their office's performance and duties. Thus, among the 17 managers responding spontaneously that their office undertakes quasi-commercial operations, the proportion of 'very positive' rises to 64.7 per cent. It is the same for the 43 managers who referred spontaneously to the specificity of their office or the nature of its intervention. Among them, 53.3 per cent had 'very positive' answers, and 37.2 per cent had 'mixed feelings'.

The capacity to understand and confront technical problems constitutes in the same way, and in the same direction, an explanatory variable. There is a division on technical issues seen in the distribution of attitudes towards technological innovation and, notably, data-processing. It is among the 'very positive' that one finds the highest proportion of man-agers saying they have had serious data-processing problems in their offices (27.6 per cent). In the same way, 54.3 per cent of them recognize that data-processing has had consequences for their personal work, against 41.3 per cent within the 'negative group'.

The more respondents emphasize their professional role, the higher the proportion of PMs. This type of cleavage can be noticed too in the various descriptions the managers give of their personal work. Among the managers obtaining the highest mark on the reliability scale for new public managers are those who referred to the implementation of new projects (45.7 per cent of 'very positive'), to the management of their office (43.8 per cent), and especially 20 officials who answered sponta-neously that they had the role of organizer (65 per cent of 'very positive' and 35 per cent of 'mixed feelings'; none were 'negative'). In contrast, as soon as the answers described work on file or a routine negotiation with other administrations, there was an increase in the proportion of 'negative' answers.

More confirmation comes from a statistical analysis of the frequency of professional contacts. Indeed, the proportion of 'very positive' is always higher where the frequency of contact with the external environment increases. There are thus 53.6 per cent 'very positive' answers among managers saying they had continuous contact with members of parliament against 41.3 per cent for those having intermittent contact and 31.7 per cent for those having none at all. The same goes for managers having frequent contact with local elected leaders (the target population here is mainly composed of heads of field offices). There are 43.9 per cent 'very positive' answers among those in continuous contact with these local politicians against 29.5 per cent for those who have no relationship with them. The same divisions apply to relationships with professional groups or users' associations. Among managers who are 'often' in contact with professional groups, 51.8 per cent gave 'very positive' answers against 30.6 per cent for those who said they had no relationship with them. Among managers who are 'often' in contact with users or users' associations, 50.5 per cent gave 'very positive' answers against only 28.7 per cent for those who have no relationship with them.

Functions of PMs and their Evaluation

The diffusion of public management tools and procedures in public administration calls for the transformation of civil servants' professional roles. New public managers may be distinguished from traditional officials on several points. First, they focus on their role as service organizers. This pattern of managerial leadership is generally associated with the definition of internal strategic plans allowing objectives to be specified, quality indicators defined and results evaluated. Their task consists therefore in pushing civil servants to explain what they are doing, the nature of their work, the problems they face and their needs. The idea prevails that the purposes of good public administration are not achieved only through correct policy implementation or straight application of legal rules.

Second, one of the most prominent characteristics of new public management is that it relates the activity of the service to its strategic environment. The targets of the service are defined with respect to the demands and expectations arising from the task environment, whether it includes users or other administrative services. This strategic perspective is generally based on surveys identifying users' needs as well as on scheduled meetings with the various actors concerned.

A third characteristic is the attention devoted to the professional training of officials. The new public manager is as much an educator as a strategist.

One of the greatest rigidities of French public administration is that the careers of officials are generally determined by their initial training and by the rank at which they leave training institutions. The modernization policy aims at strengthening professional training operations so as to adapt civil servants to the needs of services. As has been stressed, the policy of modernization has not been accompanied by a change in the public service statute. There has not been a general change in personnel management techniques. Nevertheless, personnel management within the higher civil service has developed in recent years within the sectors most committed to modernization, notably within the Infrastructure Ministry, the Postal Service and France Telecom. At the Infrastructure Ministry, managers have been subjected to systematic evaluation procedures, including an annual assessment of their results based on an interview with their hierarchical superiors. This evaluation has been organized in the context of contracting-by-objectives between the various administrations. The diffusion of evaluation techniques is very gradual and at the moment it affects only a minority of managers (Rangeon, 1992). These evaluations do not replace but are additional to the usual procedure of *notation* (points system). However, a majority of PMs want to expand such mechanisms because they think career planning is inadequate and that their personal efforts are poorly rewarded.

Our statistical survey highlights the fact that there is a strong demand for the development of individual performance evaluation. When asked whether managers would accept having their pay based on an annual evaluation, 91.9 per cent of PMs accept evaluation as opposed to 66.4 per cent for the 'negatives'. One of the most important obstacles to the development of managerial techniques is the fact that the organization of careers has not been transformed. Modernization has not fostered a general transformation of higher civil servants' career paths and promotion procedures. It results in a phenomenon of 'freezing': only managers with good career prospects invest in modernization. Those who expect their future career to be poor prefer not to invest in a modernization process where individual advantages are not clearly discernible. The results of the survey are clear on this point. In practice, as career prospects diminish, the proportion of 'very positive' declines from 59.2 per cent to 23.7 per cent, whilst the proportion of 'negatives' climbs from 7.4 per cent up to 34.2 per cent (Table 7.8).

Another obstacle is related to the fact that the managerial culture of PMs clashes with the bureaucratic culture of traditional officials. A phenomenon of misunderstanding can be observed between PMs who want to introduce administrative strategic planning so as to make their personnel

Table 7.8 *PMs and their perspectives of career*

	NPM (%)	Mixed feelings (%)	Negatives (%)
Very good	59.2	33.3	7.4
Good	48.4	37.3	14.1
Poor	37.7	35.3	27
Very poor	23.7	42.1	34.2
SR	37	36.2	26.7

more accountable, and more 'classical' managers who seem to be sceptical or indifferent. Management development implies therefore great pedagogical effort. PMs have to convince not only their subordinates but also their colleagues and their hierarchical superiors of the advantages of public management, including fewer conflicts with staff or trade unions, improved service efficiency and increased user satisfaction.

This cultural difference can be examined through answers to the question: 'In your opinion, what are the main factors of success in a civil servant's career?' New public managers emphasize technical know-how and professional aptitude, whereas traditional managers prioritize political support or personal relationships. As a general rule, however, higher civil servants very rarely cite 'results', which demonstrates a strong scepticism about the effect of modernization on their career path (Table 7.9).

THE NEW PUBLIC MANAGERS AND POLITICS

The PM group is a social category, not an institutional one. Consequently the relationships they maintain with politicians depend on their hierarchical

Table 7.9 *PMs and factors of professional success*

	Knowledge (%)	Aptitudes (%)	Mentor (%)	Political support (%)	Patience (%)	Professional results (%)
NPM	70.5	67.6	24.3	19.5	17.6	2.9
Mixed feelings	63	23.9	26.1	23.9	18.5	1.1
Negatives	53.3	61.7	34.6	40.2	20.6	0.9

level. Most heads of departments in central ministries, for example, are appointed on political criteria by the government. That is less frequent for service managers or assistant service managers. However, it is worth analysing the reactions of PMs to politicization of the civil service.

PMs and Politicization of the Civil Service

Table 7.10 *PMs and the nature of their function*

	NPM (%)	Mixed feelings (%)	Negatives (%)
Position implying to agree with the government policy	51.2	31.9	16.7
Position implying only professional know-how	38.7	38.5	22.8

More than representing a pure and simple conversion to managerial values, modernization policy tends to integrate them into the bureaucratic strategic universe as part of the resources, notably political, that are at the disposal of some managers. The proportion of 'very positive' managers is larger among those who think that their position requires an agreement with government policy (51.2 per cent) than among those who think it requires only technical, neutral competence (Table 7.10).

Do PMs have a different perception of the politicization of the civil service? The answer is yes. First, fewer PMs stress civil service politicization. When higher civil servants are asked: 'Is the civil service more politicised today than it was a few years ago?', the answers shown in Table 7.11

Table 7.11 *PMs and the politicization of the public service*

	The civil service is more politicized (%)	Nothing has changed (%)	The civil service is less politicized (%)	No answer (%)
NPM	39.5	51.4	6.2	2.9
Mixed feelings	51.6	40.8	6	1.6
Negatives	56.1	39.3	3.7	0.9

are obtained. These answers are explained by the fact that PMs are especially concentrated within field offices. That implies a twofold consequence: on the one hand, they work within a socially complex universe, implying compromises with elected local leaders, users and other administrations, and they know that they are responsible for implementation of a government policy; on the other hand, they are less exposed to political constraints and pressures than their colleagues who work in Parisian ministries. They have less contact with the political world. Fewer of them than in the 'mixed feeling' or the 'negative' group have experienced the world of ministerial *cabinets*. Many more of them have experienced professional life in a private-sector business firm (Table 7.12).

Table 7.12 *PMs and their professional experience*

	Previous experience in a ministerial cabinet (%)	Previous experience in a business firm (%)
NPM	19.5	12.4
Mixed feelings	21.7	8.7
Negatives	22.4	9.3

Modernization and Political Commitment

Do PMs have closer relationships with politicians? Are they more politicized than their more 'traditional' colleagues? There is no general answer to this question because the situation varies greatly from one sector of the administration to another. Nevertheless, it is possible to measure the involvement of PMs in the political debate with the help of some indicators. Overall, it appears that PMs are more politically committed than their

Table 7.13 *PMs' political commitment*

	Belong to a political party (%)	Belong to a political club (%)
NPM	7.6	23.8
Mixed feelings	6.5	15.2
Negatives	8.4	15.9

colleagues. Fewer of them participate actively in a political party but many more, on the other hand, are members of political clubs (Table 7.13).

This difference can be explained by the fact that active participation in a political party is likely among officials working in Paris, who are more likely to give a 'negative' answer on new public management. In contrast, the fact that the PMs are more frequently involved in political clubs indicates they are more likely to be actively thinking about the future of their profession outside public administration. Projects about reform of the state or the public service are generally raised, proposed and discussed within these political clubs (such as the 'Public Service' association, where civil servants sharing socialist values meet) before these projects became part of government policy. Table 7.14 shows PMs are more generally on the left of politics. The proportion of officials feeling politically close to the Socialist Party is clearly higher. This proximity to the Socialist Party is explained not only by the fact that officials questioned during the survey had been more frequently appointed by Socialist governments but also by the fact that various Socialist governments have developed the most systematic administrative modernization programmes. In contrast, political parties belonging to the parliamentary right (UDF should be *Union Démocratique pour la France* – and RPR – *Rassemblement pour la République*) have always favoured structural reforms aimed at reducing the number of civil servants as well as contracting-out of public services to private organizations.

CONCLUSION

The outlook for new public management in French public administration is favourable. However, this evolution is taking place within the traditional

Table 7.14   *The political proximity of PMs*

	Parti Socialiste (%)	Mouvement des Radicaux de Gauche (%)	Reassemblement pour la République (%)	Union Démocratique pour la France (%)	No answer (%)
NPM	39	4.3	10	4.8	35.7
Mixed feelings	29.9	3.8	10.9	6	41.8
Negatives	23.4	4.7	15	8.4	41.1

framework of a public service whose main rules have not changed. Modernization policy has had important cultural effects on a large proportion of higher civil servants. Up to 80 per cent of civil servants have been involved in modernization projects, and up to 70 per cent of them think that this policy has improved the situation to a greater or lesser extent. Nevertheless, the policy has not led to a radical transformation of professional roles and careers. The modernization process is not a homogeneous phenomenon. Commitment to modernization, and perceptions of its negative and positive effects, are distributed along lines that divide the administrative universe. PMs are concentrated in two particular types of public administration. First are those that already entail business and industrial operations in a competitive world (France Telecom, the Postal Service). In this context, the transformation of administrative managers into real public managers is confronted with technical as well as political constraints. There is a barrier to the transformation of public services into quasi-commercial activities that governments have not wanted to cross. Telecom or Postal Services still have to implement government policies which fit their overall industrial or economic policies. The desire to protect users implies too that private-sector practices must be kept at arms' length. Second, PMs are found particularly in field offices, where government policies are implemented, in association with multiple partners. Field office managers do not share the same social background or the same professional past as their colleagues working in central administrations or in the *grands corps*.

The adoption of managerial values and culture is, it appears, effective only at the periphery of the state. Public management is not a simple technical question and does not call only for a change of mental attitudes. It involves important social issues within public administration concerning the recruitment, training and careers of officials. It leads to a questioning of the nature of relationships between administration and politics in a country where the overlapping of the two universes has always been the rule. It is here that the limits of the strategy adopted in the 1980s appear. The quiet modernization of public administration does not allow the debate concerning the future role of the state to be concluded (Rouban, 1994b).

The move towards the new public management is not therefore irreversible. Structural reforms could be pursued in the near future that call for the devolution of central government welfare tasks to local government and private and public sector organizations, working through contractual arrangements. The state would then act more as an expert or a referee than as a manager. This type of evolution would imply that legal questions, not public management, would be enhanced. Some higher civil servants, especially those members of the *grands corps*, would certainly prefer this kind of reform. It would protect their traditional culture and offer a way of escaping more radical criticism.

References

Blanc Christian, (ed.) (1993) *Pour un état stratège, garant de l'intérêt général*, Documents pour la préparation du XIème Plan, Paris: La Documentation Française.

Picq, Jean (ed.) (1994) *L'Etat en France – Servir une nation ouverte sur le monde*, Paris: Rapport de la mission sur les responsabilités et l'organisation de l'etat.

Quermonne, Jean-Louis (1987) *Le Gouvernement de la Cinquième République*, Paris: Dalloz.

Rangeon, François (ed.) (1992) *L'évaluation dans l'administration*, Paris: PUF.

Rouban, Luc (1993) 'France in search of a new administrative order', *International Political Science Review*, 144, 403–19.

Rouban, Luc (1994a) *Les cadres supérieurs de la fonction publique et la politique de modernisation administrative*, Paris: La Documentation Française.

Rouban, Luc (1994b) *Le pouvoir anonyme, les mutations de l'état à la française*, Paris: Presses de la Fondation Nationale des Sciences Politiques.

8 Germany

Manfred Röber

The present debate on public management and public managers in Germany stems partly from the financial constraints which federal, state and local authorities are facing. Without the dramatic financial problems, politicians, top administrators and unions would be less willing to modernize the traditional bureaucratic system. As well as financial problems the public sector also has to deal with other challenges such as shifts in public duties from regulatory functions to public service delivery (requiring different organizational structures), demographic changes (the proportion of people over 60 will nearly double in the next three decades), with changing values (from materialism to post-materialism), and with an increasingly competitive international environment.

The old bureaucratic structures and system of public service in Germany have come under great pressure as a result of these challenges. Any discussion of administrative reform in Germany now recognizes that the whole system of public administration will have to be reformed fundamentally if it is to survive as an effective public service. Simple linear cutback-management together with cosmetic changes, which was the predominant approach in the past, will no longer work. As in many other Western countries (Reichard, 1993; Koch, 1994) the reform approach is dominated by models of private and public management. One of the key elements of a management-oriented modernization of the public sector is the need for a new type of administrator who will have more in common with a modern manager than with a traditional bureaucrat.

The development of public management in Germany has not been uniform because German administration is extremely varied and complex. Central government only plays a modest part in the direct administration of public services. Many public duties, such as education and police, are administered by the states (*Länder*) which have considerable political and administrative power, whilst other public duties (e.g. social services) are administered by local authorities. As a consequence the impact of public management and public managers varies throughout Germany and at different levels of public administration. The administrative structure in the Federal Republic of Germany is, apart from the principle of 'separation of powers', which distributes legislative, executive and judicial powers among separate institutions, moulded by two principles. First, federalism, which defines the *Länder* as members of the Federation yet retaining a sovereign state power of their own, and second, local government, which mainly operates on two levels, that of the local authorities and of the counties (Wagener, 1990).

THE TRADITIONAL PUBLIC SERVICE IN GERMANY

The German system of public administration is characterized by the classical bureaucratic model with strong emphasis on legality and proper fulfilment of regulatory functions (*Ordnungsaufgaben*). This model is based on the Weberian ideal type of bureaucracy with a tall hierarchy of positions, functional specialization, strict rules, impersonal relationships, and a high degree of formalization. The requirements of this model have influenced the education and training of the classical German bureaucrat. With changing public tasks within the welfare state, the functions of the state in general and of bureaucracies in particular have changed towards service orientation.

There is growing consensus among politicians, administrators, and scholars that a more service-oriented system of public administration cannot be delivered using the organizational principles appropriate for the traditional regulatory functions (*Ordnungsaufgaben*). Contingency theory suggests that a service orientated public administration needs a different – more-business-like – management approach with flexible and innovative structures. But the repercussions on the administrative system in general, and on recruitment, education and training, appraisals, payment and promotion of civil servants in particular, are still the subject of an intense debate among practitioners as well as scholars of public administration (Bischoff and Reichard, 1994). Changes are under way, but so far the drive for reform has not overcome the resistance of the traditional bureaucrats committed to the old model.

The public service in the Federal Republic of Germany has been shaped by historical traditions as well as by the changing tasks of public administration. Generally in the German public service we distinguish between civil servants (*Beamte*) and public employees which consists of office employees (*Angestellte*) and manual workers (*Arbeiter*). The term 'public servant' will be used as a generic term to cover civil servants as well as non-manual public employees. According to Art. 33 IV Grundgesetz (Federal Constitution) several posts are reserved for civil servants, mainly those with regard to law and order functions. Between the two groups of public servant some differences exist as indicated in Table 8.1.

Elements of the status of the civil servant in its present form were established at the end of the eighteenth century. The following features still belong to the traditional principles of a professional civil service (*hergebrachte Grundsätze des Berufsbeamtentums*):

- lifetime occupation and an appropriate salary according to the maintenance principle (*Alimentationsprinzip*);
- loyalty;
- political neutrality and moderation;
- dedication to public service;
- no right to strike;
- subjection to special disciplinary regulations.

The civil service in Germany is relatively standardized. There is a civil service framework law (skeleton law) which shapes the civil service laws of the federation and the 16 states. Consequently there are no major differences between federal, state and local levels or between regions.

In 1992, there were 6.6 million (3.5 million men and 3.1 million women) employed in the public sector, 18 per cent of the total working

Table 8.1 *Differences between civil servants (Beamte) and public employees (Angestellte) in Germany*

Civil servants	Public employees
Labour conditions based on public law	Labour conditions based on private law
Strict duties and sanctions and 'special' disciplinary regulations	Same duties but no disciplinary regulations
Specific pay, health-care and pension system	Pay and social security benefits comparable with the private sector
Specific pre-entry training	Recruitment with limited pre-entry training
Cadre system with promotion career pathway	Position system with limited career prospects

population. There were only 355 000 civilian staff in the federal administration. The main administrative power lies with 2.5 million public servants at the state level and 2.1 million at the local level. In addition 641 000 public servants work for German Telecom and 434 000 for the Federal Railways. Both institutions have already been privatized but, according to interim regulations, employees still have the same rights and duties they had before. Finally, 352 000 people are employed in agencies like the Federal Labour Corporation and the Federal Insurance Corporation for Salaried Employees.

After considerable increases in the 1960s and 1970s the number of public servants remained constant at about 4.6 million during the 1980s. With unification the figure jumped to 6.6 million, but because of severe financial contraints the size of the public sector workforce has already been reduced and is expected to fall further. One reason is the overmanning found in the old GDR system compared with West-German standards. Another reason is the emphasis of federal and state governments on lean administration as a tool to enhance the German position in global competition in the world market.

Of a public workforce of 6.6 million, 32 per cent are civil servants and 68 per cent are public employees. In comparison with other European countries Germany has a large civil service because many of the functions which are fulfilled in other countries by public employees, like teachers, university staff, social workers, etc., are executed by civil servants in Germany. Those civil servants who work as general administrators are generally regarded as classical bureaucrats enjoying job security and a wide range of fringe benefits (Naschold and Pröhl, 1994).

The ratio of civil servants to public employees is lower in the new *Länder* reflecting the fact that the process of establishing the legal status of civil servants only started after 1989 in East Germany and is not yet complete. As the trend is to take the West German administrative system as a blueprint for public administration in East Germany (Reichard and Röber, 1993; Schröter and Röber, 1994) the proportion of civil servants in East Germany is likely to equal West Germany in the future.

The main impetus for new public management (NPM) in Germany has come from the local level where only 8.5 per cent of staff are civil servants – compared to 44 per cent at the state level and 35 per cent at the federal level. This might suggest that the legal status of public employees lends itself to greater awareness of and readiness for NPM. The employment contracts of public employees, for example, are more flexible than those of civil servants.

However, what was in the past a clear distinction between civil servants and public employees has become narrower in practice. Public employees share nearly all of the rights and benefits that civil servants have, including security of tenure for those working for more than 15 years in the public sector. It has been argued that the regulations in the German public service law for civil servants provide even more opportunities for flexible modernization of public administration than the strict regulations in the collective agreements for public employees negotiated between public employers' associations and trade unions. Therefore one cannot assume that a high percentage of public employees would improve the prospects for NPM. The fact that the management-oriented reform process has started at the local level can be put down to other causes.

One important element of the traditional principles of the professional public service is the career structure. The career structures of the German civil service are vertically categorized into four classes (cadres):

- administrative class (*höherer Dienst*)
- executive class (*gehobener Dienst*)
- clerical class (*mittlerer Dienst*)
- sub-clerical class (*einfacher Dienst*)

Each class contains different grades (see Appendix) and each grade is related to a fixed basic salary plus increments every two years on the basis of a seniority allowance. The B-grades belong to a different pay group which exists for very senior and top civil servants. Their salaries do not contain any increments for seniority; the amount of income is irrespective of the officer's age or length of service. The distribution of grades follows the rule that each class contains a fixed allocation of a maximum number of posts at each grade, e.g. not more than 4 per cent of the posts in the executive are to be classified as grade A13 S.

The debate on public management and public managers focuses on the levels of the executive and the administrative class. To enter the executive class the Abitur-examination (A-Level) is required. Education for the general non-technical cadre and for certain other services (tax officers or policemen) takes place in colleges for public administration. Each state (*Land*) and the Federation have their own colleges and are responsible for the selection of candidates. Students have the status of civil servants and receive a salary from government. In most colleges of public administration emphasis is on developing legal skills and qualifications; economics, business administration and social sciences play only a minor part in the curriculum. Successful students graduate with a Diploma of Public Administration (*Diplomverwaltungswirt*) and normally remain in the civil service.

A condition for entering the administrative class is a university degree (normally in law) and two years' preparatory service (*Referendariat*) with practical stages in different public agencies and private institutions. About 10 per cent of the total public workforce belongs to the administrative class, 22 per cent to the executive class, 40 per cent to the clerical class, and 28 per cent to the sub-clerical class. Percentages vary between the federal, state and local levels. The state level has more public servants at the administrative and executive level, largely due to the large group of professionals like teachers and policemen who are appointed by the states. In contrast there is less than 1 per cent of public servants in the administrative class in German Telecom and the Federal Railway. In agencies of the indirect state administration (i.e. public corporations, institutions and foundations) nearly 60 per cent are in the clerical class, as they are largely executive agencies.

The traditional curriculum for the executive and the administrative class puts great emphasis on legal education and little on management. The same is true for the continuing in-service training for civil servants and public employees, carried out at both federal and state levels by administrative academies (*Verwaltungsakademie*). The debate on an emerging type of public manager cannot be restricted to education and training issues alone; one must also recognize that new public managers with their management attitudes and skills will only be able to work successfully in the context of an appropriate organizational structure. The old bureaucratic structures also require reform to permit the transition from traditional bureaucrat to new public manager.

IDENTIFICATION OF THE NEW PUBLIC MANAGERS AND THEIR CHARACTERISTICS

At present the term public manager is only used in state-owned enterprises, like municipal undertakings organized under private law as public utilities or transport undertakings. The German core public administration at the federal, state and local level is still dominated by the classical bureaucrat.

The main impetus for a management-oriented reform of the German bureaucracy has come from the local level where the context of local authorities' behaviour has changed more than that of the Federation and the states. In this respect the situation in Germany is quite different from the UK where central government put pressure on local government to change. There are some challenges which affect all three levels of German administration, such as financial contraints and changing attitudes of public servants to more cost-consciousness.

Nevertheless, there are some problems which only local authorities have to face and which have resulted in a change in the context of local government. These include high rates of unemployment with more people depending on social welfare benefits, which are provided by local authorities. Local authorities, not state or federal administrative bodies, have to deal directly with the problems of citizens. Citizens have also become more demanding and self-confident in their relationship with public services, many of which are provided by local authorities. Local government is therefore under much greater pressure to introduce improved services for citizens. Furthermore, due to increasing competition for production facilities, local authorities are involved in conducting policies of regional economic development, and have to provide new models of services for business communities.

Traditional structures of local authorities are unable to meet all these requirements and new organizational and managerial structures are required (Janning, 1994). The traditional structures reflect the classical Weberian model of bureaucracy with functional specialization often resulting in the separation of responsibilities for resources and programmes. The management of resources (personnel, finance) is the responsibility of central core units whilst the management of service delivery rests with professional programme units, e.g. adult education, youth welfare, promotion of economic activities, housing. In practice the heads of programme departments have only very limited control over their resources. Decisions on resource allocation are mainly taken by the core bureaucrats.

The main effects of the traditional model are that professionals in the programme sections have no incentives to act cost-effectively and do not think in cost-effectiveness terms. Neither do they feel responsible for the efficiency of their programmes. Heads of department have no incentive to save money because they are not allowed to use savings for more important tasks. One result is that when new public duties arise departments ask for more money and more personnel, and do not think about strategies to readjust their budget according to new developments. Professionals do not feel responsible for the budget, and core bureaucrats do not feel responsible for the programme. The only people who can take comprehensive responsibility are at the very top (mayor or the council). However, they often know too little about the details of a problem or programme to take responsibility. In the end there is a non-congruence of tasks and responsibilities and nobody feels responsible for anything. This effect has been accurately described as 'a system of organized irresponsibility' (Banner, 1991). Market orientation is extremely low; therefore adaptation of programmes to new demands and the channelling of resources to problem areas, where they are needed, normally come far too late.

There is a growing consensus amongst practitioners at the local level (Janning 1994; Reichard, 1994a) that the system of centralized resource management will be unable to meet future challenges to local government and there is a readiness for management-oriented reforms. The initial debate on public management and public managers in Germany came from a report by the 'Joint Local Government Agency for the Simplification of Administrative Procedures' (*Kommunale Gemeinschafts-stelle für Verwaltungsvereinfachung* – KGSt, 1991). The KGSt is an independent consultancy agency organized by voluntary membership of municipalities, counties and local authorities with more than 10 000 inhabitants (Banner, 1979 and 1987). Following the Tilburg model in the Netherlands (Schrijvers, 1993) the KGSt has made a proposal for a modern system of local government. (KGSt, 1993; Banner, 1991 and 1994; KGSt, 1991). In response to the criticism of muddled political and administrative responsibilities the KGSt argues for *clear-cut responsibilities between politics and administration*, a system of *contract management*, *integrated departmental structures* and an emphasis on *output control*. Councillors will decide on strategies, priorities, objectives and performance standards. Within these policy frameworks and based on contracts, with well-defined objectives, performance standards and appropriate budgets, each department will have the responsibility for all aspects of management required to fulfil its tasks. Output-oriented management will combine the activities of administration into easily comprehensible 'products', specified in terms of quantity, quality, target group and costs. Budgets will be linked to the output products rather than inputs.

In German local government, citizen and customer orientation is still relatively weak. Comprehensive approaches like the Citizen's Charter in the UK (Cm 1599, 1991) do not exist. The KGSt promotes *quality management* as another very important element of output control which must be improved (Bertelsmann, 1993; Hill and Klages, 1993a and 1993b) with the use of regular consumer surveys, analysis of complaints and staff involvement through quality circles.

Compared with other European countries, particularly the UK with its system of compulsory competitive tendering, local authorities in Germany have little experience of direct *competition* with other public authorities or private firms. Even the use of performance indicators, as a means of comparing different local authorities, has started only recently (*interkommunaler Leistungsvergleich*). Such a system of inter-communal benchmarking may be the first step to quasi-markets and to a system of full competition among public and private suppliers of services. Competition will probably become one of the key factors in the modernization process, especially at the local level, as it would make little sense to introduce company-like management structures without establishing a conducive company-like competitive environment.

Some larger cities and towns have already started to reshape their traditional bureaucratic structures to more management-oriented systems (Reichard, 1994a). Although no single modernization blueprint exists, the prevalent trend follows at least some of the elements of the KGSt model outlined above. The transition from the old bureaucratic model, in which local authorities provided all services directly to the public, to a model of contract management will require a new administrative culture and a shift from the traditional bureaucrat to the public manager.

In contrast to local government the situation at the federal and state levels is quite different where administrations are less management-oriented and less cost-conscious. They are not exposed as much to the demands from people, markets and quasi-markets as local authorities are. Therefore at the federal level there is no strategic approach towards modernizing the whole system. The Federal Government clings to the traditional principles of a professional civil service. The only aim is to change some of the extremely bureaucratic and dysfunctional elements of the civil service. This is clear from the conceptual paper on further developments in the civil service (Perspektivbericht) published in 1993, and subsequently approved in 1995 by the Federal Minister for the Interior (*Eckpunkte*, 1995). It proposes to strengthen the achievement principle, to improve mobility, and to provide some incentives for posts which face recruitment problems due to competition with the private sector.

At the state level there is some move to reorganize the bureaucratic system. In Baden-Württemberg, for example, efforts have been made to modernize the state administration and introduce new systems of personnel management (*Neue Führungsstruktur*, 1985; Klotz and Mauch, 1994). More recently these ideas have been taken further both by a commission in Baden-Württemberg's State Ministry of Interior (Verwaltung 2000, 1993) and the Staatsministerium Baden-Württemberg (Staatsministerium, 1994). The latter published results of an investigation into performance-oriented pay systems. Other interesting reform projects are under way in the city states which combine state and local functions. In Berlin, for example (Röber, 1995), an ambitious reform project started at the end of 1994 with the following elements:

- defining and clarifying products and outputs;
- introducing a new system of cost accounting;
- designing a system of contract management;
- improving personnel management within the framework of public service law, especially the statute relating to civil servants;
- providing training courses for administrators to familiarize them with the new system and to change their traditional bureaucratic attitudes towards management-oriented attitudes.

A growing consensus is emerging that the traditional emphasis on law qualifications and training is no longer suitable for the public bureaucracy (Widder, 1994). As public administration becomes more and more service-oriented, in a competitive environment, the qualifications of staff will have to be changed towards problem-solving competences, initiative, autonomy, professional leadership and customer orientation. However, public managers must not only be successful in economic terms but also in their political sensitivity. Thus the new public manager cannot simply be a copy of the successful private manager.

General Personnel Management

Human resources in the public sector have not traditionally been rewarded for achievement or personal development. Although the federal constitutional court has said that, according to Art. 33 of the Basic Law, professional efficiency is part of the traditional principles of the professional civil service, the public perception is of a civil service with permanent employment, with promotion on the basis of seniority and security of social position – and not with efficiency and effectiveness.

In the early 1970s the Federal Government of SPD-FDP, which was dedicated to far reaching reforms, established a 'Commission for the Reform of Public Service Law' (*Studienkommission für die Reform des öffentlichen Dienstrechts*) which proposed uniformity of legal status for all public servants (civil servants, public employees, workers) and a modern personnel management approach. In 1976 the Federal Government presented its *Aktionsprogramm zur Dienstrechtsreform* which contains some of the recommendations of the *Studienkommission*. However, apart from minor changes to salaries and vertical mobility, none of the recommendations have been put into practice. The modernization debate re-emerged in the late 1980s, as a response to claims of inefficiency and demands for privatization, and was influenced by privatization and deregulation programmes in the USA and the UK. The approach taken to modernize the public sector and to improve public management can be seen in part, therefore, as a response to the privatization campaigns (Naschold, 1993).

The interest in modernizing the public sector diminished, temporarily, after 1990 with the unification process in Germany. The opportunity to introduce a new reformed system of public administration in East Germany was not taken and the old Western model of public adminsistration was the blueprint for the administrative structures in the former GDR (Reichard and Röber, 1993; Schröter and Röber, 1994).

Once the political turmoil of unification settled, the problem of public sector modernization reappeared on the political agenda. Severe financial problems and the fundamental changes in the context of public administration, identified above, called for a new approach to personnel management and a new type of public administrator. The new human resources approach at the federal and state levels has focused around recruitment, appraisals, performance-oriented salaries, promotion, temporary executive duties, style of leadership, and mobility.

Recruitment

Each ministry or department at the federal, state and local authority level has the right to recruit its own staff. Each post has to be advertised and recruitment is generally based on merit combined with seniority – although there are some political appointments (*Ämterpatronage*) (Dyson, 1979; Derlien, 1985). Many of those who join the civil service are risk averse, attracted by job security and not all are achievement-oriented. These 'bureaucrats' have been recruited by 'old' bureaucrats with similar characteristics. The result is a workforce which is generally less efficient and effective than that in private enterprises (OECD, 1990; Naschold and Pröhl, 1994). Concepts of comprehensive recruitment strategies, like personnel marketing (KGSt, 1992), are still rare.

The personnel structure in public administration is also very strongly moulded by a dominance of lawyers (*Juristenmonopol*). A consequence of this is that decisions tend to be based on the criterion of legality and not on criteria of expediency, customer service or efficiency. For this reason there are proposals to reduce the dominance of lawyers and to recruit more economists and management experts to the civil service.

In the past administrative reformers hoped that the influx of business management experts into public administration would change the awareness towards efficiency and effectiveness more or less automatically. However, the recruitment of more people with professional backgrounds from economic and social sciences has had no major effect. Administrators, irrespective of their professional education, refer to the traditional criteria of decision-making because they do not have any incentives to behave in a more management-oriented way, unless the rules and the culture of the administrative system are changed.

Private management experts cannot be easily transplanted into the public sector because they must work in a system of complex political requirements. Public managers have to weigh up different possibilities according to political and policy requirements as well as economic ones. And they must know the scope of bureaucratic action and be familiar with administrative culture (Stewart and Walsh, 1992; Gray and Jenkins, 1995).

At the federal and state levels, in particular, there is still a dominance of public servants with law qualifications. Specialists can be found in areas such as health (doctors) or transport (engineers), but this is not evidence of an emerging new type of public manager. To date, only a few recommendations to change recruitment policies towards new public managers can be found (Schleswig-Holsteinischer Landtag, 1994). At the local level the situation is different. Local politicians and chief executives have complained for some time that those trained for the executive and administrative class no longer meet the new requirements (Reichard, 1994b). Some local authorities have changed their recruitment policy and recruit more candidates with a professional managerial background, but there is still a lack of qualified management experts even in those cities which have started to reorganize their city administration on the general lines of the KGSt model.

Training

Politicians and top civil servants are beginning to realize that a new type of administrator is needed, especially at the executive or middle management level of the public administration system. The curriculum in the training schools is still dominated by constitutional, administrative and private law, with only a few colleges of public administration having courses in economics, business administration, political and social sciences. Another obstacle to a stronger management orientation is the legal status of the students. The double status of student and public servant with job security socializes them at an early age to those attitudes of civil servants which are not conducive to public management.

Local authorities have been pressing for substantial changes in the curriculum of the colleges for public administration (cf. *Deutscher Städtetag*, 1992; KGSt, 1993a), but many of the Ministries for the Interior, whose training departments are responsible for changes of curriculum, are very cautious about changing the old system. They adhere to the traditional principles of the professional civil service and their reservations against a management-oriented modernization of the civil service are very strong. Their refusal to change the whole system in the direction of public sector management has been tempered in some instances with approval for several pilot projects of public management courses in the colleges (especially for the executive level). In these courses much more emphasis is put on education in management combined with classes in law, social sciences and political science. Such pilot projects have been started in Northrhine-Westfalia, Bavaria, Berlin, Baden-Württemberg and Brandenburg (Bischoff and Reichard, 1994; Reichard, 1994b; Mundhenke, 1993; Pippke, 1994; Richthofen, 1990 and 1993).

In the long run the aim should be to integrate the internal colleges of public administration into the general university and *Fachhochschule* system and to provide a curriculum which covers a wider range of subjects from private to public management. Such a change will be one of the prerequisites for more openness and a higher mobility between the private and the public sector (Pippke, 1994).

While the aim of innovation at the executive level is to improve the economic knowledge and management skills of civil servants and public employees, the reforms at the administrative level are much more directed towards leadership training. At present, civil servants are promoted to higher levels in the hierarchy without any management or leadership training. In many cases they do not change their attitudes and behaviour at all. Many regard themselves as the best specialist in their department and hesitate to delegate decision-making to lower levels of the hierarchy.

Developments in leadership training are taking place in some of the states (Walther, 1991; Göck, 1993; Hager, 1994), providing younger, most promising, higher civil servants with special training courses. One of the best-known courses in Baden-Württemberg lasts for 15 months and includes case-study-oriented theoretical courses, a placement in a private company and a placement abroad. A similar course is held in Bavaria every two years and a new programme started at the *Hochschule für Verwaltungswissenschaften* in Speyer in 1991. The main features of all these courses are their interdisciplinary approach, practical orientation,

international focus and strong emphasis on management skills. These programmes now provide a pool of highly qualified civil servants who can be
deployed to suit the personnel strategies of their ministries.

Appraisals

One of the prerequisites for modern public management is a meaningful
appraisal system which does not exist in German bureaucracies. In most
authorities appraisals take place every three or four years. The assessors,
normally the immediate superiors, do the appraisals and nearly all civil
servants get high gradings. As a result, appraisals are considered to be
meaningless. The Federal Minister of the Interior recently proposed that
quotas for gradings should be introduced (*Eckpunkte*, 1995, p. 2).
However, it is necessary to go a step further to meet the requirements
of the NPM and to have a system of annual personal appraisals
(Schleswig-Holsteinischer Landtag, 1994, p. 112; Verwaltung 2000,
1993, pp. 39ff).

Promotion and Pay Incentives

In the absence of meaningful appraisal there is no basis for pay and promotion incentives, although several commissions have recommended performance-oriented pay systems (Perspektivbericht der Bundesregierung,
1993;   Staatsministerium   Baden-Württemberg,   1994,   Schleswig-
Holsteinischer Landtag, 1994; Schedler, 1993). The classic reward strategy, of promotion to a higher position, has not worked for some time
because of lower manpower requirements and reduced budgets in the
1990s, as compared to the 1970s. The resulting promotion blockage produces frustration among civil servants with consequent impacts on motivation and performance-oriented behaviour.

   Many initiatives are already under way to introduce performance-
related pay (PRP). The Federal Minister of the Interior (*Eckpunkte*, 1995)
is recommending restructuring of the system of seniority allowances so
that at the beginning of a civil servant's career the seniority allowances
will rise faster than at the end of their career and that they can be accelerated or slowed down in relation to the performance of each civil servant.
Far-reaching ideas to abolish the system of seniority allowances completely and to use this money for performance-oriented salaries are also
under consideration. These moves towards an element of PRP have
aroused the suspicions of the trade unions who fear that supervisors may
use their power in an arbitrary fashion.

Temporary Executive Duties

In the German civil service it is practically impossible to downgrade a civil servant for poor performance. This has repercussions for the overall efficiency and effectiveness of public bodies. The impact is greatest and most detrimental at senior management level. Proposals for temporary executive duties, or short-term appointments, have been made in both Baden-Württemberg (Neue Führungsstruktur, 1985) and Berlin (Enquete-Kommission, 1984). There, commissions recommended that top civil servants be paid extra salary for holding a particular post, e.g. heads of departments in ministries, presidents of higher state authorities. Every five years a decision to reappoint would be taken on the basis of performance. In the case of poor performance civil servants would return to their status position (career grade) and normal salary.

These recommendations were aimed at top civil servants who were unable to meet the demands of executive duties or whose motivation and/or performance has declined. However, Baden-Württemberg's state government chose not to implement the proposals for fear of challenges in constitutional and civil service law. Although the proposal failed, the debate marked a great step forward in acknowledging leadership problems amongst traditional bureaucrats. It paved the way for the recent proposal of the Federal Minister of Interior (Eckpunkte, 1995, p. 1ff) to promote civil servants to top jobs for a two-year probationary period before confirming the position. Greater flexibility in promotion, based on 'leadership qualities', has an impact on changing the attitudes and behaviour of senior officers from traditional bureaucrats to public managers.

Mobility

Another problem discussed by reform commissions is limited mobility in public administration. Most civil servants never work outside the public sector and many have never left their department or section in which they started their career. This lack of mobility tends towards 'tunnel vision' and the demotivation of civil servants who wish to gain experience in different fields of activity. Low mobility also limits incentives for exceptional performance.

To counter this problem, the administrative reform commissions, e.g. in Baden-Württemberg, Hamburg and Berlin (Röber, 1991) have recommended a systematic strategy of job rotation especially for executives, in conjunction with personnel development procedures and systematic career planning for younger civil servants. To increase flexibility in the public sector the Federal Minister of the Interior recommended, in April 1995, temporary assignments of civil servants to another authority for up to five years. It also recommended increasing vertical mobility from the executive to the administrative class.

Inflexible regulations in German public service law account in part for low mobility and for the absence of a performance-oriented personnel policy. However, while the restrictions of the present civil service law are very rigid and 'resistant to modernization', the implementation of many procedures and decisions conducive to performance-oriented behaviour and to greater mobility of civil servants is feasible, given the political will to proceed in that direction.

AUTHORITY, RESPONSIBILITY AND ACCOUNTABILITY OF CLASSICAL ADMINISTRATORS AND PUBLIC MANAGERS

The fundamental principle of the civil service is written in Art. 33 (4) and (5) of the Basic Law for the Federal Republic of Germany:

(4) The exercise of public authority as a permanent function shall, as a rule, be entrusted to members of the public service whose status, service and loyalty are governed by public law.

(5) Public service law shall be based on the traditional principles of the professional civil service.

The traditional principles of the professional civil service can be interpreted as a code of administrative ethics which require civil servants to be impartial, correct, honest, and loyal to their democratically elected employer who represents the public interest (this also applies to public employees). In theory the traditional principles of the professional civil service also incorporate the achievement principle, but in practice that principle remains indeterminate and diffuse. Poor performance does not normally result in punishment, although civil servants who fail to meet (unwritten) minimum standards of quality will not be promoted. Once promoted, however, there is practically no chance to downgrade a civil servant.

Civil servants have to act in a party-politically neutral way, but they are allowed to be party members, to work in parties, and to stand for elections. According to the principle of incompatibility of mandate and office at the same level of government, civil servants (and public employees) cannot become members of a parliament or council which controls the administrative body to which they belong – unless the elected member takes temporary retirement. However, they can become council members or members of parliament of a different level of government. In general there has been a tendency towards the 'bureaucratization' of parliaments and councils which affects the notion of separation of powers substantially. According to a survey in 1983, up to 50 per cent of the members of state parliaments and about 35 per cent of the members of the federal diet belonged to the civil service (Derlien, 1985).

A small number of senior civil servants have the status of 'political' officials (*politischer Beamter*). At the state level the permanent secretaries belong to this group while at the federal level permanent secretaries and deputy secretaries (i.e. the heads of divisions) are political officials. They are normally well-qualified career civil servants (Derlien, 1990a and 1990b) who are politically sympathetic to the minister. Where political and professional judgements lead to disagreement between minister and political official, the latter can be temporarily retired. In such cases they receive generous pensions to compensate them for the risk involved. The temporary retirement of political officials often happens when the government changes and new ministers want to appoint senior civil servants in whom they have confidence (Derlien, 1985). The institution of the political official seems to be widely accepted as an instrument to control the bureaucracy in a politically effective manner.

At the federal and state levels civil servants, as well as public employees, are accountable to ministers who, in turn, are accountable to parliament, although in the Federation and in most states, unlike in the UK, a formal ministerial responsibility to parliament does not exist. That means that a single minister cannot be dismissed by a motion of no confidence in parliament (Sontheimer, 1993). As there are a wide range of models in local government across states, the situation at the local level is much more complex. In general, public servants are responsible to the chief executive officers of local authorities who are elected either by voters directly, e.g. mayors in Bavaria, or by the council, e.g. mayors in Schleswig-Holstein and chief executives in Northrhine-Westfalia.

Mayors and chief executives are accountable to the council which consists of local politicians. There are considerable doubts whether local politicians can exercise effective control over the chief executive officer and his professional staff. Similar doubts exist at the federal and state level with regard to the role of members of parliament. In practice the position of top administrators is extremely powerful. The impact of the introduction of new public management on the power relationship between the legislature and executive is an important and still open question (Wollmann and Reichard, 1995). On the one hand it could increase the power of the executive body because it has more discretion to implement programmes and to manage resources. On the other hand it could strengthen the position of the legislative body which can set, monitor and control well-defined targets with regard to client groups, quantity, quality, price and costs.

Public servants are responsible to citizens, who can make complaints about their work through an official procedure (*Dienstaufsichtsbeschwerde*). Action against civil servants, however, can only be taken in cases of illegality or failure to follow administrative procedures correctly. Appeals are heard at different administrative levels and, ultimately, people can present their case to an administrative court. Again, these courts can only check the legal correctness of an administrative decision. The changing values and expectations of people are leading to demands for higher standards of service, and comparisons will be made between organizations in both the public and private sector. Such developments are leading to a re-examination of the relationship between the public servant and the citizen. Public services administrators at all levels of the hierarchy will in future be forced to think and behave much more as public managers than as classical bureaucrats.

Financial accountability has traditionally required a high degree of centralization to meet the requirements of political accountability. Budget control by audit committees of legislative bodies and by independent auditor's offices at the federal and state levels mainly focuses on the formal correctness of the budget and on single, sometimes very small and unimportant items of expenditure. The NPM gives managers greater freedom to manage their budgets. Some German local authorities have already changed their budgetary procedures to a decentralized system of block grants. In such an approach, financial control focuses more on performance than on probity. The role of the auditor's offices will also have to change, concentrating much more on elements of preventive management advice and consultancy (e.g. Auditor General of Canada, 1988).

RELATIONS BETWEEN BUREAUCRACIES AND POLITICS

The changes in responsibilities will undoubtedly affect the traditional linkages between bureaucracies and politics.

Classical Administrators and Politics

In theory there is a separation of legislative, executive and judicial powers among institutions (Wagener, 1990) and between elected politicians and appointed public servants. In practice, at all levels of government, political and administrative spheres overlap. Top civil servants have a very strong position in the politico-administrative decision-making process. With their professional expertise, they often influence the debate on political alternatives and determine political decisions. Therefore the role of high-ranking officers in the German policy-making process has changed over time, moving away from the ideal type of the 'classical bureaucrat' towards that of the 'political bureaucrat' (Aberbach *et al.*, 1990; Derlien, 1990b and 1994). The comparative work on administrative élites by Putnam (1973) and Aberbach *et al.* (1981) demonstrated that their work was clearly shaped by political and social problems and programmes. The political bureaucrat is an important element in politico-administrative decision-making and has become a highly functional part of the political system in Germany.

This development has been the subject of heavy criticism. Public choice theorists, for example, see the potential for promoting bureaucratic self-interest (Niskanen, 1971). There are also strong reservations about a further erosion of political power in favour of administrators. Therefore it comes as no surprise that in the course of the debate on public management in Germany politicians as well as some academics are afraid that accountable management could weaken the influence of politicians further. Aucoin (1990, p. 117) has argued that 'mechanisms must be found to reassert the primacy of the elected politician over the bureaucrat with respect to both budgets and policy' because the elected politician is at least responsible to voters.

New Public Managers and Politics

The debate about public management, not only in Germany, focuses on the redistribution of power. Devolving the power to manage to public servants implies loss of power in the hands of elected representatives. Alternatively, politicians may strengthen their position if they concentrate on important strategic issues and on output-oriented performance indicators. The outcome of that debate is still uncertain. Traditionally, strategic political management has been largely neglected by elected representatives. Especially at local level, party-politicized councils have intervened more in matters of implementation.

The model of NPM places emphasis on precise political objectives and clearly defined responsibilities for legislative and administrative bodies. If politicians are not willing to refrain from single issue interventions and to focus on formulating goals and setting targets, accountable management may already be jeopardized at an early stage of administrative modernization. And if high-ranking administrators think that accountable management restricts their discretion only to cost-cutting strategies, whilst at the same time curbing their role as political bureaucrats, they will almost certainly oppose NPM too.

What is needed is a new type of managerial bureaucrat who respects the primacy of elected politicians and also has a respected role as a political bureaucrat. Some think this is like trying to square the circle, but it only reflects the great demands on administrators who will have to work as public managers in future.

CONCLUSION

In summary, one cannot say that there is a broad movement from public administration to public management in Germany. It is only in local government that some top administrators have became 'more "managerial" and less "administrative" in their attitudes' (Banner, 1987, p. 21), as a result of the budgetary crisis at the beginning of the 1980s. At present more and more municipalities and local authorities are introducing modern systems of management-oriented local government (Reichard, 1994a). The situation at the federal and state levels is, to date, less promising. Hardly the triumphal march of public managers into public administration!

Public managers can still be found in state or municipal undertakings, normally organized under private law or as public agencies (*Anstalt des öffentlichen Rechts*). In local authorities a growing number of top administrators see themselves as public managers, although they do not yet have the power and discretion to act as such. In the long run, developments in the context of local and state government will undoubtedly change the consciousness, attitudes and behaviour of public servants towards managerialism. But at present it is too early to say that the trend towards new public managers is irreversible. There are still too many beneficiaries of the old bureaucratic system who will resist quick and radical changes. One of the crucial questions in the entire process of administrative modernization is whether the traditional bureaucratic workforce is willing and able to meet the new requirements stemming from a new public management.

The likelihood of change in this direction, however, is relatively high. One reason is that, under the pressure of increasing financial constraints, public management has a higher electoral profile and position on the political agenda. Furthermore, as financial pressure on the public sector increases, it will be necessary to work much more cost-effectively in the future. Finally, developments in the European Union will require public authorities to work in a competitive environment which, in turn, necessitates the introduction of NPM systems.

One has to be very careful, however, not to throw out the baby with the bathwater. The German system of public services achieves relatively high standards, as far as regulatory functions are concerned. The aim must be to preserve those parts of the traditional system which fit the regulatory functions and reform those elements of the traditional bureaucratic structure which are stumbling-blocks to a modern service-oriented system of public administration. If German politicians and top administrators fail to modernize the public sector they will not be able to sustain the system because it has become too expensive. The effect of failure to modernize would be cuts in service delivery, especially hard for those who have to rely on public services. This prospect must act as a warning that in practice there is no alternative to the modernization of the public sector. German bureaucracy is condemned to modernization.

Appendix   *The class and career structure of the German civil service*

B 11	Permanent Secretary	
B 7	Deputy Secretary	Administrative class =
B5 to B6	Under-Secretary	*höherer Dienst*
A16 to B4	Assistant Secretary	
A 15	Senior Principal	
A 14	Principal	
A 13	Higher Executive Officer	

A 13 S	Higher Executive Officer	
A 12	Executive Officer	Executive class =
A 11	Clerical Officer	*gehobener Dienst*
A 10	Senior Clerical Assistant	
A 9	Clerical Assistant	

A 9 S	Clerical Assistant	
A 8	Senior Clerical Secretary	Clerical class =
A 7	First Clerical Secretary	*mittlerer Dienst*
A 6	Second Clerical Secretary	
A 5	Assistant Clerical Secretary	

A 5S	Assistant Clerical Secretary	
A 4	*Amtsmeister*	Sub-clerical class =
A 3	*Hauptamtsgehilfe*	*einfacher Dienst*
A 2	*Oberamtsgehilfe*	
A 1	*Amtsgehilfe*	

References

Aberbach. J.D., Derlien, H.-U., Mayntz, R., and Rockman, B.A. (1990) 'American and German federal executives – technocratic and political attitudes', *International Social Science Journal*, 1, 3–18.

Aberbach, J.D., Putnam, R.D. and Rockman, B.A. (1981) *Bureaucrats and Politicians in Western Democracies*, Cambridge (Mass): Harvard University Press.

Aucoin, P. (1990) 'Administrative reform in public management: paradigms, principles, paradoxes and pendulums', *Governance*, 115–37.

Auditor General of Canada: Attributes of well-performing organizations. Extract from the 1988 annual report, Canadian Publishing Center Ottawa, Canada 1988.

Banner, G. (1979) 'Organizing for local government efficiency in Germany', *Local Government Studies*, May/June, 55–71.

Banner, G. (1987) 'Political, structural and technological aspects of financial management in German local government', paper presented to the seminar on Improving the Financial Management of Local Authorities, organized by the Steering Committee for Regional and Municipal Matters (CDRM) of the Council of Europe, Strasbourg.

Banner, G. (1991) 'Von der Behörde zum Dienstleistungsunternehmen', *Verwaltungsführung/Organisation/Personal* (*VOP*), pp. 6–11.

Banner, G. (1994) 'Neue Trends im kommunalen Management', *Verwaltungsführung/Organisation/Personal* (*VOP*), pp. 5–12.

Bertelsmann Foundation (1993) *Democracy and Efficiency in Local Government*, vol. I: Documentation of the International Research, Gütersloh.

Bischoff, D. and Reichard, C. (eds) (1994) *Vom Beamten zum Manager? Herausforderungen und Perspektiven der Verwaltungsausbildung*, Berlin: Hitit.

Cm 1599 (1991) *Raising the Standard: The Citizen's Charter*, London: HMSO.

Derlien, H.-U. (1985) 'Politicization of the civil service in the Federal Republic of Germany: facts and fables' in Francois Meyers (ed.) *Politicization of Public Administration*, Brussels: International Institute of Administrative Sciences, pp. 1–38.

Derlien, H.-U. (1990a) 'Wer macht in Bonn Karriere', *Die Öffentliche Verwaltung* pp. 311–19.

Derlien, H.-U. (1990b) 'Continuity and change in the West German federal executive elite, 1949–1984', *European Journal of Political Research*, pp. 349–72.

Derlien, H.-U. (1994) 'Karrieren, Tätigkeitsprofil und Rollenverständnis der Spitzenbeamten des Bundes – Konstanz und Wandel', *Verwaltung und Fortbildung*, pp. 255–74.

Dyson, K. (1977) 'The West German "Party-Book" administration: an evaluation', *Public Administration Bulletin* 25, Dec., pp. 3ff.

Eckpunkte einer Reform des öffentlichen Dienstrechts (1995). papier des Bundesministeriums des Innern, 12 April.

Enquete-Kommission (1984) *Schlußbericht der Enquete-Kommission zur Verwaltungsreform vom 30.5.1994*, Drucksache 9/1829 des Abgeordnetenhauses von Berlin vom 21: June.

Göck, R. (1993) *Führungskräftefortbildung. Konzept und Umsetzung am Beispiel der Führungsakademie Baden-Württemberg und des Führungskolleges Speyer*, Baden-Baden: Nomos.

Gray, A. and Jenkins, B. (1995) 'From public administration to public management: reassessing a revolution?' *Public Administration*, pp. 75–99.

Hager, G. (1994) 'Führungskräftefortbildung im föderalen Vergleich', *Verwaltungsführung/Organisation/Personal (VOP)*, pp. 56–60.

Hess, A. (1983) 'Berufsstatistik der Mitglieder des 10. Deutschen Bundestages', *Zeitschrift für Parlamentsfragen*, pp. 486–9.

Hill, H. and Klages, H. (eds.) (1993a) *Spitzenverwaltungen im Wettbewerb: Eine Dokumentation des I. Spcyercr Qualitätswettbewerbs*, Baden-Baden: Nomos.

Hill, H. and Klages, H. (eds.) (1993b) *Qualitäts- und erfolgsorientiertes Verwaltungsmanagement. Aktuelle Tendenzen und Entwürfe*, Berlin: Nomos.

Janning, H. (1994) 'Rahmenbedingungen neuer Steuerungsmodelle und dezentraler Organisationsstruktur in der Kommunalverwaltung', *Verwaltungsführung/Organisation/Personal (VOP)*, pp. 239–45

KGSt (1991) 'Dezentrale Ressourcenverantwortung: Überlegungen zu einem neuen Steuerungsmodell', *KGSt-Bericht*, 12.

KGSt (1992) 'Einführung in das Personalmarketing', *KGSt-Bericht*, 11.

KGSt (1993a) 'Das neue Steuerungsmodell: Begründung, Konturen, Umsetzung', *KGSt-Bericht*, 5.

KGSt (1993b) 'Ausbildung und Entwicklung von Personal mit betriebswirtschaftlichem Aufgabenschwerpunkt', *KGSt-Bericht*, 10.

Klotz, E. and Mauch, S. (1994 (1995) 'Personalmanagement in Baden-Württemberg: Die Implementierung einer Konzeption in der Landesverwaltung', *Verwaltungsführung/Organisation/Personal (VOP)*, pp. 232–38, 336–46 pp. 28–31, 116–19, 179–81, 210–20.

Koch, R. (1994) 'Senior civil servants as entrepreneurs: towards the impact of new public management concepts on personnel management', no. 26 der Beiträge zur Verwaltungswissenschaft, Universität der Bundeswehr, Institut für Verwaltungswissenschaft, Hamburg.

Mundhenke, E. (1993) 'Zunkunftsaspekte der Verwaltungsausbildung: Fachhochschulen für Öffentiliche Verwaltungen im Umbruch', *Verwaltungsführung/Organisation/Personal (VOP)*, S. 82–5.

Naschold, F. (1993) *Modernisierung des Staates: Zur Ordnungs- und Innovationspolitik des öffentlichen Sektors*, Berlin: Editions Sigma.

Naschold, F. and M. Pröhl (eds) (1994) *Produktivität öffentlicher Dienstleistungen: Dokumentation eines wisscnschaftlichen Diskurses zum Produktivitätsbegriff*, Gütersloh: Bertelsman Verlag.

Neue Führungsstruktur Baden-Württemberg: Bericht der Kommission (1985) *Band I. Leitbilder und Vorschläge.*

Niskanen, W. (1971) *Representative Government and Bureaucracy*, Chicago.

OECD (1990) *Public Management Developments: Survey 1990*, Paris.

Perspektivbericht (1993) *Bericht der Bundesregierung über die Fortentwicklung des öffentlichen Dienstes*, Bonn: Internal Paper of Federal Government.

Pippke, Wolfgang (1994) 'Fachhochschulen für öffentliche Verwaltung im Wandel', *Verwaltungsrundschau*, S. 289–95.

Putnam, R.D. (1973) 'The political attitudes of senior civil servants in western Europe: a preliminary report', *British Journal of Political Science*, pp. 257–90.

Reichard, C. (1993) 'Internationale Trends im kommunalen Management' in G. Banner and C. Reichard (eds) *Kommunale Managementkonzepte in Europa: Anregungen für die deutsche Reformdiskussion*, Cologne: Editions Sigma.

Reichard, C. (1994a) *Umdenken im Rathaus: Neue Steuerungsmodelle in der deutschen Kommunalverwaltung*, Berlin: Kohlhammer.

Reichard, C. (1994b) '"Public Management" – ein neues Ausbildungskonzept für die deutsche Verwaltung', *Verwaltungsführung/Organisation/Personal (VOP)*, S. 178–84.

Reichard, C. and M. Röber (1993) 'Was kommt nach der Einheit? Die öffentliche Verwaltung in der ehemaligen DDR zwischen Blaupause und Reform', G.-J. Glaeßner (ed.) *Der lange Weg zur Einheit*, Berlin: Dietz pp. 215–45.

Richthofen, D.V. (1990) 'Verwaltungsmodernisierung in deutschen Städten durch Aus- und Weiterbildung', *Zeitschrift für Beamtenrecht*, S. 70–5.

Richthofen, D.V. (1993) 'Auf dem Weg zum öffentlichen Manager? Neuere Entwicklungen in der Ausbildung für das mittlere Management der Kommunalverwaltung', *Der Städtetag*, S. 589–92.

Röber, M. (1991) 'Auf der Suche nach betriebswirtschaftlich orientierten Anreizsystemen in neueren Konzepten zur Verwaltungsreform', in G. Schanz (ed.) *Handbuch 'Anreizsysteme in Wirtschaft und Verwaltung'*, Stuttgart: C.E. Poeschel pp. 1103–28.

Röber, M. (1996) 'Eine neue Verwaltung für die Hauptstadt? Verwaltungsreform in Berlin zwischen Anspruch und Wirklichkeit', in W. Süß (ed.) *Hauptstadt BERLIN, Band 3: Metropole im Umbruch*, Berlin: Nomos.

Schedler, K. (1993) *Anreizsysteme in der öffentlichen Verwaltung*, Bern, Stuttgart, Wien: Paul Haupt.

Schleswig-Holsteinischer Landtag (1994) *Bericht der Enquete-Kommission zur Verbesserung der Effizienz der öffentlichen Verwaltung*, Drucksache 13/2270, 2 November.

Schrijvers, A.P.M. (1993) 'The management of a larger town', *Public Administration*, pp. 595–603.

Schröter, E. and Röber, M. (1994) 'Regime change and administrative culture: role understandings and political attitudes of top bureaucrats from East and West Berlin, unpublished paper.

Sontheimer, K. (1993) *Grundzüge des politischen Systems der neuen Bundesrepublik Deutschland*, 15th ed, München/Zürich: Piper.

Staatsministerium Baden-Württemberg (Hrsg.) (1994) *Möglichkeiten für eine leistungsgerechtere Besoldung im öffentlichen Dienst: Ergebnisse einer Expertenanhörung zur Reform des öffentlichen Dienstrechts am 18.11.1993 in Stuttgart*, Stuttgart.

Stewart, J. and Walsh, K. (1992) 'Change in the management of public services', *Public Administration*, pp. 499–518.

Verwaltung 2000 (1993) *Strategisches Personalmanagement für die Landesverwaltung Baden-Württemberg: Schriftenreihe der Stabsstelle Verwaltungsstruktur, Information und Kommunikation. Band 11.* Herausgegeben vom Innenministerium Baden-Württemberg, Stuttgard.

Wagener, F. (1990) 'The external structure of administration in the Federal Republic of Germany', in K. König, H.J. von Oertzen and F. Wagener (eds) *Public Administration in the Federal of Germany*, Boston: Deventer.

Walther, H. (1991) 'Konzepte der Führungskräfteentwicklung in der öffentlichen Verwaltung', *Verwaltungsarchiv*, pp. 54–80

Widder, G. (1994) 'Verwaltung 2000: Die Kommunalverwaltung im Wandel', in *Möglichkeiten für eine leistungsgerechtere Besoldung im öffentlichen Dienst.*

Ergebnisse einer Expertenenhörung zur Reform des öffentlichen Dienstrechts am 18.11.1993 in Stuttgart, Stuttgart: Herausgegeben vom Staatsministerium Baden-Württemberg.

Wollmann, H. and Reichard, C. (eds) (1996) *Kommunalverwaltung im Modernisierungsprozeß*, Basel: Burkhaüser.

9 Ireland

Mary Coolahan and Sean Dooney

The public sector in Ireland consists of the civil service – those employed to serve the institutions of state, namely the president, the judiciary, the prime minister and other ministers, the attorney general and the comptroller and auditor general – local government, the regional health authorities, state-sponsored organizations – such as trading bodies like Aer Lingus and non-trading ones like the Tourist Board – the *Garda Siochana* (police), the defence forces and teachers in primary and secondary schools. This chapter examines the emergence of new public managers in Ireland and some of the factors affecting their roles and responsibilities.

THE STRUCTURE AND FUNCTIONS OF IRISH PUBLIC SERVICES

The civil service is the most important part of the public service because it is closest to ministers and government and, therefore, most immediately involved in the making of policy. Moreover, its supervisory influence extends to the various other parts of the public service, on whose activities it impinges in one way or another, whether in matters of policy, finance, organization, pay or personnel management. It is at the 'hub of the wheel' of government. The numbers of personnel employed in the public sector are shown in Table 9.1. The numbers employed in 1995 and ten years

Table 9.1 *Public sector employment in Ireland, 1995*

Civil service	31 461
Garda Siochana	11 421
Defence forces	13 015
Education	56 993
State-sponsored bodies (non-trading)	8 116
Health services	64 000
Local authorities	27 200
Total public service	**212 206**
State-sponsored bodies (trading)	**63 061**
Total public sector	**275 267**

previously are almost the same, though they have fluctuated in between, because of periods of retrenchment for budgetary reasons and of expansion to improve services. Table 9.2 shows trends in the exchequer pay and pensions bill as a percentage of GNP since 1987.

The forces of change in Ireland and the sources of policy are political, administrative, external and appellate. Demands emanating from the public are articulated through the media, through meetings with public representatives, pressure and interest groups, the programmes of political parties, the public service itself, the European Union (EU) and other international bodies, the decisions of the courts and administrative tribunals of various kinds. These lead to policies which often mirror those in other western European countries in areas like unemployment, incomes, crime, drugs and the environment. Ireland, though still conservative in some social areas, such as divorce and abortion, has of course, the same general problems as other countries.

In writing about the public services, it is important to recognize that the new Irish State, when it was established in 1922, had to agree a form of government and a system of administration to serve the government in the post-British period. The Ministers and Secretaries Act 1924 established departments of state and assigned each of them to a minister. The Act is also the legal basis for the Irish civil service. It empowers ministers to appoint officers to their departments and also largely determines the way in which those officers perform their duties. Each minister, as head of a department, is a 'corporation sole with perpetual succession' which means

Table 9.2 *Trends in exchequer pay and pensions as a percentage of GNP in Ireland, 1987–95*

Year	Exchequer pay and pensions bill (£ million)	GNP (£ million)	Bill as a % of GNP
1987	2759	18 963	14.5
1988	2845	19 995	14.2
1989	2914	22 161	13.1
1990	3160	23 962	13.2
1991	3382	25 324	13.4
1992	3750	26 693	14.0
1993	4087	28 563	14.3
1994	4355	31 050	14.0
1995	4619	33 575	13.8

that the acts of departments, including the acts of any of their civil servants, are the acts of ministers, for which they alone are accountable. Legally, unless there is an exception in law, as there is in the case of the Office of the Revenue Commissioners with regard to the determination of tax liabilities, no civil servant can make a decision. In effect, the minister *is* the department: civil servants have no separate existence. Every decision from a government department comes, strictly speaking, from the minister. The current Programme for Government (December 1994) includes, however, the following provision.

> In co-operation with the public service, reform of the Ministers and Secretaries Act, 1924 will be undertaken with a view to, *inter alia*, the separation of policy and executive functions of Departments, and clearly highlighting all areas of direct ministerial accountability in matters of policy and practice so as to allow for the delegated exercise of power and responsibility.

The existing system has had a major impact on the way in which the Irish civil service functions. It is the minister who is answerable to parliament, and ultimately to the electorate, for all the activities of the department. And, as the minister may be questioned in parliament, the discretion and freedom of action of civil servants are limited. Officials are reluctant to make decisions unless they are reasonably satisfied that these are the decisions which their minister would, personally, have made had the issue been brought to his/her notice in the first place. A higher priority is therefore often put on avoiding mistakes which might embarrass the minister rather than on giving the customer the best possible service. The result is that the dominant concerns of civil servants, as in the 'old' UK civil service, have been legality, equity and the impartial application of rules rather than customer service, economy, efficiency and effectiveness. That situation is now changing.

In local government, responsibility for the entire system rests with the Minister for the Environment, with the state being responsible for 100 per cent of the capital expenditure of local authorities and for almost half of their current expenditure. There are 29 county councils and, in addition, there are corporations in the large cities, town commissioners with limited responsibility in some of the large towns, and urban councils in others. Their functions are divided into reserved functions, discharged by elected members, and executive functions, performed by the city or county manager. Reserved functions relate to the adoption of estimates, the fixing of annual rates on property and the adoption of development plans. Executive functions include all those functions not reserved.

Each local authority has a manager under a system of management introduced in 1942. Managers are appointed by the local authority on the recommendation of the Local Appointments Commission. Internal promotion to manager, from within an authority, is not permitted but nearly all managers are persons who have served in local authorities, usually in an administrative grade but sometimes in a technical one. Some counties have assistant managers. Managers appointed since 1991 are appointed for a seven-year term.

Under the Management Acts there is an exact legal division between the functions of the manager and those of the elected council. The intention is that the council should have a full-time administrator to discharge all day-to-day business, leaving it free to concentrate on policy. In practice the position is somewhat blurred. For example, the adoption of development plans is a function reserved to the council, as is the preparation of annual estimates. In both these areas, however, the preparation is done by the manager. So, while councils make the decisions, these decisions are influenced by the advice of their managers. Evidence suggests, in practice, that managers exercise the dominant role in Irish local government – in housing, roads, environmental protection, sanitary services and so on – under the various policy directives of central government.

Responsibility for health policy lies with the Minister for Health and is set out in legislation. Implementation of this legislation is a matter for eight regional health authorities, and these services are almost entirely funded by the state. Each health authority has a chief executive officer who has responsibility for day-to-day activities.

The Minister for Justice is responsible for the administration of justice, security of the state, preservation of law and order, operation of the courts, prisons and proper functioning of the national police force. General management of that police force is the responsibility of a Commissioner, who is directly responsible to the Minister for Justice. Command of the defence forces is exercised by the government through the Minister for Defence.

State-sponsored bodies (trading and non-trading) referred to in Table 9.1 are autonomous public bodies. They are neither temporary in character nor purely advisory in function but were created by government to perform specific tasks. Shortly after the Irish Free State was set up in 1922, and after the passing of the Ministers and Secretaries Act 1924, it became clear that the rigidity of the civil service system was unsuitable for the running of certain commercial operations which were becoming necessary. If such tasks, desirable in the national interest, were to be undertaken by the state, then it would be necessary to loosen the direct control of ministers. Thus, in order to cut through the red tape that often constrains speedy direct action by government, the first of the commercial bodies, the Electricity Supply Board, was set up in 1927. Others such as Aer Lingus, *Bord na Mona* (the Turf Board) and *Coras Iompair Eireann* (the National Transport Company) followed. There are now about 25 trading state-sponsored bodies, where ministers set broad policy guidelines and are responsible to parliament for these, but are not concerned with day-to-day execution. Ministers appoint the boards of directors but staff are not civil servants. These public bodies are part of the system of government: the Minister for Finance is the shareholder and government is ultimately responsible for their performance. They are expected to achieve commercial results within a competitive framework and to operate in the market place, without state help.

In addition to the bodies set up for trading purposes, others have been established to carry out a wide range of non-trading activities. They include agricultural, industrial, educational and other bodies, such as *Teagasc* (the Agricultural Development Authority), the Industrial Development Authority and the National Council for Educational Awards. The reasons for establishing these as separate bodies derive from a tacit acceptance by ministers and the public generally that certain functions are best performed by bodies with a single remit, outside the civil service with its existing organization and constraints. Such organizations are funded almost entirely by the state, though they generate some small income from services. Until recently, there was a tendency to set up a new body to meet each new need or opportunity as it arose. More recently, especially in the case of non-trading bodies, their *raison d'être* is being looked at closely, with a view to exercising greater control and more economy.

The management of state-sponsored bodies varies and is determined by practical considerations, whilst the recruitment procedures/organizational structures, staff grades and operational systems of government departments and local authorities are identical. State-sponsored bodies also have freedom to adopt those structures and practices most suitable for the efficient performance of the duties assigned to them. The freedom which they have in matters of pay and conditions is, however, gradually being controlled by the Minister for Finance, acting through individual ministers. This is to ensure that all public servants have the same broad conditions of service in the areas of pay, leave, superannuation and so on. Perquisites are frowned on, such as entertainment allowances, cars and insurance policies.

The Review Body on Higher Remuneration in the Public Sector recommends, and the government normally approves, the remuneration of chief executives of state-sponsored bodies. In some cases the Review Body permits boards to pay their chief executives 10 per cent above or below the recommended rate and also to pay bonuses in circumstances for which guidelines are prescribed.

The new public manager, in the narrow sense of the term, is mainly found in the local authority and state-sponsored sectors and to a lesser degree in the health boards because, while broad policy is prescribed by the government or by individual ministers for these sectors, the bodies are then authorized to implement that policy themselves. In the civil service, classical public administration continues in that managers assist in the formulation of policy by making recommendations to ministers and are then also responsible to their ministers for its implementation when that falls to their departments. In that sense, the focus of this study is on managers at the top three levels in local authorities, state-sponsored bodies and health boards.

It would be wrong to exclude the civil service totally, however, since the techniques, practices and attitudes of what is referred to as the new public management are increasingly appreciated and applied in all parts of the public service. Besides, the programme of the government currently in office provides for the reform of the Ministers and Secretaries Act 1924, with a view to separating the policy and executive functions of departments and 'clearly highlighting all areas of direct ministerial accountability in matters of policy and practice, so as to allow for the delegated exercise of power and responsibility', as indicated above.

Attempts to combine aspects of classical public administration with a general management perspective are based on the premise that managers in the public and private sectors face many common problems and are engaged in activities which are in many ways similar. Since government is judged, however, not on managerial criteria but on social, political, cultural and economic achievements, subject to some overall limitation upon total demands for taxation, the efficiency and effectiveness with which government departments conduct their business is not the dominant factor in determining the flow of funds towards them and such bodies have not, generally, been compelled to employ those kinds of management systems common to the private sector. Besides, public management does not have a high electoral profile. Developments in public management such as the separation of the civil service into core departments and executive agencies, which have occurred in some other countries, such as in the UK, have not happened in Ireland to the same extent. Here the classical model continues, by and large, to operate with highly centralized management control being carried out at a global aggregate level, separating the control of expenditure from those activities which generate that expenditure.

There are, however, some indications of a movement towards a 'new public management', based on international experience. Accountability processes in the Irish public sector through the minister, parliament and ultimately the electorate are steadily being modified and there is an attempt at incremental reform. Among the reasons for this relatively slow progress towards public management are: a reluctance on the part of parliament to free large areas of government administration from day-to-day control; disinterest by parliament in the topic; a multi-seat proportional representation system; lack of will in political parties; deficiency of management culture in the senior civil service; under-investment in management training in the civil service; the absence of an independent body to review a reform programme; problems caused for a small civil service by membership of the EU; economic difficulties in Ireland; and an inherent conservatism.

THE NEW PUBLIC MANAGERS

Despite the inhibiting factors referred to above, a new type of public service manager is increasingly to be found throughout the Irish public service, though it is difficult to quantify precisely how large that group is. A new emphasis on economy, efficiency, effectiveness and excellence is permeating the public service and such developments are changing the climate of public-service management.

The Public Services Organization Review Group, which reported in 1969, made major recommendations concerning the organization of government departments involving the separation of policy and execution. Policy was to remain with ministers in much smaller departments, and execution was to be assigned to satellite bodies/agencies. In 1985 a Government White Paper promised that, where departments had a sufficiently large volume of executive work, ministers would be enabled by legislation to transfer such work to executive offices. Progress has been slow in giving effect to these and other public service reforms because of two basic, yet related, reasons. First, there has been a real need to move on to what were regarded as more pressing items of government business. Second, there has been a somewhat hesitant enthusiasm for change at administrative level, brought about largely by the fact that public managers did not own the decisions involved in the reform process.

There has, however, been a movement towards more accountable management and performance measurement. Undoubtedly the influence of these has been more marked in market-driven public enterprises, in particular among those which compete in the international market place. Elsewhere, the deep-rooted conservatism of the civil service and the constraints placed upon it by the concept of the minister as a 'corporation sole' have resulted in a slower acceptance of, and a greater resistance to, change. Political concerns and the absence of quantifiable or qualitative work targets have also been major inhibiting factors. Still, the prevailing administrative circumstances are more conducive to change.

Similar considerations, though not to the same extent, apply in the case of the local authorities and regional health boards, which are almost entirely financed by central government which, despite an increasing use of block grants, exercises a fairly tight control on the expenditure of monies allocated. Also the defence and security forces are closely monitored both in their programmes and their expenditure by their parent Departments of Defence and Justice and by the Department of Finance, which monitors expenditure across the entire public service.

In general, officials who might be described as new public managers are from the middle/upper-middle socio-economic stratum. Their educational qualifications are generally a degree or equivalent in public administration, management, engineering or economics. The most senior posts in the civil service are now held by officials who reached them through the rigorous competitive system of the Top Level Appointments Committee. This Committee comprises secretaries of government departments and persons distinguished in the private sector. It makes recommendations concerning those civil servants to be appointed to the posts of secretary and assistant secretary, by the government and ministers respectively.

Table 9.3   *Civil service managers in Ireland, 1995*

Title	Number	Sex		Average age	Annual remuneration (maximum) (£)
Secretary of Department	16	1	Female	46	75 000
		15	Male		
Assistant Secretary	92	7	Female		51 000
		93	Male	47	
Principal Officer	331	63	Female		41 000
		268	Male	47	
Assistant Principal	972	416	Female		31 000
		511	Male	42	

These officials regularly get together in networks to discuss, analyse and plan resolutions to the various management issues confronting the public service.

Top managers in local government are almost exclusively male and generally have lower salaries than civil servants. But a few county/city managers have higher remuneration than indicated, reflecting variations in individual levels of responsibility and the scale of operation of the authority for which they are responsible.

Table 9.4   *Local authority managers in Ireland, 1995*

Title	Number	Sex	Annual remuneration (£)
County and city manager	34	Male	47 000
Assistant to manager	19	Male	40 000
County secretary/ finance officer	57	Male 54 Female 3	33 000

In the absence of detailed empirical research, in-depth biographical information is not available on managers in the state-sponsored body sector. Observation of the system, however, suggests that they are generally between the ages of 35 and 50, come from the same social background as the civil service managers and have similar educational qualifications. There are no female chief executives in state-sponsored bodies and under-representation is common throughout all higher levels of management in public bodies. By law there is no discrimination of any kind against women in the public service and officials of both sexes compete, with equal chance, for all posts. However, prior to Ireland's joining the European Community in 1973, female public servants had to retire on marriage and this may be a reason for the relatively few women in senior posts.

In considering the remuneration of senior managers in state-sponsored bodies, the Review Body on Higher Remuneration in the Public Sector has identified three categories depending on the responsibility attaching to the post, staff numbers and the significance of the body nationally. The salaries recommended range from £40 000 to £70 000 a year. Chief executives of the trading bodies command the highest levels. In some cases a car is provided, which includes private use; in other cases a charge is made for such use. Particulars of the remuneration packages for managers below the level of chief executive are not available.

Legal Status

Civil servants hold office at the 'will and pleasure' of government which means, in practice, that they have lifetime employment and may be dismissed only by the government of the day. Read literally, this provision would mean that a civil servant could be dismissed for any or no reason and that fair procedures need not be followed. In practice, the official is informed why dismissal is being contemplated and given the opportunity to put his/her side of the case. Those employed in the local authorities, health boards, police and army also have lifetime employment but may be dismissed by the appropriate minister, if statutory grounds for removal from office obtain and fair procedures are followed. In recent years, those appointed to the most senior level, head of a government department or a county/city manager, may not hold office for a period of longer than seven years. A slight, but noticeable, tendency is emerging, especially in the case of specialist technical vacancies such as architects, engineers, accountants, to appoint persons on a contractual basis. This tendency is more discernible at higher levels in the state-sponsored bodies sector. It is generally accepted that such developments are a reflection of moves towards the creation of a cadre of 'new' public managers.

Recruitment and Selection

All recruitment to the public service is based on merit and open competition. Recruitment to all levels of the civil service, and from middle-management upwards in the local authority and health areas, is conducted centrally by two bodies operating under statute, the Civil Service Commission and the Local Appointments Commission. The former body also selects those for initial appointment to the police. Recruitment to state-sponsored bodies is conducted by the organizations themselves, often through the use of specialized recruitment agencies. In such cases, the normal procedure is for the recruitment agency to place an advertisement for the vacant post and also to carry out preliminary interviews, shortlisting the applicants. Those on the shortlist are then interviewed by a sub-committee of the Organization's Board of Directors. All appointments are on merit.

As indicated earlier, all managers in the civil service are recruited at school/university level and are then promoted on merit through the hierarchy. Specific qualifications for promotion are rarely prescribed but those entering the competitions at the level of principal officer and upwards, which are advertised internally throughout the civil service, must be recommended by the heads of their departments and are expected to have well-developed and proven management skills, have displayed qualities of organization and leadership and be active, innovative and good at communication. An academic qualification is not sought specifically. For positions at assistant principal officer level, there are qualifying written tests and an interview. In nearly all instances, competitions are conducted from amongst existing civil servants by the Civil Service Commission.

In local government, appointments to middle and senior posts are made following competitions organized by the Local Appointments Commission, a three-person body, established by law, of whom the chair is the Ceann Comhairle (Speaker) of the Dail (Parliament). Specific qualifications are not prescribed but those applying are expected to have a satisfactory knowledge of Irish public administration and administrative experience at a high level, including experience in the organization and control of staff. In practice, most of the posts advertised are secured by persons who have served in local authorities and are familiar with the vast corpus of local government law. The appointment of the chiefs of the security and defence forces are made directly by the government, with internal appointments being made following selection board procedures. Conditions of service, including pay and related matters, are prescribed by appropriate ministers under guidelines laid down by the Minister for Finance.

The appointment of public managers in all areas reflects a strong emphasis on political neutrality, a fact supported, recognized and protected by public servants and politicians alike. Public servants seek to serve successive governments with equal degrees of independence and impartiality. There are no moves to change this situation.

In tertiary education, the Institute of Public Administration, a national agency for the advancement of public-sector management, offers undergraduate, postgraduate and professional programmes in public management, public policy studies, business studies, accountancy and computer technology, all devised as part of the professional development of serving Irish public servants. A significant number of graduates of the Institute and similar type programmes are now emerging at the most senior levels of government.

Developments in Remuneration

As part of the control of national finances, the Minister for Finance has statutory control over the remuneration of the civil service and that of the non-trading state-sponsored bodies, defence forces and *Garda Siochana*. In the case of local authorities and health boards there are, in practice, non-statutory arrangements which enable the minister to have *de facto* control. The Minister for Finance is party to schemes of conciliation and arbitration, for all grades, except the highest, which operate throughout the public service. Pay scales for top-grade civil servants are recommended by the Review Body on Higher Remuneration in the Public Sector, which also makes recommendations concerning the salaries of the Taoiseach (Prime Minister), ministers, members of parliament, judges, county managers, and chief executives of health authorities and of state-sponsored bodies. These recommendations are subject to the approval of the government.

Performance-related pay does not apply in the civil service, except in one grade, or in the local authority or health areas, and there are no imminent moves to introduce it. The one grade to which it does apply is that of assistant secretary, where there is a scheme of performance bonuses. The secretary of each department identifies for each assistant secretary objectives for the year ahead. Payment is made on the basis of the achievement of these objectives. The only other public-sector, area in which performance bonus applies is chief executives of state-sponsored bodies, as already described.

It is difficult to evaluate pay relativities between the public and private sectors in the absence of reliable income figures for the private sector. However, analysis of available data suggests that pay levels are broadly comparable, with public-sector pay levels being slightly below those of the private sector, reflecting perhaps the value attached to permanent status in the former. At senior management level, public-sector pay rates are considerably lower than the comparable private-sector remuneration package.

Inherent in the new public management is a strong emphasis on systematic evaluation. In the civil service and local authorities, pay scales provide for a number of annual increments awarded, in practice, on the basis of a minimum level of satisfactory service. All officials in the same grade receive the same level of increment, with no provision for reward for any higher level of satisfactory service. Non-award of increment is rare. Heads of government departments have flat salaries. Thus, the pay structure is much less flexible than pay arrangements in ordinary commercial employment. Whilst the White Paper, *Serving the Country Better* (1989), announced the introduction of merit pay, this has not yet been introduced. It must be added that merit pay has not been welcomed either by public servants or their unions, both groups referring to difficulties in performance assessment and to the risks of favouritism in implementing it.

Career Progression

Promotion systems are based on merit, although seniority occasionally plays a part. In the civil service, promotions to the highest posts are made by ministers or, in the case of heads of departments, by the government, on the basis of recommendations from the Top Level Appointments Committee which interviews candidates. In other cases, promotions are also by selection board. Candidates must be serving civil servants. Heads of departments may serve for a period of not more than seven years and, if 55 years or older at the time of appointment, they must retire after five years' service. Within local authorities and health boards, the top three grades are filled by the Local Appointments Commission. Vacancies for chief executives in state-sponsored bodies are also normally filled by open competition in the manner described. Throughout the entire public service promotion by selection board is the norm.

There is little mobility between the various parts of the public service and hardly any between the public and private sectors. There is considerable mobility within the civil service such as from one department of state to another but little or none between the civil service and local authorities or health services. Entry to civil service recruitment grades is either from school or university and all posts above these grades are filled by promotion. Only within local government does mobility occur, because of the statutory obligation to advertise posts. There are no moves to alter these existing practices.

Training and Development

Training facilities are widely available throughout the public service. Individual government departments have their own internal training units, the Department of Finance trains all middle and senior management grades across the Civil Service and the Institute of Public Administration provides training for all parts of the public service. Training facilities provided by the Irish Management Institute are also used along with specialized facilities provided by universities and other similar institutions both at home and abroad. Typical courses provided by the Civil Service Training Centre in the Department of Finance, and by the Institute of Public Administration, include undergraduate and postgraduate courses in management and business studies, accredited part-time and block release courses in finance, accountancy and information technology, and short courses in various aspects of management development and relevant skills.

Even where specific programmes of staff development are not provided, incentives are often in operation which encourage staff to pursue educational activities including degree courses. These include schemes for the refund of fees, study and examination leave, scholarships, schemes of appraisal and mobility. In the past ten years or so, because of world recession and financial problems besetting the Irish economy, there has been, first, an embargo and, latterly, tight restriction on recruitment to the public service. While this has militated against the release of staff for all but essential training and development programmes, there is a strong appreciation of the importance of training and development and a recognition that both result in a positive orientation towards public management. Many of the new public managers have undergone considerable training, both on and off the job, though most have never worked outside the public sector.

AUTHORITY, RESPONSIBILITIES AND ACCOUNTABILITY

The Ministers and Secretaries Act 1924 designates the minister in charge of a government department as that department's legal personality, on whom, with few exceptions, legal powers are conferred. To be validly exercised, all powers must be exercised under the minister's direction, a system of individual responsibility of ministers to parliament which is in sharp contrast to systems which obtain elsewhere. This Act underpins the Irish civil service system and imposes obvious limitations on public management where civil servants are concerned. Its provisions, as indicated above, are now under review with a possible amendment including the extent and limitations of ministerial accountability and liability.

Civil servants, who are heads of offices, are accountable to the parliamentary system, through their ministers, whilst others are accountable to the administrative system, through hierarchical schemes. Duties are performed through a system of implicit delegation from minister to secretary and so on down through the various ranks. In the same way, heads of other public bodies are accountable to their councils or boards of directors. There is a wide variety of reporting procedures, including meetings, written reports, informal contacts, review of budgets and estimates and the monitoring of work schedules.

Public managers are also accountable to the law, having no special immunity from prosecution in either civil or criminal courts. There is no system of administrative courts, and cases involving officials are heard in the ordinary courts. These courts cannot, however, intervene provided that a public authority entrusted with discretion keeps within its powers and commits no open breach of natural justice. Administrative appeals tribunals in Ireland cannot be said to constitute a formal system. They have been established by individual ministers on a more or less *ad hoc* basis and there are inconsistencies in their composition, procedures and areas within which they operate.

Ireland has an Ombudsman whose remit covers government departments and offices, local authorities, health boards, telecommunications and the postal services, with provision for extending the list by ministerial order. In his own words the Ombudsman sees his role as 'being concerned not only with the legal aspects of a complaint but also with the question of equity and fair play'. His assistance may be sought directly by citizens.

While formal definitions of the authority, responsibility and accountability of the public manager do not exist, it is accepted that the public service manager operates in an environment radically different from that of the past. Factors contributing to attitudinal change include the financial constraints under which modern government operates and the changing expectations which the public and politicians have of public servants. Besides, the complexity of modern government demands both mechanisms of accountability and clearer guidelines as to the authority and responsibilities of the public manager. As a result, there is a marked trend towards 'management-by-contract' with letters of undertaking, quasi-legal obligations and framework documents, setting out broad strategies in various policy sectors. This is more the situation in the competitive public enterprise sector where such systems are well developed, but it is also becoming the situation, though to a much lesser extent, within the civil service. There, emphasis on the '3Es' – economy, efficiency and effectiveness – is growing. There is also increased emphasis on other 'Es': excellence, ethics, environment and a European dimension.

That part of the public service which is most actively, indeed almost exclusively, involved in the making of policy is the civil service. Civil servants analyse problems, define the issues involved and devise suitable solutions. Having examined all aspects of the problems laid before them, they advise ministers of the various alternatives available, making recommendations as to the preferable course of action. Ministers and government then make choices and the civil service ensures that whatever policy is chosen is implemented. The stage has not yet been reached where policy-making and managing can be clearly differentiated.

Administrative control in public authorities is exercised through the hierarchy within and through the Department of Finance, which plays a key role particularly with regard to financial control over the public service as a whole. A system of delegated administrative budgets, recently introduced, is helping to encourage the development of a new public management culture throughout the civil service. Under this arrangement the Minister for Finance and the minister in charge of a line department enter into a formal agreement, usually covering a three-year period, whereby heads of government departments have delegated authority to decide on the amount of monies to be spent on the various components of their departmental budgets. Thus, emphasis is shifting from control of individual items of expenditure towards control of the overall size of the allocation to departments. These arrangements allow management to achieve greater efficiency and effectiveness and encourage greater delegation of authority in relation to administrative costs. They also encourage medium to long-term planning of civil service administrative costs and encourage greater delegation of authority in relation to such costs within departments.

Until recently, evaluation within the Irish public service has depended on auditing and accounting which ensured that funds were spent in the way authorized, and that spending complied with administrative regulations. The Comptroller and Auditor General (Amendment) Act 1993, however, extends the powers of that constitutional officer to carry out examinations of the economy and efficiency of operation of government departments and certain other publicly funded bodies. Because of the current widespread acceptance that more than a financial regulatory audit is now required, and because it is also generally accepted that terms such as economy, efficiency and effectiveness do not readily fit into neatly defined categories, the new Act requires that the Comptroller and Auditor General (CAG) must also now be concerned with the adequacy of management effectiveness. While the CAG is not required to carry out reviews, since this is left to departments and other public bodies, he/she reports to Parliament on the adequacy or otherwise of management systems. In effect, the Act provides that the public bodies concerned are now obliged to have adequate management systems in place. All of these bodies are also subject to value-for-money examination, at the CAG's discretion.

PUBLIC MANAGERS, CLASSICAL ADMINISTRATORS AND ETHICS

The principles of management for, and the priorities of, both the new public manager and the classical administrator are, to an extent, similar. However, a major difference exists regarding the operating environment.

While there has been some development in the role and responsibilities of the public manager, the fact is that the public manager operates in a political environment. Public-sector strategic executions and planning can be inhibited as a result of inconsistent policies arising from national circumstances, the changing and evolving policies of the EU and, to some extent, stop-go policies of government.

Private-sector management models are not directly transferable to the public sector because of the distinguishing characteristics of that public sector. These include:

- The prime purpose of a public service is to serve the public, to seek the common good; the activities of public servants are fixed by law and these are not judged on a profit basis.
- Public authorities have coercive powers; hence there is a need to provide for consultation, objection and appeal.
- Public administration is carried on in a 'glass bowl', in that there must be a high degree of transparency;
- The public sector has an organization culture determined by socio-political aims with consequent difficulty in measuring much of its work;
- The public service manager works for, with and under the direction of politicians;
- The public sector balances the various demands made upon it. Moreover, the manner of execution often owes more to political factors than to bureaucratic rationality.

Changes in the public service, arising from the demands of a modern economy and of an increasingly educated and sophisticated electorate, put pressures on public servants, which in Ireland are evolutionary rather than revolutionary, and such pressures are threatening the traditional strengths of the public service such as political neutrality, loyalty to the democratically elected government of the day, evenhandedness and fairness to all, discretion and the avoidance of the limelight and dedication to the national interest. Whilst there is a strong appreciation of what is called the public service ethic, such an ethic is not written down in a code of conduct. There are some written guidelines, which seek to ensure that public servants perform their duty honestly and impartially and avoid situations which compromise their integrity. These standards relate to such matters as government contracts and purchases from, or sales to, government departments, engagement in outside occupations, involvement in politics and the acceptance of gifts.

One of the more important challenges facing public administration in Ireland today is to protect tradition by adapting old practices to modern conditions in such a way as to respect and reflect those values which form the cornerstone of the Irish tradition. Public servants in Ireland are ever-conscious of the fact that the most frequently used informal remedy of those who wish to have a grievance against the administration investigated and, if appropriate, redressed is to approach a politician, usually their member of parliament, to use influence with the relevant minister or decision-maker. Such approaches, 'clientelism', are, indeed, frequently encouraged. Parliament has long regarded itself as a watchdog against government, and the handling by its members of individuals' problems could be regarded as an extension of this viewpoint. In the Irish system of multi-seat constituencies, where members of even the same party are in competition with each other for election, there are tangible benefits to be gained from interest in all issues affecting constituents and constituencies. Thus, the public manager must be ever-vigilant not to move too far from the policies and opinions of his/her political masters.

THE NEW PUBLIC MANAGEMENT AND POLITICS

In Ireland, civil servants at middle and senior management levels have always been prohibited from participating in party politics. It is accepted that it is in the public interest that civil servants should be politically impartial, and confidence in such impartiality is an essential part of the structure of government. This situation is one which is rarely questioned by either government or civil servants.

A recent development (1993) has been the appointment by ministers of programme managers whose task it is to assist ministers in managing and co-ordinating the achievement of the objectives of the published Programme for Government. The role and function of the programme manager is distinct from that of departmental secretary and senior line manager. Where the latter have responsibility for the development of policy proposals, the overall management of programmes, and have charge of their departments generally, the programme manager has the specific task of providing administrative support and assistance to ministers in managing and co-ordinating the achievement of the objectives of the programme of the three-party government, to identify problems and remove dissension. To this end, programme managers meet weekly as a group, and each programme manager reports regularly to the chair of the group, the programme manager of the prime minister, to review progress.

Part of the task of each programme manager is to oversee the implementation of the government's legislative programme. They also work as individuals with their ministers in dealing with specific projects. These programme managers have been recruited by ministers from outside the public service and their appointments are co-terminous with those of the ministers. These new arrangements are being monitored closely but it is too early yet to reach any definitive conclusion about the success or otherwise of the development.

While public managers and politicians in Ireland come from the same socio-economic background, in general they tend not to frequent the same networks after appointment to their chosen occupations. Indeed, in so far as the civil service and local services are concerned, great care is taken to preserve detachment and independence. Though the occasional manager in the public enterprise sector may align publicly with the political master of the day, each group usually takes great care not to trespass on the territory of the other. Though public servants have an active role in the formulation of policy, this is done on a non-partisan basis. The public servant seeks to provide frank, independent and informed advice, on the basis of experience, not calculated to advance the political fortunes of the party in power. In doing this, public servants are not unaware of the minister's role as a member of a political party and, on occasion, find it necessary to perform a delicate balancing act. Politicians accept this situation and, in general, take care not to cause embarrassment for officials in the implementation of policy.

CONCLUSION

The advent of new public management to Ireland seems to be already changing the climate and culture of public-sector organizations. While there has been no fundamental structural change in the machinery of government, a more results-oriented approach is developing. Relations between the new public manager and politics remain unchanged, both sides seeming to be happy with the present situation: the new public manager has continued to be averse to politics, seeing that area as best left to political advisers, programme managers and the private offices of politicians.

Despite the inhibitions referred to earlier, there is nevertheless a movement away from classic public administration to public management in Ireland. In February 1995, a Minister for State was appointed with the specific task of developing the Strategic Management Initiative (SMI) set in train by the previous Prime Minister in 1994. The primary objective of the SMI is to put in place, in each department and public service agency, a management process focused on ensuring continuous improvements in the performance of the civil and wider public service in relation to the contribution they can make to national development, provision of services to the public and the efficient and effective use of resources. A second aspiration is to ensure a greater focus on improving the delivery of services with a view to making them more customer-oriented. Departments are now commencing the process of concentrating aims and strategies into specific objectives to inform the day-to-day work of staff.

The pace of change, social, economic and political, and the growing impact of international factors, increasingly demand that public management structures and systems in Ireland, be flexible, responsive and capable of delivering value for money. The new initiatives are intended to embrace a critical assessment of existing practices, along with the many assumptions and rigidities, which have grown up in areas of the public service over the years. Hopefully this will facilitate the carrying through of necessary reforms to ensure that the public service is able to meet the challenges of the coming decades effectively and with confidence.

At present, the new public sector managers are located mainly in the public enterprise sector. However the world-wide agenda of public sector renewal and reform is now being actively pursued in Ireland, with the thrust coming from both the political and the administrative arms of government. Most senior officials in Ireland's public service are very aware of developments taking place elsewhere in the field of public management and of the advantages to be gained from advancing the practice of effective public management. There is therefore an irreversible trend towards public management, if at a somewhat slower pace than its advocates wish.

References

Advisory Committee on Management Training (1988) *Managers for Ireland*, Dublin: Stationery Office.

Boyle, R. (1993) *Administrative Budgets in the Irish Civil Service*, Dublin: Institute of Public Administration.

Carvill, D. (1993) 'Things old and new – the Comptroller and Auditor General (Amendment) Act 1993', *Seirbhis Phoibli*, 14, (2).

Dooney, S. and O'Toole, J. (1992) *Irish Government Today*, Dublin: Gill & MacMillan.

A Government of Renewal – A Policy Agreement between Fine Gael, the Labour Party, Democratic Left (1995) Dublin: Government Information Services.

Industrial Policy Review Group (1992) *A Time for Change: Industrial Policy for the 1990s*, Dublin: Stationery Office.

Institute of Public Administration (1995) *Yearbook and Diary*, Dublin: IPA.

Local Government Reorganisation and Reform (1991) Dublin: Stationery Office.

Ministers and Secretaries Act, 1924 (No 16), Dublin: Stationery Office.

Moore, P.J. (1991) 'Administrative budgets – a new era for civil service managers', *Seirbhis Phoibli*, 12 (2).

Murphy, K. (1993) 'Managing the Irish public service in the 1990s', *Seirbhis Phoibli*, 14 (2).

National Economic and Social Council (1990) *A Strategy for the Nineties: Economic Stability and Structural Change*, no. 89, Dublin: Stationery Office.

National Economic and Social Council (1993) *A Strategy for Competitiveness, Growth and Employment*, no. 96, Dublin: Stationery Office.

O'Toole, B.J. (1994) 'Permanent secretaries, public administration and public management', *Public Policy and Administration*, 9 (1).

Parliamentary Debates – 24 January 1995, col. 1521.

Public Services Organization Review Group (1969) *Report*, Dublin: Stationery Office.

Review Body on Higher Remuneration in the Public Sector (1992) *Report no. 32*, Dublin: Stationery Office.

Serving the Country Better – A White Paper on the Public Service (1989) Dublin: Stationery Office.

Stewart, J. and Walsh, K. (1992) 'Change in the management of public services', *Public Administration*, 70, Winter.

10 Italy

Carlo D'Orta and Valerio Talamo

Since the early 1990s, Italy has been experiencing a period of intensive administrative reforms. Though a number of aspects remain uncertain, the newly constructed system is characterized by five fundamental pillars:

- reform of structures, including ministries, public bodies and corporations, and other branches of public administration;
- reform of administrative procedures, with a case-by-case review to determine whether the present model is still valid and capable of meeting the objectives set;
- reform of administrative controls, focusing on efficiency and quality in terms of results of administrative activity, rather than on its conformity to rules;
- reform of the budget structure of the different branches of public administration;
- reform of public employment and, within this context, the public management corps.

With regard to the first three pillars, the underlying idea is to simplify the administration in terms of organization, functions and procedures for action. Regarding the fourth pillar, the purpose is to tie the activities of the major internal departments of each branch of public administration to precise budget objectives. The key concept of the fifth pillar is the transition of public-sector personnel management from a bureaucratic to a business model.

Legislative decree no. 29, 3 February 1993, together with a number of the provisions of law no. 537, December 1993, particularly article 3, represent the instruments through which reform of public-sector employment has been implemented. The new rules and regulations are applied in their entirety only to the administrative corps of central government ministries. However, the underlying principles of the reform provide an outline for a model of public-sector management which is valid, following appropriate modifications, for other branches of public administration, as well as public corporations and organs of local government.

There are two essential characteristics of the new model. First, there is a distinction between the role of political bodies and the bureaucracy. The former is responsible for providing overall guidelines and monitoring the results of administrative operations, whilst the latter handles operational and administrative activities. Second, a business-management approach is being introduced into the operating methods of public-sector management, based on managing budget objectives, greater flexibility in the organization of work and personnel and the assumption of responsibility for the results of administrative operations. The effectiveness of this new model can only be measured in the light of actual operating experience over the next five to ten years.

THE NEW PUBLIC MANAGERS

Reform of industrial relations involving employees of different branches of public administration, enacted through legislative decree no. 29, 3 February 1993, brings to completion the process of privatization of public employment. It marks the transformation from industrial relations governed by unilateral, authoritative acts to a system essentially organized on a contractual, bilateral basis. In particular, the reform decree follows a policy concerning legal status which brings Italian public employment fully in line with the European-wide transformation of public administration. This is geared towards a business-management model, with restructuring of relations between the political and administrative spheres. It is against the backdrop of this transformation that the reform of the public administrative corps is taking place, with decisive powers of management and organization being granted to managers.

As the role of the public manager changes, there is a growing convergence between private-sector and public-sector approaches (Carinci and Carinci, 1993). Indeed, legislative decree no. 29 contemplates a mixed model structured on two different levels. First, public functions and administrative organization, on the strength of the prerogative included in the Constitution (art. 97), are regulated according to standard public-sector procedures (art. 2.1, legislative decree no. 29). Second, work and relations with employees fall under the private-sector model. The two levels constantly interface, reciprocally influencing each another. This makes it easier to appreciate the delicate role of the public manager, whose job is to co-ordinate work activities with the administrative operations of public offices (cfr. 3.1.1.).

To perform this function, the manager uses powers of both a public-sector and private-sector type, with the latter being similar to those held by private employers. Managers are placed in charge of offices, from which they can issue any sort of administrative or operational provision, with the sole limitation being the financial resources allocated in the budget. Managers are also responsible for the results of operations under their control and for observing the general directives received from the political body, which sets programme goals, overall guidelines and objectives.

These brief initial observations clearly demonstrate the key role of the management corps within a public administration which is operating 'by objectives'. In a similar framework, it is managers who, in personifying the organization, personify the employer (Zoppoli, 1993) and to whom the most significant powers involving the organization of work are granted. Such an operation is made possible through the new rules and regulations which have been stipulated regarding the relationship between politics and the administration. This is based on the clear-cut distinction between power to establish guidelines and monitor results (a prerogative of the political body) and actual operating powers (assigned to the management corps).

In the light of these considerations, the relationship between the political body and the management corps is no longer hierarchical but involves issuing broad directives. Managers are not subject to an authority which issues orders but merely to directives handed down from above. This opinion is supported by almost all scholarly opinion, with the exception of Albenzio (1994). These characteristics of independence and managerial responsibility are, however, fully evident only in the uppermost ranks of the renewed public-management corps (general directors and similar positions). Following a strategy which has been criticized by the majority of the experts (Zoppoli, 1993; D'Alberti, 1994; D'Alessio, 1993; Cassese, 1993; Albenzio, 1994; Albanese and Torricelli, 1993; Carinci and Carinci, 1993), a split has been established within the management corps between general directors and lower-level management personnel. In fact, the status of general directors is still regulated under a statute based on administrative law. Lower-level managers are subject to normal labour law and therefore to collective bargaining as well. Their legal status is regulated under a statute based on private law.[1]

There would appear to be a hierarchical relationship between the two managerial rankings (D'Alessio, 1993) or a relationship which, at the very least, significantly limits the autonomy of lower-level managers. The margin for making decisions on the part of the latter would seem to be reduced to a merely administrative role within bounds which have been predetermined by the general director, with little possibility for participation in the decision-making processes determining the organization of work and the managing of resources (Albanese and Toricelli, 1993). It is safe to say, therefore, that legislative decree no 29, 1993, the fourth reform of Italian public employment,[2] has identified the general director as that corresponding to the 'public manager' position borrowed from the private sector (Zoppoli, 1993). With this assumption, our analysis focuses primarily on top-ranking managers within the public administrative system.

CHARACTERISTICS OF PUBLIC MANAGERS

Numbers

It is generally agreed that administrators in the public sector are too numerous, are not highly motivated and are frustrated by a levelling of compensation. The excessively high number of public administrators has led to a confusion of duties and responsibilities, an overlapping of roles and a dilution of the role of the administrator (Romangnoli, 1988). An analysis of the management corps as a whole, in both the public and private sectors, shows continuous expansion throughout the period 1971 to 1991. According to a 1993 estimate by the Italian Federation of Corporate Managers (CIDA), the percentage of managers for every 1000 workers employed rose from 4.6 per cent in 1971 to 12.2 per cent in 1991. The expansion of the management group appears to be closely related to the growth of service-industry activities and public employment, areas in which roughly 25 per cent of all managers are employed.

At the end of 1992, there were 547 general directors in government ministries and 5087 at other levels. Together, the 2 management categories accounted for some 2 per cent of full-time personnel employed. At the same time, the number of general directors in independent state enterprises was 54, whilst lower-level managers numbered 655, accounting for 0.25 per cent of full-time staff employed in this area, a rise of 123 since 1986. In non-economic public bodies, there were 88 general directors and 1664 lower-level managers, corresponding to some 3 per cent of all employees. Within this sector of public administration,[3] there was a decrease of 765 in the number of managers employed during this period.

In regional governments and local government bodies, higher-ranking administrators totalled 3009, whilst those in lower ranks totalled 14 190 or 2 per cent of all employees in this sector.[4] Finally, in the school sector, there were 14 074 administrative personnel (principals, educational directors, directors of conservatories and holders of equivalent posts) or 1.4 per cent of full-time employees.

Female Managers

The presence of women managers varies significantly in different sectors of public administration, with the highest levels found in schools, where women accounted for 43 per cent of educational directors, 28 per cent of principals and 28 per cent of conservatory directors (all figures rounded). In local government, women represented 16 per cent of management personnel and 17 per cent in government ministries. In non-economic public bodies, women account for 11 per cent of management personnel but for only 4 per cent in independent public corporations (see Table 10.1).

The presence of women in the ranks of top management is almost insignificant. Women general directors account for 4 per cent of all general directors in government ministries, 4 per cent in independent public corporations, 4 per cent in public bodies and agencies, and 9 per cent in local and regional government and agencies. Compared with the private sector, however, the percentage of women in the public management corps is generally higher. Access to management positions in public administration, despite the progress made over the last decade, remains an almost exclusively male prerogative, especially at top levels, and in a number of specific sectors.[5]

Geographic Origin

One of the traditional characteristics of Italian public employment is the predominance of staff from southern Italy and the Latium region. The traditional southern Italian origin of public employees is confirmed by the geographic origin of administrative and managerial personnel. An analysis of the data on public functionaries accepted for managerial training programmes, as well as candidates admitted to the recruitment course for administrative functionaries, organized by Italy's Advanced School of Public Administration, shows a clear predominance of students coming from the regions of southern and central Italy, as opposed to the north (see Table 10.2). The southern Italian origin of the upper echelons of the bureaucracy is reflected in the educational and cultural background of these employees which is mainly in the humanities and legal studies. This is more deeply rooted in the traditions of southern and central Italy, which lack the influences of the industrial culture typically found in the north (Cassese, 1983).

Table 10.1 Number of managers by gender and managerial ranking in Italy, 1992

	Total managers	Men AV	%	Women AV	%	Upper-level managers	Men AV	%	Women AV	%	Lower-level managers	Men AV	%	Women AV	%
Ministries	5634	4685	83.2	949	16.8	547	523	95.6	24	4.4	5087	4162	78.0	925	22.0
Independent enterprises	709	680	95.9	29	4.1	54	52	96.3	2	3.7	655	628	95.9	27	4.1
Public agencies and corporations	1752	1552	88.6	200	11.4	88	85	96.5	3	3.5	1664	1467	88.2	197	11.8
Regional and local government bodies	13809	11590	83.9	2219	16.1	2947	2674	90.7	273	9.3	10862	8916	82.1	1946	17.9
Schools (principals)	9473	6841	72.8	2632	27.8										
Schools (educational directors)	4571	2563	56.8	1954	43.2										
Schools (conservatory directors)	80	58	73.0	22	27.0										

Note: AV = Absolute Value
SOURCE: General Accounting Office.

Table 10.2 *Geographic origin of the participants in courses organized by the Advanced School of Public Administration in Italy, 1991*

	% of participants in management course	% participants in course for recruitment of management personnel
North	4.6	3
Centre	26.2	53
South	69.2	44

SOURCE: documents of the Department of Public Operations and the Advanced School of Public Administration for the year 1991

Education and Training

In order to reform the public administrative corps along managerial lines, nothing less than a cultural revolution would appear to be necessary in the training and background of public management personnel. The typically humanistic and legal training of public managers – a side-effect of the predominantly southern Italian origin of personnel – lies at the root of an administrative culture with a high concentration of legalistic elements. According to research performed on a test group in 1989 by the Centre for Studies on Social Investments (CENSIS), 64 per cent of management personnel in state organizations and major public-sector bodies hold law degrees. The inclusion of all degrees in any of the humanities raises the figure to 72 per cent. Graduates in economics and statistics, on the other hand, account for only 14 per cent of the total. As much as 40 per cent of management personnel possess an adequate knowledge of French or English, but only 6 per cent have a similar knowledge of German.

Data on management training and recruitment for management-level officials, held at the Advanced School of Public Administration (ASPA), confirm the above. Among graduate entrants as management functionaries 87 per cent had arts degrees and 67 per cent law degrees. The percentage fell to 53 per cent for participants in management courses, with 46 per cent holding law degrees. The percentage of those with knowledge in information technology (IT), at 14 per cent, was low, whilst only 19 per cent had a professional specialization. Initiatives involving training and refresher courses for managers and administrative personnel are run either by the ASPA or on an independent basis by individual branches of the public administration. In 1992, 55 per cent of training activities of the

ASPA were for managers and administrative functionaries – some 1594 personnel in total.

Intensive training in advanced professional skills were carried out, in 1993, by a number of ministries, including the Ministry of Finance (1734 managers and junior managers), the National Flight Assistance Agency (330 managers and junior managers), the National Workmen's Compensation Institute (640 managers) and the National Institute of Statistics (540). Almost all branches of public administration include IT in their training, whilst the largest number of participants at the ASPA were on courses on the European Union. Further examination of these statistics, however, produces a contradictory overview. The professional culture of the upper echelon of the bureaucracy, which has yet to advance beyond the old model, shows cultural and practical shortcomings. Efforts are under way to make up for lost time. It is acknowledged that the traditional legal/arts preparation must be supplemented, with both knowledge of European law and training in IT. Shortcomings still persist, moreover, when it comes to enriching professional skills with knowledge of economics or business strategy (D'Alberti, 1994).

Age, Recruitment and Careers

Analysis confirms the underlying ageing of Italy's public-management corps. Only 20 per cent of state general directors are under 50, and 28 per cent are over 60. The average age is 58 for directors, 54 for lower-level male managers and 53 for women. Entry into management-level positions essentially takes place through competitive procedures, falling into two categories: competitive examinations for staff already in public employment and open competitive examinations. Appointment to the position of general director, on the other hand, is granted through a decree issued by the President of the Republic, in response to a resolution reached by the Cabinet on the proposal of the minister responsible. These appointments maintain their traditionally political nature.

In the past, recruitment to lower-level managerial career paths was based on seniority and there was no lateral entry. The average seniority qualifications for entry into the initial managerial level (first-category manager) was about 20 years' service for men and 19 for women, and for entry into general director level, some 25 years' service. A recent legislative decree (no. 29, 1993) has introduced access for individuals outside public administration to the initial level of its different branches.

Staff Mobility

In general, the career path of public employees remains within the same branch, with transfers between different branches occurring only rarely. It is also rare for public administrators to move into the private sector. According to CENSIS research in 1989, 60 per cent of state management personnel have always served in the same branch of work, whilst 21 per cent have been employed at universities or research centres and 6 per cent in public agencies and corporations. Only 3 per cent of state management personnel have been employed by public or private business enterprises. An analysis of the data published in the report presented annually by the Italian Prime Minister to parliament on the state of public administration shows, for 1993, that only in government ministries have there been significant transfers of personnel between one branch and another, to fill temporary or command positions (see Table 10.3).

Pay Rewards

Compensation of general directors is set down in a decree issued by the President of the Republic, in response to a resolution passed by the Cabinet, following a proposal from the Minister of Public Operations and Minister of the Treasury (art. 2, Law 216, 1992). Three different levels of compensation are distinguished by letters of the alphabet: A (ambassadors); B (class 1 prefects); and C (other general managers). In the case of the lower-level management personnel, pay is set through collective bargaining. This is carried out separately from other employ-

Table 10.3   *Personnel on loan and provisional in Italy, 1993*

		Ministries	*Enterprises*	*Non-economic public bodies*	*Research organizations*
General directors	A	8	0	0	0
	B	10	0	0	0
	C	233	5	0	9
Lower-level directors		538	7	5	38

SOURCE: Report on the State of the Public Administration for the year 1993.

ees, in each of the eight *comparti* of public administration. In the case of general directors, there is a single salary scale which includes all payments.

Other management personnel receive two types of compensation: salary and operational pay, with the latter relating to assigned duties and responsibilities (art. 24 of legislative decree no. 29, 1993). The ranking of different functions and responsibilities is set down in a ministerial decree. Since the end of 1992, the average pre-tax compensation of a B-level general director in a ministry, not including the pension and social security benefits paid by the employer, was equal to 151 340 000 lira per year, paid out in 13 instalments (see Table 10.4). The compensation received by a B-level general director in an independent state enterprise, on the other hand, was equal to 147 828 000 lira per year, a figure slightly lower than the compensation paid to a manager at the same level in a semi-state organization (165 680 000 lira). For lower-level management personnel, the annual, pre-tax, per capita compensation runs from a minimum of 73 355 000 lira (local government bodies and corporations) to a maximum of 112 433 000 lira (health-care).

In general, there has been a fall in the rate of salary increases for public employees since 1990, due largely to the failure to renew labour contracts. This followed a major growth in compensation in the period 1987–90, equal to almost 11 per cent per year, though the consumer price index rose by an average of only some 6 per cent. The limited growth of compensation levels has also had an effect on the upper echelons of the bureaucracy. Comparative analysis of compensation in the private sector clearly demonstrates that managers in all branches of public administration continue to be paid at lower levels than private-sector managers. This is demonstrated by a recent estimate by CIDA-based data for 1991, provided by the Ministry of Finance. On average, pre-tax compensation of public-sector management personnel accounts for 84 per cent of their total income. In some cases, salaries earned as public employees are supplemented by independent activities, particularly in education (22 per cent) and health-care (12 per cent) and where personnel are permitted to carry out professional activities in addition to those performed as public employees.

On the whole, the role played by compensation in linking individual performance to specific objectives is insignificant in the public sector. Adequate, objective systems for evaluating and monitoring productivity are still lacking. This contrasts with the private sector, where a growing role is played by systems evaluating the performance of managers, with supplementary compensation tied to the results achieved.

Table 10.4 *Annual pre-tax compensation of personnel in lira in Italy, 1994*

Ranking	Ministries	Independent enterprises		Universities	Public bodies	Local govern-ment bodies	Health-care			Research organizations		
		A	B				Admin	Medical	Other	Admin	Research	Technology
General director B	151 340	147 828			165 680							
General director C	106 910	120 682	141 282		133 053				127 901			
Lower level managers	84 732	86 592	100 477	81 867	101 968	73 355	81 678	112 433	88 842	84 815	82 345	98 098

SOURCE: State General Accounting Office, 1994.
NB 2400 lira ≃ £1.00.

POWERS AND RESPONSIBILITIES

One of the most important innovations introduced by legislative decree no. 29 is the attempt to transform the administrative corps into a group of managers and, at the same time, abandon the traditional bureaucratic model in which the management role merely involved guaranteeing the legitimacy of administrative decisions. Within the new approach, the public manager becomes a 'manager of human and material resources for the purpose of achieving objectives set by the political body, whose position is characterized (but not limited by) the determination of the end purposes of the organization' (Zoppoli, 1993).

The political body and upper echelon of the public administration are responsible for issuing guidelines and monitoring results, whilst management has the task of conducting the administrative and financial operations effectively. In effect, the range of the manager's independent duties and responsibilities has been extended, placing them on the same functional level as that of the private manager. In particular, the reform of 1993 has established the public manager as the point of contact between private- and public-sector approaches, between the special needs of the public organization and those relating to the new privatized system of industrial relations. It is the responsibility of the manager to combine the pursuit of the public interest with an efficient, correct use of resources, whilst respecting the legality of administrative acts. The main duties of public managers, therefore, relate to the internal organization of public bodies and the managing of personnel, but they also have powers of control and discipline.[6] Furthermore, public managers contribute to the formulation of policies through powers involving activities performed in the enactment of the public administration's external policies.[7]

All activities regarding the managing of public employees are the responsibility of public managers. In fact, managerial activities not the responsibility of the manager are explicitly mentioned.[8] In the same way, the manager is assigned all the powers involving the internal organization of offices, both of people and the offices' activities[9]. The public manager has the task of co-ordinating the work activities of employees with the administrative activities of public office. In performing this function, the manager uses powers identical with those in the private sector involving the managing of people and resources.

This consideration makes it possible to clarify relationships between the new public-sector management and trade unions. Before 1993, the decision-making powers of managers were paralysed by the 'system of obligatory agreements', which had to be reached on either a national or decentralized level with trade unions. The assignment of managerial power involving the organization of labour within the unit has led to a revision of this approach. Except in the case of rewards, none of the issues regarding union organization or personnel management are any longer subject to compulsory collective bargaining. A form of union participation remains, consisting of obligatory procedures supplying information. In such cases, managers are required to supply information or to discuss issues, upon request, with union organizations. Managers, though fully retaining independent, decision-making authority, can judge it worthwhile to continue discussions till agreement is reached (Russo, 1994).

The distribution of responsibilities between the bodies governing the branches of the administration and the management corps does not mean that the two spheres are isolated from each other. Nor does it lead to a situation in which the upper echelon of the bureaucracy risks being relegated to tasks involving nothing more than implementation. The reform, giving due consideration to the fact that the political and the bureaucratic spheres must operate side by side, does not establish a one-way command procedure, as happens in a hierarchical system, but it lays out a model characterized by co-operation between the two areas (D'Orta, 1994a).

As the manifestation of the working relationship between the political and administrative spheres, upper-echelon management plays a role of stimulating and co-operating in the formulation of guidelines. The general director is empowered to make requests and proposals regarding all the acts falling under the jurisdiction of the political body, in this way participating in the establishment of the criteria which will be used as guidelines for the operational activities themselves.

The move in the direction of interaction between the political body and managers is in contrast to the experiences of the past, when the public-management corps had limited participation in political decision-making and their role was essentially one of implementation and enactment. This reflected the traditional, special relationship between the Italian bureaucracy and political authorities. This was centred around the handing-out of favours, a structural separation between the bureaucracy and the political class, resulting in the isolation of the upper echelon of the bureaucracy, plus a number of the socio-geographic characteristics of the management corps.

Cassese (1983) has used the formula of the 'security-for-power' trade-off to explain why the bureaucracy has turned away from a role in political decision-making, waiving, as a result, the exercise of an active role which would have generated responsibility. It is widely acknowledged that, in Italy, public employment serves as 'the lone escape valve from situations

of depression in the private market' (CNEL, 1981). This had two consequences. First, there was the heightened 'southernizing' of the civil
service, as the critical unemployment conditions in southern Italy led
people to seek public-sector jobs as a means of economic security.
Second, that yearning for security lies at the root of 'the proprietary view
of one's job'.

All issues of personnel management are given constant attention by the
bureaucracy. In this way, the groundwork is laid for an unspoken
exchange: the 'political class' does not interfere with the careers or the
status of public functionaries, who, in turn, refrain from assuming an independent role and allow themselves to be excluded from decision-making
procedures and fill a role in which they passively enact the directives
decided by political bodies. Two serious distortions result from this. The
political class continues to be involved in administration, which should be
left to the management corps. The bureaucracy, on the other hand, with
the tacit approval of the political bodies, entrenches itself in a defensive
position, placing obstacles in the way of whatever innovations might
undermine its own prerogatives and, in doing so, essentially condemns the
administration to an immobile stance (Cassese, 1983). The hope is that the
reform of 1993, more complete than previous efforts, will lead to a real,
though inevitably lengthy, process of transformation.

One of the measures accompanying the transformation from a bureau-
cratic-administrative culture to a managerial-administrative one is the
granting to managers of autonomous spending powers, within the limits of
budgets allocated by ministries and distributed under the framework of
legislative instructions, which are based on the needs and objectives of the
different offices. In this way, managers draw on the budgets of their
branch of the administration, in order to organize their decisions
rationally. In the old system, the spending power of managers was exercised within predefined sums set for each function. The introduction of
budget objectives eliminates the paradox represented by the figure of the
'fake manager' or managers lacking adequate funding and discretionary
powers (Rusciano, 1990). This makes the introduction of managerial
responsibility for operational results possible (D'Orta and Meoli,1994;
D'Orta,1994b)

EVALUATING MANAGERS

The point at which management evaluation is performed represents one of
the two innate acts in the relationship between the political authorities and

managers, with the former being responsible for providing guidelines and then monitoring the results achieved. This is not the first time that managers have been held responsible for operational results. But the legal instrument used to govern such responsibility (Presidential Decree no. 748, 1972) failed because of a number of factors. One was a failure to identify the bodies assigned the task of performing the controls. At the same time, there was no definition of the parameters against which evaluations were to be measured. The new procedures call for *ad hoc* bodies or evaluation teams, which will define the parameters and will report to the administrative body in question. These bodies take the form of staff offices and maintain a functional relationship with the bureaucratic leadership and trust with the political leadership (D'Orta, 1994b).

One criticism of the new system is the inadequate independence of the bodies assigned to do the monitoring. Their decisions are not binding on the body responsible for the political guidelines but merely oblige it to state the reasons for any options judged to be out of line. Further, the composition of evaluation teams does not appear to satisfy the requirement of independence, given that the members include managers from the branch being examined. This approach is justified on the need for knowledge of the structural peculiarities and problems of the branch in question. However, there is a risk that monitoring of operations becomes 'self-controlled monitoring' (D'Auria, 1993).

The monitoring of operations carried out by teams, within a single procedural model, has a dual purpose. On the one hand, it supplies information for establishing guidelines and eventually correcting these as a result of a review. In addition, monitoring serves as the basis for penalties being imposed in the case of more serious operational shortcomings. The issue of so-called 'managerial' responsibility, therefore, is closely tied to controls on the activities of the offices. The manager is now held responsible not for the individual acts of the operations being managed, but for the overall achievement of the objectives set, as well as observing the general directives laid down by the body issuing the guidelines.

The monitoring carried out by evaluation bodies involves a series of elements: the results of administrative and financial operations; the achievement of objectives; the efficient management of public resources; the impartiality and proper performance of administrative activities; and working within the general directives laid down. In terms of managerial responsibility for results, a distinction must be made regarding disciplinary responsibility. This is invoked when the manager's behaviour is not in line with the legal rules governing the activities of public employees. Managerial responsibility, on the other hand, revolves around a judgement of economic, and not merely legal, legitimacy, and stems from evaluating operational results in light of the objectives set and resources employed. An adverse judgement of performance means that the individual is seen to lack the qualifications for managerial functions, above and beyond any violations of the rules or regulations of professional behaviour.

Two types of penalties are imposed upon managers, when they are judged to be responsible for shortcomings. The first, which can be applied to managers in all ranks, involves making the manager available for transfer for up to a year, with the loss of all supplementary pay. The second, which involves serious or repeated shortcomings, varies according to the legal status of the manager, whether the office is regulated by public law or private law. The measure contemplated for general directors is early retirement for work-related reasons, whilst lower-level managers are subject to termination of employment.[10]

The overall monitoring system, as summarized above, seeks to introduce a system of control of administrative outputs and results, in place of the traditional system rooted in formal legality (D'Orta, 1994a). Preliminary controls of legitimacy are maintained only for the most significant administrative acts. This use of techniques borrowed from the world of business is not easily implemented, nor, for that matter, can it ever be fully put into effect. This is due not only to a public-law statute being retained for general directors, but also because a total privatizating of the public management corps is simply not possible. This is on account of the fact that the foundations underlying the power of upper-echelon management in business enterprises, and their connection with the business owner, are distinct from the ties between public managers and political bodies (D'Alberti, 1990b).

POLITICS AND PUBLIC MANAGERS

The relationship between the political sphere and the administrative one is a critical factor in the development of a modern, democratic and efficient system for governing public affairs. The history of Italian public administration has been marked by different types of relationships between political and bureaucratic bodies, ranging from the original, and openly hierarchical model (the Cavour law of 1853 for the Kingdom of Sardinia), to the model laid down by the decree establishing the public administrative corps (Presidential Decree no. 748, 1972). This was based on an initial separation of powers stipulated through rules and regulations but never enacted practically, given the frequent overlapping and interference on the part of the political sphere in the area theoretically reserved for the bureaucracy.

Given that a system based on the absolute supremacy of political bodies over administrative ones would be irrational and, at the same time, that it is impossible to establish a strict separation between the two spheres, present guidelines represent a more realistic attempt at transforming the upper-echelon bureaucracy in the direction of managerial practices. The aim is to forge a relationship based on mutual collaboration between the two areas. The need for reciprocal interaction, for the *continuum* existing between politics and administration, is acknowledged, and a new model of relations is established, replacing hierarchical command with one of direction.

In the place of the power to give orders, a typical feature of a hierarchy, the bodies responsible for issuing political guidelines are granted, by the reform of 1993, the power to direct and monitor, whilst the management corps is empowered to handle financial and administrative matters. As a result, the powers of intervention held by the political body in administrative issues have been considerably reduced. For that matter, the exercise of the power to issue political-administrative guidelines is subject to rules of procedure and precise deadlines (D'Orta, 1994c). Procedural activities begin with the formulation, within two months of the approval of the budget, of the guidelines by the political body. These guidelines are issued, after consideration of proposals put by management personnel, in the form of general directives, programmes and projects for administrative activities. Following application of the guidelines by the managers, an overall evaluation of activities is performed (see Figure 10.1).

The operational responsibilities of public managers, regarding financial, technical and administrative affairs, are their exclusive prerogative and are protected from interference by the political sphere. This means that the powers of managers are not subject to substitution by those of the political body (D'Orta, 1994a). The exclusion of political bodies from powers of administrative activity is, however, mitigated by the possibility of superseding individual acts falling under the jurisdiction of the management corps. In order to prevent abuses of ministerial power superseding the acts of managers, a number of limits have been established. As a result, the issue of measures calling for such acts to be superseded is permitted only when all of the following conditions exist:

- when the measure affects an individual act and not a series of powers assigned to the jurisdiction of managers;
- when specific motives of necessity and urgency exist;

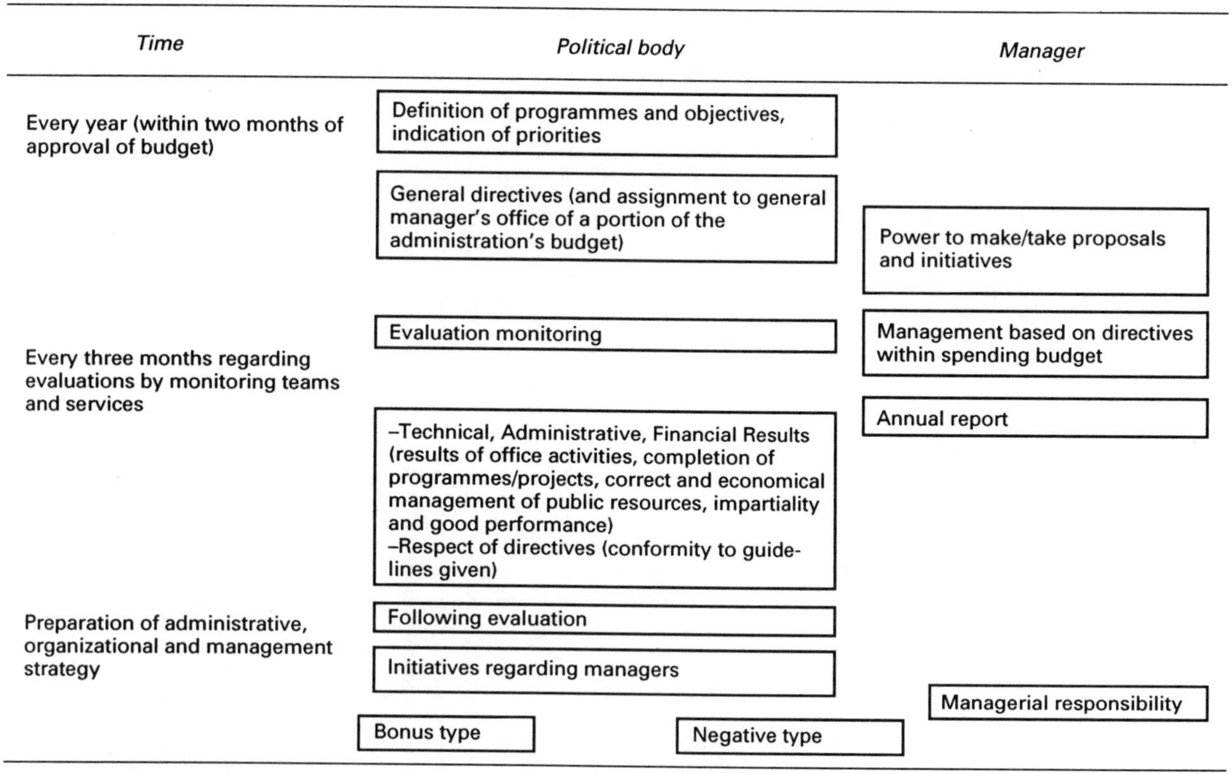

Figure 10.1 Activities of a general manager: relationship with political body

Time	Political body	Manager
Every year (within two months of approval of budget)	Definition of programmes and objectives, indication of priorities	Power to make/take proposals and initiatives
	General directives (and assignment to general manager's office of a portion of the administration's budget)	Management based on directives within spending budget
Every three months regarding evaluations by monitoring teams and services	Evaluation monitoring	Annual report
	–Technical, Administrative, Financial Results (results of office activities, completion of programmes/projects, correct and economical management of public resources, impartiality and good performance) –Respect of directives (conformity to guide-lines given)	
	Following evaluation	
Preparation of administrative, organizational and management strategy	Initiatives regarding managers	
	Bonus type Negative type	Managerial responsibility

* when the written measure superseding the act, which is to be communicated to the Cabinet, expressly lists the motives behind the measure.

The power to supersede the acts of managers, therefore, merely represents a stop-gap measure within the system and should be considered as an option to be used only under extraordinary conditions and to be applied only when the manager has not been able to handle the matter. Otherwise, it would represent a technically irregular and unauthorized means of nullifying the acts of managers (D'Orta, 1994c). In any event, measures superseding the acts of managers represent the only form of intervention open to the political authorities in administrative issues. Indeed, the logic of the new system demands the elimination of other powers of intervention in practical administrative activities granted under previous procedures. These include the power to nullify, revoke or cancel the acts of managers.

The reforms have maintained the predominantly political nature of top public employees. A number of limits have been established to keep the discretionary power on the appointment of general directors within bounds. On the whole, the limits are generic in nature. Thus the professional skills of the candidate must be sufficient for the tasks to be performed. In some cases, there must be appointment of experts with particular qualifications or of managers at lower levels with at least five years' experience. Shortcomings in the process of appointments could be remedied by formulating a set of rulings by the Council of State restricting and channelling the discretionary power granted to political bodies. In particular, there is an obligation to provide the reasons for the choices made, as well as an express indication of the criteria used in comparing different candidates.[11]

There is traditionally little exchange between the management corps of the public sector and the country's politicians. Over the last sixty years, the number of managers entering politics from public administration has been very limited, despite the fact that Italian law provides the possibility of leave of absence for public employees chosen to hold elective office. In more recent years, however, the trend has been reversed. In the Xth legislature (1987–92), public managers and functionaries accounted for a total of 4 per cent of the members of parliament. In the XIth legislature (1992–94), the figure rose to 6 per cent. In the last two legislatures, two so-called cabinets of technical experts have been formed, many of whose members have been chosen from the upper echelons of the bureaucracy, meaning that the members of the government are not tied directly to political parties. Finally, a significant number of university professors and teachers have been members of parliament in the last two legislatures.

Taken as a whole, this professional category represented 20 per cent of the members of the Xth legislature, with 9 per cent university professors and 11 per cent teachers, and 21 per cent of the members of the Chamber of Deputies and 14 per cent of members of the Senate in the XIth legislature.

THE SPREAD OF THE NEW MODEL INTO OTHER SECTORS

The model of the public-management corps laid out by legislative decree no. 29, 1993, having been designed on the basis of the structural character-istics of the ministries and independent state administrative bodies, can be applied directly, and in full, only to these organizations. Nevertheless, the characteristics of the reform serve as a valid prototype for all branches of public administration, which are also required to bring their structures into line with the new provisions. In other words, the fundamental principles of the reform apply to all branches of public administration, though, at the same time, the peculiar characteristics of different sectors are safeguarded, based on the existence of spheres of independence protected under the constitution. These include regional governments and provinces with legislative autonomy. There is also the different type of relation between the function of issuing guidelines and that of actual administration which exists in a number of branches whose highest-ranking administrators are not chosen on the basis of direct political representation. These include non-economic public agencies and corporations, universities and research corporations.

In any event, the principle of the distinction between the guideline and the management functions is fully applied in every branch of public administration. In light of this, an analysis must be made of the com-patibility of the rules and regulations governing the different sectors with the new model. In a number of public bodies, provisions have already been adopted which are in line with the principles of the 1993 reform. In health-care, a corporate-type organizational model has been adopted for the major hospitals and local health-care boards (Usls). Under this model, the general director has been granted power to represent the Usls, together with full administrative independence, within the framework of the rela-tionship of trust with the body providing political direction – in this case regional government.

In non-economic public bodies and agencies, a number of organizations have been restructured through a series of initiatives, with the distinction always being made between bodies with responsibility for issuing guidelines and bodies assigned administrative tasks. In all these cases, the management corps is granted broad, independent administrative authority. It is also held responsible for the results of the operations under its control. In other sectors of public administration, however, the new principles governing management personnel must still be transformed into practical provisions. In local government, for example, Law no. 142, 1990, had already granted managers powers involving administrative operations and acts representing commitments on the part of the administration towards third parties. They provided power to preside over commissions for tenders and competitive examinations and responsibility for contract procedures and signing of contracts. Taken as a whole, however, these powers are much more limited than those granted to public managers by the reform of 1993. The distinction between the guideline and management functions has been only partially enacted, compared with the approach contained in legislative decree no. 29, 1993.

CONCLUSION

The organization of Italian public administration is governed by two fundamental constitutional principles. The first is the principle of guarantee, and consists of the obligation of public administrators to respect the law or the principle of legality in their operations. It seeks to safeguard the right of interested parties to participate in administrative proceedings and in the formulation of administrative decisions, to enact multiple forms of administrative control over the acts of public administrators, and to guarantee the possibility of appealing against decisions of the administration before a special court. The second tenet can be defined as the principle of effectiveness-efficiency. This means that public administrators must operate to realize the objectives assigned by the law in the best and most economically efficient way possible.

In the past, the first principle always overshadowed the second, meaning that public administration has been more concerned with the procedures of administrative activity than with its objectives. What is more, the very principle of guarantee has been understood and applied in a formalistic fashion. For the classic public employee, the important thing is to function in a way that is formally correct with respect to the law, as well as all the other rules governing administrative activities. The classic public employee attempts to avoid all responsibility. As a result, all choices, all discretionary judgements, are avoided whenever possible. This has the consequence that the purpose of the activities of public administration, i.e. services provided in the interest of the public in the most rapid and useful way possible, is almost always forgotten.

The reforms initiated in the 1990s are meant to preserve the principle of guarantee, an essential element in the activities of public administration, but they also represent an attempt to achieve a working balance between the principle of guarantee and the principle of effectiveness-efficiency. To this end, efforts are being made to:

- eliminate any rules governing the activities of public administration which appear to be unnecessary in respecting the principle of guarantee;
- simplify the organization, procedures and controls of public administration in order to make its operations more rapid;
- create a situation in which the bureaucracy assumes responsibility for the results of its operations.

The challenge requires a thorough-going change in the approach of public employees to their work. But the managerialization process has only just begun and it will be some years before a judgement can be given of its lasting effects.

Notes

1. There are three different levels within the job ranking of general director, identified with the following letters of the alphabet: A (ambassadors); B (class 1 prefects, General State Auditor, general directors of independent public corporations); C (other general directors).
2. The first three 'reforms' consisted of: decree no. 3 issued by the President of the Italian Republic on 10 January 1957 (unified text of the provisions regarding the statute for civil servants); decree no. 748 issued by the President of the Italian Republic on 30 June, 1972 (*Disciplina delle funzioni dirigenziali nelle amministrazioni dello Stato*); and the general law on public employment (law no. 93 of 29 March 1983).
3. Italian public employment is subdivided into eight macro-sectors ('comparti') which group together homogeneous or similar branches of the public administration (health-care, ministries, schools, universities, non-economic public bodies, independent public corporations, regional governments and local government bodies and research bodies).
4. This sector also witnessed a slight decrease, totalling 114 units, in the overall number of administrators in the period from 1986 to 1992 (source: Italian Department of Public-Sector Operations).
5. In the construction sector women managers account for 3.3% of the total number of active managers, while the figure in the commercial sector is

10.9%, with figures of 5.1% in the manufacturing industry, 5.7% in agriculture, and 4.7% in banking and insurance (CIDA estimate for 1993). Regarding the growth rate for management personnel in the public sector, in 1987 the figure for the presence of women in the area of government ministries was equal to 9.7%, the figure for autonomous state corporations was 2.7% and the figure for secondary state bodies was 10.9% (source: Report on the state of the public administration for the year 1987).

6. An example of these powers is the monitoring function through which general directors control lower-level managers, with the power to replace the manager in cases of inertia, as well as the power to propose disciplinary measures for managers and the power to discipline other employees.

7. The managers are responsible for all administrative, technical and financial operations, including the adoption of acts which constitute agreements between the public administration and third parties.

8. Among other things, management personnel are responsible, under the provisions of legislative decree no. 29(1993), for assigning supplementary economic compensation, as well as higher levels of responsibility, to public employees.

9. Among other things, the managers establish the structure of the work schedule, evaluate the productivity of the different offices, set the work loads, coordinate the activities of those in charge of different procedures, and set the hours in which the offices are in service and open to the public.

10. The few procedural instructions provided by legislative decree no. 29 on the subject of judging management responsibility regard the manager's right to respond and the indication of the body with jurisdiction over the issuing of the measure laying down the penalty (in the case of branches of the state administration, the minister issues rulings affecting lower-level managers, while the government Cabinet issues those involving general directors; in the case of the other branches of the public administration, the upper management of the branch handles the matter).

11. The decision cannot be based on an evaluation of a similarity of personal or political ideas, but must consist of 'the collection of objective data regarding the likelihood that the individual will perform the public duties with success for a period which is not connected with developments affecting the government cabinet or coalition'. The Italian Council of State, section VI, sentence no. 393 of 16 March 1993.

References

Albanese, A. and Torricelli, A. (1993) 'La dirigenza pubblica' (The public-sector management corps), *Giornale di diritto del lavoro e delle relazioni industriali.*

Albenzio, G. (1994) 'Il punto sulla privatizzazione del pubblico impiego dopo gli interventi correttivi del d.lgs 29/1993' (An up-date on the privatization of public employment in the wake of the corrective measures contained in legislative decree 29/1993), *Rivista italiana di diritto del lavoro,* 1.

Carinci, F. and Carinci, M.T. (1993) 'La privatizzazione del rapporto del lavoro' (The privatization of the work relationship), *Diritto e pratica del lavoro,* 15, pg. III.

Cassese, S. (1983) *Il sistema amministrativo italiano* (*The Italian Administrative System*), Bologna: Il Mulino.

Cassese, S. (1993) 'Il sofismo dell privatizzazione del pubblico impiego' (The sophism of the privatization of public employment), *Rivista italiana di diritto del lavoro*, 1.

Cecora, G. and D'Orta, C. (eds) (1994) *La riforma del pubblico impiego* (*The Reform of Public Employment*), Bologna: Il Mulino.

CENSIS (1987) *XXI rapporto sulla situazione sociale nel paese* (*XXI Report on the Social Situation in the Country*), Milan: F. Angeli.

CENSIS (1991) *Le pubbliche amministrazioni negli anni 90, un'indagine sull'alta dirigenza dello Stato* (*the Branches of the Public Administration in the 1990s, A Survey of the Upper-Echelon State Managers*), Milan: Franco Angeli.

Cerilli Zanganelli (1992) *Dinamica occupazionale e retributiva nel pubblico impiego* (*Employment and Salary Trends in Public Employment*), Bologna: Il Mulino.

CIDA (1994) '*Rapporto sulla dirigenza in Italia, 1993*' (*Report on managers in Italy, 1993*), *Lavoro e sicurezza sociale*, 2.

CNEL (1981) *Rapporto su tendenze e prospettive nel pubblico impiego* (*Report on Trends and Prospects for the Future in Public Employment*).

D'Alberti, M. (ed.) (1990) *La dirigenza pubblica* (*Public Managers*), Bologna: Il Mulino.

D'Alberti, M. (1994) 'L'alta burocrazia in Italia' (The upper echelons of the bureaucracy in Italy) in D'Alberti (ed.), *L'alta burocrazia* (*The Upper Echelons of Bureaucracy*), Bologna: Il Mulino.

D'Alberti, M. (1990) 'Per una dirigenza pubblica rinnovata' (For a renewal of the public management corps), in D'Alberti (ed.), *La dirigenza pubblica* (*The Public Management Corps*), Bologna: Il Mulino.

D'Alessio, G. (1993) 'Organizzazione amministrativa e dirigenza pubblica nel decreto legislativo 3 febbraio 1993' (Administrative organization and public managers in the legislative decree of February 1993) in Naccari, A. (ed.) *La riforma del lavoro pubblico* (*The Reform of Public Employment*), Rome: Ediesse.

D'Auria, G. (1993) 'Il nuovo pubblico impiego e i controlli amministrativi' (The new public employment and administrative controls) in *Giornale di diritto del lavoro delle relazioni industriali*.

D'Orta, C. (1994a) 'La riforma delle dirigenza pubblica' (The reform of the public management corps), in Rusciano Zoppoli (ed.) *L'impiengo pubblico nel diritto del lavoro* Turin: Giappichelli.

D'Orta, C. (1994b) 'Controllo di gestione e responsabilita dirigenziale nelle recenti riforme della pubblica amministrazione' (Monitoring of operations and management responsibility in the recent reforms of the public administration, *Rivista trimestrale di scienza dell'aministrazione*, 4.

D'Orta, C. (1994c) 'La sopraordinazone dei ministeri secondo il d.lgs 3 febbraio 1993, n. 29, Poteri di avocazione, annullamento e decisione dei ricorsi gerarchici sugli atti dei dirigenti' (The command powers of the ministries according to legislative decree no. 29 of 3 February 1993, Powers to Supercede, Nullify and Make Decisions on Hierarchical Appeals Involving the Acts of Managers), *Foro amministrativo*, 5.

D'Orta, C. (1994d) 'La riforma della dirigenza: dalla sovrapposizione alla distinzione fra politica e amministrazione? '(The reform of the management corps: from an overlapping to a distinction of politics and administration?), *Rivista trimestrale di diritto pubblico*, 1.

D'Orta, C. and Meoli, C. (1994) *La riforma della dirigenza (The Reform of the Management Corps)*, Padua: Cedam.

Glannini, M.S. (1984) 'Considerazoni sulla legge-quadro sul pubblico impiego (Considerations on the unified law regarding public employment), *Politica del diritto*.

Glannini, M.S. (1979) 'Rapporto sui principi problemi della pubblica amminis-trazione' (Report on the main problems of the public administration), *Lavoro e diritto*.

Gragnoli, E., (1993) 'Problemi e limiti della privatizzazione' (Problems and limitations of privatization), *Il Progetto*.

Indirizzi per la modernizzazione delle amministrazioni pubbliche, (Guidelines for the modernization of the Public Administration), Prime Minister's Office (1993) Department of Public Operations.

Rapporto sulle condizioni delle pubbliche amministrazioni (Report on the conditions of the Public Administration), Prime Minister's Office.

Relazione del Governo sullo stato della pubblica amministrazione, anni 1992 e 1993 (Report of the Government on the State of the Public Administration).

Romagnoli, U. (1988) 'Le vicende della dirigenza amministrativa' (Developments Affecting Administrative Managers), *Lavoro e diritto*.

Rusciano, M. (1990) 'La dirigenza amministrativa fra pubblico e privato' (Administrative managers between the public model and the private model), Bologna: Il Mulino.

Russo, C. (1994) 'Il pubblico impiego fra ieri e domani' (Public employment between yesterday and tomorrow) *Edizioni Lavoro*.

Virga, P. (1993) *Il pubblico impiego dopo la privatizzazione (Public Employment following Privatization)*, Milan: Giufrré.

Zoppoli, L. (1993) 'La dirigenza del pubblico impiengo privatizzato' (The management of privatized public employment), M. Rusciano and L. Zoppoli (eds) *L'impiego pubblico nel diritto del lavoro*, Turin: Giappichelli.

11 The Netherlands

G. Oosterhuis and T.P.W. van der Krogt

Government in the Netherlands has three levels: *central, provincial* and *local*. Central government consists of 13 ministries and some additional advisory units. Some of the ministries have concentrated all their staff in the city of the Hague, the main residence of the Netherlands government. Other departments have extensive field administrations with regional and local units. Examples of the latter are the Ministry of Finance, the Ministry of Public Works and the Ministry of Defence. Central government employed about 225 000 people, including 112 000 in the armed forces, in 1993. At provincial level, there are 12 provinces with most of their tasks in the field of co-ordination, planning (socio-economic structure, infrastructure, environment, health, recreation) and control (finances). The provinces employ around 13 000 public servants. The size and the tasks of the provinces are currently under discussion because of the recent rise of city-provinces and regional authorities. At local level there are 636 municipalities ranging from 981 to 724 195 inhabitants. Forty municipalities have more than 60 000 inhabitants and seven more than 150 000. Finally, there are 111 water boards with a water-quantity and/or water-quality regulation task.

Municipalities and provinces are ruled by elected councils, whose members perform their duty on a part time basis. The chairpersons of these councils (the mayor and the Queen's commissioner respectively) are not chosen but appointed by the Crown, on the advice of local representatives and the Home Office. The daily governing of municipalities and provinces is done by a college consisting of the chair of the council and two to six elected members (aldermen) who perform this task on a half time or full time basis.

The division of governmental activities in the above three levels is a legacy of the country's federal past, before 1795, and the Municipality Act 1851. The Municipality Act 1985 roughly prescribes the same tasks and responsibilities for all municipalities, irrespective of their size and number of inhabitants. This leads to diseconomies of scale in the small ones and underestimates the typical big-city problems of the large ones. Small municipalities are coping with this problem by designing intercommunal organizations. Since 1984 this regionalization process is facilitated and standardized by legal arrangements.

A typical example of regionalization is the reorganization of the police forces. Until 1994, every municipality with over 40 000 inhabitants had its own local police force. In the remaining parts of the country police tasks were fulfilled by local units of a federal police corps. Since 1994, there are 25 regional police forces and one central unit, formed after a merger, regionalization and simultaneous reorganization of the federal and municipal police.

Other tasks have also been transferred to regional authorities. One of the most striking problems is lack of coordination and planning. The authority of the respective regional bodies is strictly limited to their specific functions and geographical boundaries of the specialized authorities differ. This situation is partly due to the unwillingness of politicians to create an official level of government between provinces and municipalities, directly chosen by the people.

As to the bigger cities, a discussion is going on as to whether 'city provinces' should be formed mainly for town and economic planning tasks. At the moment, city-provinces are being created in the regions of Amsterdam, Rotterdam and the Hague. Mergers of small municipalities are also taking place, often 'forced' by the province and/or central government, in order to improve their effectiveness and efficiency. In 1994 the Union of Municipalities in the Netherlands (VNG) published a report in which a minimum of 40 000 inhabitants was seen as necessary for a viable municipality. Under pressure from the majority of the members of the Union this figure was later changed to 18 000.

In total approximately 500 000 men and women are working in government, which is almost 9 per cent of the working population. Table 11.1 provides a overview of the numbers of employees in the civil service of the Netherlands.

In the Netherlands the majority of people working in education, culture, health-care and social welfare are not employed by government. For example, education which employs 274 000 people, is run by private, non-profit organizations. These were established in the first half of the twentieth century by associations which were Roman Catholic, Protestant, humanist or socialist. From the 1970s most of these organizations merged into non-denominational non-profit organizations and their main source of income is government subsidies. Similar non-profit organizations run the health service and their funds come from health insurance. Besides these organizations there are a number of tripartite organizations, governed by government, unions and employer unions, that run the unemployment

Table 11.1   *The civil service in the Netherlands, 1993*

Central	General Affairs	371
	Home Affairs	2 937
	Foreign Affairs	2 910
	Economic Affairs	5 262
	Finance	1 702
	Finance (revenue service)	30 304
	Justice	20 293
	Agriculture	11 585
	Education	3 382
	Social Affairs	2 516
	Public Works	4 374
	Public Works (dikes, roads, waterways)	10 074
	Public Housing and Planning	7 287
	Health / Culture	7 251
	Defence	112 000
	Other	1 891
	Subtotal (central government)	224 000*
Provinces		13 000*
Municipalities		189 000*
Intercommunal organizations		21 000*
Water boards		7 000*
Police		38 000*
Other		8 000*
Total:		500 000*

*approximately.

benefits and pension schemes, and, since 1993, the Regional Employment Exchange. These non-governmental organizations are changing rapidly. Business-like management is being introduced on a large scale, mostly forced by central government. In all fields mergers are being forced to create a big enough scale for professional management. If these organizations were within government, their leading officials rightly could be called public managers.

THE CONTEXTS OF PUBLIC SECTOR CHANGE IN THE NETHERLANDS

As in most other western European countries, the reform of the civil service in the Netherlands started in the late 1970s when national government was facing serious budgetary problems (Ringeling, 1993). These problems were caused in part by a fast-growing number of people not participating in the labour market due to unemployment, physical disabilities or age, who were taking an increasing share of national income. At the same time the welfare state was consuming large proportions of GNP. A lot of people were employed by an ever-growing public apparatus to take care of others 'from the cradle to the grave' . The so called collective sector had become too extensive, compared with the market sector. The public debt and the budgetary deficit grew rapidly, with the result that interest payments took a growing share of the budget each year. Cutbacks became inevitable. Under two successive Christian Democrat-Conservative administrations (1982–89), the welfare state and the government apparatus were reorganized. Central government passed the buck partly to provincial and local government, which depend on central government money for about 80 per cent of their revenue. First pro rata cutbacks were used for several years but this yielded unsatisfactory results. In the late 1980s and early 1990s three different strategies (Korsten, 1994) were developed to overcome the crisis. What follows is a description of the strategies and their effects on the level of society (macro), public organizations (meso) and individual senior civil servants (micro).

At the *macro level* the issue of the *retreating government* was raised. Central questions discussed were: What are the central or essential tasks of government and should government do all the things it does? The outcome of this debate, also known as the 'core activities discussion', can be summarized as follows: First, government should be smaller but better. Second, policies should be made by relatively small 'core departments', leaving implementation to private or privatized organizations because these can be more effective and efficient. In the process of decentralization the government structures of Sweden and Denmark were taken as examples. Developments in the United Kingdom, such as Next Step agencies, are also being followed with great interest (Kickert, Mol and Sorber, 1993). The organization of central government has been the object of official studies since 1971. Several advisory bodies and special committees have drafted reports on this subject (Kickert, 1993). The discussion has already yielded some remarkable results.

Both at central and local level more and more activities are hived out to private firms. Sometimes units of government have been privatized, including personnel, and contracted in again. Different public enterprises have been privatized (e.g. Dutch Railways) and some now have a stock market quotation such as the Royal Dutch Post and Telecommunication (KPN). Several agencies have been created already and more will follow.

There are also plans to privatize the pension fund which administers all the pensions of people working in government and education (ABP) which is one of the largest institutional investors in the world.

In 1993 the joint secretaries general of all ministries wrote a report on *The Organization and Functioning of the Government Service*. This identifies strengths and weaknesses of central government. The weaknesses are: the size of the central apparatus, the costs of decision-making, the agenda overload, the 'pillarization' of the departments, and the lack of attention to policy execution. In response they have advocated the formation of 'core departments', separate agencies for policy execution, more collaboration amongst departments and privatization as optional solutions (Secretarissen Generaal, 1993).

On the *meso level* public organizations are concentrating on the issue of *efficient and effective management*: A popular view is that government itself should be managed like a business, no longer oriented towards inputs but towards outputs and clients. Politicians should control 'from a distance' or 'at arms-length'. Units engaged in the implementation of policies should have more autonomy. Discussion on the meso level has led to increasing demands for training in management techniques developed in the market sector. Government, central as well as local, has learned how to improve its efficiency (Spijker, 1992). 'Business-like' government became popular, especially among liberal and conservative politicians. The introduction of all kinds of business techniques and the language that goes along with it (like 'clients' instead of 'citizens', 'output', 'products' and 'markets') were seen as absolutely necessary and unproblematic. First of all, government was forced to improve the financial control systems in order to prevent units exceeding their decreasing budgets. In local government result-oriented budgeting and management by contract became popular. The system of contract management has been applied also to the recipients of public subsidies. It is seen as a prerequisite to obtaining public funds.

At the *micro level* discussions focus on the issue of *public entrepreneurship*: a new role for government in society. The ideas behind public entrepreneurship have been made popular by the Americans Osborne and Gaebler (1992). New ideas about the position of government in society have caused an unmistakable shift in the conceptions about the civil or public servant in central and local government. The classic public servant, who loyally carries out orders given by politicians and sticks to procedures, is no longer wanted. Government needs 'public entrepreneurs', aware of the turbulent market that government is in, trained to apply business methods to control their organizations, preferably with an MBA degree, willing to take risks and being responsible for the performance of their organization. In short: government wants 'new public managers'.

THE NEW PUBLIC MANAGERS

If we stay close to the definition of public managers given in chapter 2, hardly any senior civil servants in the Netherlands meet all the criteria. This is mainly because the majority of civil servants, even when they are appointed to a certain post, have a job for life, that is until retirement on their 65th birthday. Limited-time contracts only occur in the lower ranks, e.g. researchers for the duration of a project, and in the armed forces. Moreover, some elements in the definition of public managers need further interpretation: for example, they are evaluated on their results according to well-defined criteria.

In order to collect information about public managers in the Netherlands, a questionnaire was sent to personnel directors of all ministries. They were asked to identify – according to our criteria – the public managers in their departments, and to provide some information about their specific characteristics. Out of 13 ministries 8 responded. In some cases the information was followed up with interviews. A second source of information was the periodical report on Government and the Labour Market. This report provides an overview of new directions in personnel policy and detailed figures of the workforce. This limited data still gives an impression of the state of affairs and the figures serve as a useful illustration by the sometimes limited personnel policy documents. Table 11.2 gives an overview of the departments that responded, their workforce and the number of public managers identified.

Taken together the figures in Table 11.2 illustrate that about 3 per cent of the workforce serves in the senior officer ranks. About 30 per cent of senior officers were identified as public managers, or less than 1 per cent of the civil service. Further, there is an over-representation of public managers in ministries that have their workforce concentrated in the Hague and an under-representation of senior officers and public managers in ministries with a widespread regional organization. The following managerial positions were reported: permanent undersecretary; general director; director of underdepartment; chief of staff and supreme commander in the armed forces; and chief executive of regional units.

A couple of recent developments in central services must be highlighted. The Internal Revenue Service, a unit of the Ministry of Finance, has undergone a drastic reorganization in order to become more efficient,

Table 11.2   *Public managers in some departments of central government in the*
Netherlands, 1993

Ministry	Total workforce	Senior officers	Public managers
General Affairs	371	26	8
Home Affairs	2 937	120	30
Finance	1 702	106	30*
Finance (revenue service)	30 304	267	105
Agriculture	11 585	186	30
Social Affairs	2 516	120	20
Public Works	4 374	112	35
Public Works (dikes, roads, waterways)	10 074	102	35
Public Housing and Planning	7 287	167	100
Defence	112 000	150*	40

*estimate.

client oriented and effective, with faster collection of taxes and more tax
compliance. The 280 offices of this service were, until 1990, organized
along the lines of the respective tax laws – income tax, corporation tax,
wealth tax – and the different elements of the taxation process – levying,
collection and control. Now the service is organized in 89 regional offices
in conformity with target groups, individuals, corporations and big corporations. In these offices, the separate laws and processes are integrated.
Clients have one counter for all their taxes and questions (Voigt,
1994).The service changed to a market-oriented organization, with much
attention paid to effectiveness and efficiency. The head and perhaps
subheads of the different offices are treated as public managers.

The armed forces are in the middle of a dramatic reorganization. Up to
now the Netherlands has had a system of conscription, but the armed
forces are changing to a volunteer force whilst at the same time decreasing
in size. The reductions of total strength amount to approximately 35 per
cent (army 50 per cent, air force 35 per cent, navy 25 per cent), plus an
equal share of civilian professionals. Efficiency is expected to increase,
and business-like instruments are being introduced. Covenants have been
signed, specifying the mutual expectations and obligations of supreme
commanders and commanders of specific services. This tool of management has found its way downwards in the hierarchy, and a lot of officers,
such as heads of bases, depots and facilities, are changed into public

managers. In the officer training programmes at military academies much attention is being given to administrative and business sciences. Along with these reorganizations there is a change in the operational tasks the forces have to be prepared for. The Cold War scenario has been replaced by a programme in which availability for UN operations is a central task.

Public managers can be found at all three levels of government in the Netherlands. At the local and provincial level public managers are found especially in the larger organizations and include the heads of departments, often called 'sectors', of provincial and local government. We have the impression that in most municipalities with more than 50 000 inhabitants, and in all provinces, the heads of departments meet the criteria for public managers. Probably also the town clerks of many small municipalities can be seen as public managers, if the organization uses management by contract or performance budgeting as its primary tool of management.

Finally, the regionalization process requires new public managers. The reorganization of the police forces serves as an example. After a merger of the municipal police forces, in cities above 40 000 inhabitants, and the federal police in smaller communities, 25 regional corps were established. These are controlled by a regional college consisting of all the mayors of the district. One of the mayors, in most cases the mayor of the largest municipality, is the formal executive (*Korpsbeheerder*). This mayor, responsible for public order and safety, together with the district attorney, responsible for law enforcement, controls the police, advised by the regional chief commissioner of police. The latter has much discretion with respect to the organization and operations of the police force under his command. The 25 police services are subdivided into districts. Heads of districts also have considerable freedom of action. In most cases a form of management by contract is applied. The chiefs of police and their district chiefs are clearly public managers. In other regionalized bodies, chief executives and sometimes department heads can act as public managers, especially when their expertise exceeds the capacities of the politicians and administrators of the small municipalities that established the regional body. Management by contract is very common in these cases.

CHARACTERISTICS OF DUTCH PUBLIC MANAGERS

From our data we know that most public managers in central government are between 40 and 65 years old. Length of service varies from 25 to 40 years, with a few exceptions if public managers are recruited from private enterprises. The great majority of public managers are male. The proportion of female public managers ranges between 0 and 13 per cent. This is only one illustration of the under-representation of female staff in the senior ranks in the Netherlands. Figure 11.1 illustrates this phenomenon, with figures of all ministries except Defence.

Legal Status

The legal status of most public managers is the same as that of all public servants: appointment to a position for an unlimited time, after a period of probation. However, central as well as local government is beginning to appoint managers and others 'in general service', which facilitates mobility between departments. This policy started in 1992 when the 'Intertop' project was launched in all 13 ministries of central government. The target group of Intertop were: permanent undersecretaries, general directors, and some directors of underdepartments. The idea was to create a pool of broadly experienced and highly mobile senior managers, available in central government. When a ministry has high level vacancies it is obliged to recruit from this pool first. Since July 1993, the same strategy was

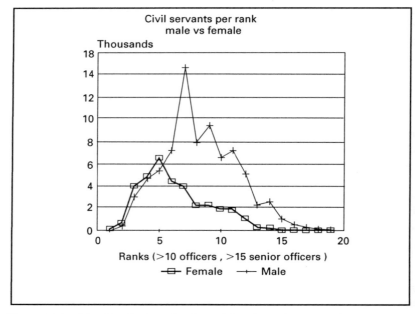

Figure 11.1   *The distribution of male and female civil servants by rank in the Netherlands*

applied to the officers of all central ministries except Defence. All these officers, about 29 700 employees, have been transferred to 'general service' and are no longer appointed to a specific ministry. The civilians in the Department of Defence and the provinces and municipalities might join this programme in the future. Another popular phenomenon is the use of 'interim managers' in government. They are hired for a limited time from consultants or specialized firms. A lot of them were public managers themselves previously. They are hired mainly to implement reorganizations.

Recruitment and Selection

The development of Intertop and the General Service should be seen as a way to stimulate mobility between departments in order to reduce pillarization. The need for these initiatives becomes clear when we regard the traditional pattern of recruitment. In most cases (80–90 per cent), managers are recruited from within the department or from other public organizations (10–15 per cent) and rarely from the private sector. In the Netherlands there are no special universities or staff colleges for public administration, like ENA in France. Public servants are recruited from all kinds of schools, depending on the prerequisites of the specific position. Vacancies are normally published in newspapers and magazines and there is open competition for posts.

Education

The education of public officials depends on the ministry. Public managers tend to have university degrees in law, economics/finance, accountancy or sociology. In more technical units specialized engineers are commonly hired. More students with a degree in public administration are being recruited now and in due course we shall find them among the public managers too. There are no specific selection instruments or criteria for all public managers or civil servants. Every organization is free to use whatever instrument they think is suitable. For managers the Assessment Centre method has become popular in recent years.

Remuneration

Salaries of public managers are determined by the same regulations as for all public servants. For some scarce categories special arrangements exist in order to retain them or to attract them from the private sector. Salaries range between ƒ100 000 and ƒ200 000 gross which is equivalent to £40 800 and £81 600 respectively. Public managers make less money than managers in the profit sector. A public manager earns approximately 50–75 per cent of the salary of a comparable corporate manager, with fewer benefits.

Evaluation

There are some initiatives to design specific evaluation methods for public managers. Management by contract and performance budgeting is being introduced, which implies that managers become responsible for a specific performance such as a specified number of products or services of a specified quality. They are being required to keep their contract, and if they fail more than once it has consequences for their position. Because management by contract and performance budgeting are in the process of being introduced, there is limited experience of its implications. About ten years ago, the Revenue Service introduced a system in which public managers were to identify the seven most crucial factors in their work and specify a target in each. This set of targets has to be updated every year and serves as a guideline for evaluation. Initially there was a tendency to evaluate only the results, but later working methods were evaluated as well. This was done because in some instances results, either good or bad, were beyond the capacity of the public manager to influence, whereas his/her working methods are his/her own responsibility.

Evaluation is a major issue in government at the moment. Many public organizations are introducing human resources management in one form or the other. In HRM, evaluation or appraisal is very important. Until recently public servants were not regularly evaluated. Only when promotion was at hand did a formal evaluation take place. Under the influence of the HRM ideas, appraisal interviews are being introduced on a wide scale. These are done at least once a year. The idea is to exchange information about the performance of employee and supervisor, to look for possibilities of improvement on the side of the employee as well as the supervisor, the job content and work processes. This means that the performances of all public servants, public managers included, are evaluated more frequently. However, currently, appraisal interviews are being introduced for lower levels only.

Career Progression

The traditional career of a public manager is that of a technical specialist who progresses through a technical hierarchy to a management position.

The traditional manager is the best professional, promoted because of his professional expertise, often without any demonstrated managerial expertise. This traditional career pattern is now changing. It is now recognized that management is a profession in its own right. When technical professionals want to become managers, they must follow management courses. Trained managers are sometimes hired for their experience in the profit sector, although the specificity of public-sector management is increasingly recognized. Another prerequisite for holding top managerial positions is experience in all the facets of departmental organization. In ministries with a central department in the Hague and regional units, such as Finance, Public Works and Defence, spells of service in headquarters and the field are necessary.

Training and Development

Many managers in junior positions follow part-time management education. A lot of courses are being offered by all kinds of organizations: in-house (ministries and larger municipalities), universities and colleges for higher vocational training and commercial educational and consultancy organizations. The courses offered by universities and colleges have to be paid for by the participants. The two largest public administration faculties in the Netherlands, Twente and Rotterdam/Leiden, both provide a two-year part-time master's programme in public management/public administration which has been available for five years. These training programmes are very popular with public managers because in most departments the philosophy still is that a manager is an expert in his field. All future managers start their careers in positions where technical competence comes first. So there is a permanent need for technical experts to enhance their managerial skills.

THE AUTHORITY, RESPONSIBILITIES AND ACCOUNTABILITY OF PUBLIC MANAGERS

In contrast to the past, public managers are engaged more in managing than in policy-making. However, there are differences between central and local/provincial organizations. In central government there is a tendency to concentrate the policy determination in so called 'core ministries' and to leave policy execution to autonomous agencies, or to decentralize these tasks to other levels of government (Van Twist and In 't Veld, 1993). So, at the central level, public managers spend less time on preparation of policies, except for advice on the practicability of proposed legislation. At the provincial and local level in the last decade reorganization has led to organizations with a 'concern-like' structure. This means a central unit for co-ordination, control and strategic decision-making, and a few sector services such as welfare and education, town planning, construction, environment and economic affairs in which policy preparation and execution are brought together. The heads of these services are clearly public managers as they are responsible for policy-making and management. When public managers are involved in policy-making, they are subordinate to the political leaders of their organization. Of course they have much influence because of their expertise and their role in the policy preparation process, and on minor points they perhaps 'make' the policy, although this is exceptional.

Even the role of departmental heads at all levels of government is becoming more managerial. Due to the societal and economic developments sketched above, they are forced to act like public managers. The continually decreasing budgets have caused an enormous emphasis on financial control and keeping to budget, but also on the issue of the accounting for products and services in quantitative and qualitative terms. In 1985, new regulations for the budget of local government were implemented. Besides some technical elements, it was prescribed that all costs on a particular policy area should be presented together. So programme costs and the costs of personnel and materials used to 'deliver' this subsidy have to be added. Further, these new directions require that data have to be produced about performance, that are the result of the activities to which the costs are related. To help municipalities with this change in budgeting, the Home Office, together with the Netherlands Union of Municipalities, created the BBI project. BBI stands for 'Policy and Control Instruments'. This project offers assistance and performance indicators. As a result, in over 300 of 636 municipalities, budgets are being transformed from input budgets to product budgets. Based on an inventory and classification of tasks that local government is performing, all products and services produced within each task are identified, and all costs are assigned to the specific products and services, producing an integral cost price. Although no comparable project exists in central government, a lot of organizational units are in a similar process of transformation.

Public managers have considerable freedom of action with respect to the allocation of financial, human, informational and organizational resources. Especially when there is management by contract, exchanges between categories are possible, although there are some limitations. Besides the total amount of money available, a usual restriction is the total number of officials on tenure in specific ranks. The manager is not free to 'buy' the support needed wherever he likes. This gives managers of internal service units the opportunity to reform their organizations and make them able to survive in competition in a free market. Most internal service units will probably be forced into privatization in the near future. In exchange for freedom of action, the public manager is obliged to give adequate information on the performance of his/her unit. Through the use of frequent management reports, higher management and/or the political executive is informed on performance compared with planned targets. Using these reports, principals can check performance and intervene when necessary. Intervention can be necessary because the organization performs less well or because external circumstances are changing.

RELATIONS BETWEEN NEW PUBLIC MANAGERS AND POLITICS

In the Netherlands there are no political appointments. For the highest positions in ministries, provinces and larger municipalities the political affiliation of the candidate is important, but being of the same political party as the politician in charge is not necessary. At central level a reflection of the current political composition is sought. At local level, the mayor and Queen's commissioners who are appointed by the Crown also more or less reflect the poltical balance of the council that they chair. Sometimes appointees are former ministers, deputy ministers or top officials, who are taken care of this way. Although the council has the right of advice, the Crown, in this case the Home Office and the Cabinet, decides. When the political colour of the politician in charge or the political body changes, the public manager, like every public servant, cannot be dismissed. The only political appointees in the Netherlands are a few political secretaries in one or two municipalities.

There are even some legal restrictions on appointments. Civil servants, employed by provinces or municipalities, are not allowed to be members of the political bodies that rule their organizations. But civil servants employed at one level sometimes are politicians at other levels. There are no constraints on political involvement of public managers either, and, although they are supposed to keep a 'low profile', some of them are active and well-informed party members. In their job they ought to be neutral and loyal. This sometimes results in conflicts of loyalty. A growing number of civil servants have strong political opinions about, for instance, environmental pollution or social justice. These opinions might even have been a major reason for their choice of a career in the public service. When policies change, in an unwanted direction, they tend to be more loyal to their beliefs than to their department.

Also in other ways high officials and public managers among them are no longer apolitical. The present labour-conservative-liberal Cabinet, the first after the Second World War without Christian-Democrats, has three ministers who were high-level civil servants up to the elections: the Minister of Justice (liberal) who was Attorney General, the Minister of Agriculture (conservative) who was Secretary General at the Home Office, and the Minister of Finance (conservative) who was head of the socio-economic Central Planning Bureau. They were all politically active in their respective parties, although not in the front line. There are also examples of higher local officials who have become mayors and of aldermen who became town clerks.

In summary, the socio-economic backgrounds of Dutch public managers are not different from those of other high-level public servants. A majority of them have college or university degrees, and come from middle-class socio-economic backgrounds. Top civil servants and politicians in the Netherlands tend to be members of the same social networks and there are few boundaries between them.

CONCLUSION

Our findings suggest that government in the Netherlands at all levels is in transition from traditional public administration, where management was a side issue, to public management. The attention to management issues is overwhelming. Government is becoming more business-like quickly. Common tools of management adopted from business are: cost-based-accounting, performance budgets, performance indicators, management reporting, quality management, certification and project management. Without specific management education, recruitment to a management position is now unlikely.

In our opinion the change from public administration to public management is irreversible. The pressure on government to be effective and efficient will remain. The change has brought remarkable benefits too. Government at all levels is doing more with less people and less money. There is a sense of a more citizen/client oriented government with more attention to people, outputs and outcomes instead of rules. Some critics say that the management issue, especially the question of efficiency, seems the only issue at stake. They point to the specificity of government, and issues like legitimacy, legality, righteousness, and legal security, as of equal or even more importance (Burger *et al.,* 1993).

There are also critiques of the 'figure-fetishism' that is part of business management and of the administration needed to operate the new management systems. It is very important to weigh the costs of producing output figures against the benefits of knowing them. If the costs are too high, knowing less or less precise information, can be much more efficient. Another critique has to do with the political character of public management. It is often difficult to express all political goals in specific quantities and qualities. Politicians sometimes do not want to be as clear and precise as prescribed by business management principles. It is not always possible to state explicitly the expected results of a certain policy. Exceptions, inconsistencies and 'sudden' changes in priorities in policy and policy implementation are sometimes necessary to reach compromises, to satisfy a particular group for the moment, or to reach results in a totally different policy sector. This is the reason politicians will not easily leave policy implementation to officials. They are afraid that these managers are not politically sensitive enough and might endanger their political effectiveness, by rigidly sticking to the agreed policy.

References

Burger, Y.D., Demenint, M.I. and Treur, N.J.H.F. (eds) (1993) *Effectief organiseren in de publieke en private sector. Tussen centrale beheersing en autonomie,* Utrecht: Lemma.

Kickert, W.J.M. (1993) 'Publiek management en organisatie' in W.J.M. Kickert (ed.) *Veranderingen in management en organisatie bij de Rijksoverheid,* Alphen a.d. Rijn: Samson.

Kickert, W.J.M., Mol, N.P. and Sorber, A. (eds) (1993) *Verzelfstandiging van overheidsdiensten,* The Hague: VUGA.

Korsten, A. (1994) 'De overheidsmanager en de nieuwe zakelijkheid' in G. Bouckaert, A. Hondeghem. and R. Maes (eds) *De overheidsmanager. Nieuwe ontwikkelingen in het overheidsmanagement,* Leuven: Vervolmakingscentrum voor overheidsbeleid en bestuur, Faculteit Sociale Wetenschappen, K.U. Leuven.

Ringeling, A. (1993) *Het imago van de overheid,* The Hague: VUGA.

Spijker, W.H.J. van 't (ed.) (1992) *Bestuursvernieuwing bij de Overheid,* Alphen a.d. Rijn: Samson/Tjeenk Willink.

Osborne, D. and Gaebler, T. (1992) *Reinventing Government,* Reading, Mass.: Addison Wesley.

Secretarissen Generaal (1993) *De organisatie en werkwijze van de rijksdienst; rapportage van de secretarissen generaal,* The Hague: Home Office.

Voigt, R. (1994) 'Reorganisatie van de belastingdienst', *M & O, tijdschrift voor organisatiekunde en sociaal beleid*, 48 (1) , 5–24.

Van Twist, J.W.M. and In 't Veld, R. (1993) *Over kerndepartementen. Een vergelijkend onderzoek naar departementale veranderingsprocessen in Groot Brittannië, Zweden, oorwegen en Denemarken*, The Hague: VUGA.

12 Spain

Salvador Parrado

Public service in Spain is still largely characterized by the classical public administration model, based on administrative law. Efforts by Socialist Governments since 1982 to establish a new public management in central government have largely failed. This chapter describes the changes that have taken place as part of the shift towards a modern democratic state in Spain and analyses the Modernization Programme (MP), announced in the late 1980s, which aimed to introduce aspects of 'new public management' (NPM) into Spanish public service. This chapter also examines the problems confronting the MP and identifies where the new public managers are. To identify and locate public managers in the Spanish system, it is necessary to contrast public administration before 1978 with recent measures to modernize its administrative structures. Although the analysis portrays a modernization programme which has largely failed, there are areas of the public sector where it is possible to see the emergence of new public managers. These are to be found in Social Security, the Tax Agency, some universities and some local authorities in the Valencia Autonomous Community.

THE POLITICAL CONTEXT

After the death of Franco in 1975, the Spanish political system underwent a political transition, covering the period 1975–78. Since then, three presidents and two political parties have governed Spanish democracy. The first two presidents from 1978 until October 1982 belonged to the *Union de Centro Democratico* (UCD), a centrist political party. Since 1982 there has been a stable period dominated by the Socialist Party, although since 1993 the PSOE (*Partido Socialista Obrere Espanol*) governs in coalition with a nationalist party. That coalition is not stable, however, as shown by the refusal of the nationalists to take a ministerial post offered by the Socialists. The PSOE was the first political party to form a government which did not participate in the transitional process to democracy. The Socialist Party's loss of the 1996 general election can be attributed to scandals which have emerged in recent years.

The Spanish political system is becoming quasi-federal in status, through a decentralization process starting with the Constitutional Law in 1978, which was further developed in 1984–85. There are currently 17 Autonomous Communities (AACC) which replicate the Spanish central state (government, public administration, parliament, etc.). The 'federal' formula states which functional competencies will remain at central level and which are devolved to regional authorities. The transfer process is uneven and still unfinished. Four AACCs which, historically, have demanded autonomy from the centre have already received control over a great number of services, whilst the remaining 13 Autonomous Communities are still waiting for the transmission of relevant services to them, like education and health. In fact, most services are being transferred from the centre to both the autonomous regions and local authorities, leaving only the functions of co-ordination and evaluation at central level.

The entry of Spain into the European Union (EU) in 1986 accompanied the relocation of internal political power and functions. The task of administrators is to integrate the Spanish economy and the public sector into the international framework as well as the regional one. In addition, with the advent of democracy, the welfare state has begun to take root in Spain. Demands for greater social benefits, however, have come at a time when economic pressures give greater emphasis to the rising costs of the welfare state. This is a universal concern throughout western Europe.

Modernization of the public sector is necessary, if the goals stated in the Constitutional Law, and in political party manifestos, are to be realized. The old model of administration is not suited to offering more and better services to citizens. The regime's administrative structures are not responsive to the demands and complaints of citizens. The old public administration model cannot meet the challenges of citizen-customer involvement in public-service delivery, the redistribution of power to the regions and localities and the demands of membership of the EU.

TRADITIONAL PUBLIC ADMINISTRATION

Before 1978, three elements of Spanish public administration facilitate an understanding of how public service evolved. These are: the structure of public administration; the framework of administrative law and public service; and the relationship between politics and administration (Baena, 1993).

The Structure of Public Administration

During the Franco regime, the system of public administration was both territorially centralized and functionally decentralized. Territorially, the principal units of government were the provinces and the municipalities (*municipios*). Both were closely linked to the centre and shared responsibility over the local area with the Ministry Delegations (field offices). At provincial level, civil governors were appointed by Franco and, at local level, mayors were selected either by the Minister of Internal Affairs (*Ministro de la Gobernacion*) or the corresponding civil governor. The Minister of Internal Affairs had the power to oversee the local administration through what was officially called 'administrative direction' (Baena, 1993). In fact, most control was carried out by Ministry Delegations.

The centralized territorial structure was accompanied by decentralization of functions at ministerial level. Ministers depended upon a ministerial team in their departments, comprising one under-secretary in charge of ministerial resources and a small number of general directors (GDs) who managed specific units. In addition to these ministerially run departments, there were other forms of functionally decentralized units, including *Organismos Autonomos* (OOAA) and Public Enterprises (PPEE). Public Enterprises, such as the railways, steel and coal companies, are run on commercial lines. The OOAAs are departmental agencies, operating under the direction of ministers but with much greater freedom for managers to manage. They have, in principle, been given budgetary autonomy but the Exchequer has tried to limit it in practice. Initially, they were presented as alternatives to decentralized territorial units of government as a means of delivering services more efficiently, thus avoiding the rigidity of strong legal supervision (Nieto, 1988; Baena, 1993). Hospitals, universities, the Spanish National Bank and harbours are some examples of OOAAs which have increased in an uncontrolled way, with the result that nobody knows their real number. However, their financial autonomy has declined and the Ministry of Finance and Treasury obtained strong control over these functionally autonomous units, as over the traditional ministries.

The creation of the Autonomous Communities or regions has been the major structural change within the post-Franco state. Political decentralization has impacted on civil servants and local government officials in a number of ways by changing the relationships between different levels of government. It has been argued that the power of officials has declined in relation to elected representatives and that the grand corps have suffered a weakening of their position (Clegg, 1987). Figure 12.1 shows the organization of the public sector in 1995.

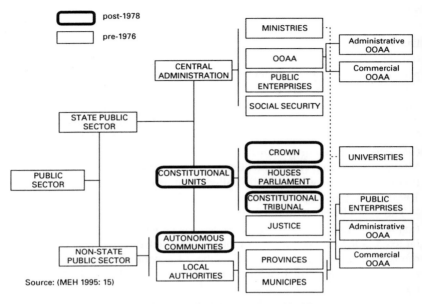

Figure 12.1   *Organization of Spain's public sector, 1938–95*

Administrative Law and Public Service

The framework of administrative law was established during the 1950s – through *Jurisdiccion Contencioso-Administrativa* 1956, *Ley de Regimen Juridico la Administracion del Estado* 1957 and *Ley del Procedimiento Adminstrativo* 1958. These pieces of legislation tried, on the one hand, to establish a legal state and, on the other, to reform public administration. The purpose of this legislation was to ensure the equal treatment of citizens but it did not greatly improve delivery of service. Systems of administration, commonly found in continental Europe, place considerable emphasis on regulation and codification of the law to ensure uniformity in the handling of cases. Lawyers dominate the higher ranks of the public service, unlike in those countries based on the UK system of administration in which interpretation of the law is more flexible.

Civil servants are found at national, provincial, regional and local levels of government. In 1964, the law relating to public servants (*Ley de Funcionarios Civiles del Estado*) was published. This demonstrated the predominance of the *corps* which from the earliest days of the civil service had been the focus of administrative life. Recruitment to the civil service is achieved only through a *corps* and each *corps* recruits through a competitive examination process. The most prominent *corps* developed a strategy to colonize governmental organizations, especially during Franco's era. No matter what the specialization of the *corps*, the goal was to gain administrative areas of work to be offered to their members. Colonization did not happen to all political and professional positions. Some *corps* retain a predetermined sector of the organization, with jobs offered to their members without real competition. These actions undermine the idea of an administrative career based on merit. An attempt was made in 1984 to reform this system by placing greater emphasis on promotion by merit. Top civil servants interviewed before the 1984 reform opposed the *corps* system when they cited other *corps* but not when they made references about their own *corps* (Beltrán, 1985).

In the local sphere, centralization of territorial units was achieved through the key posts of *secretario* (town secretary), *depositario* (treasurer) and *interventor* (auditor). They belonged to the national public service and were centrally recruited and were selected on the basis of their legal knowledge. The *secretario*, for instance, must assess whether the decisions taken by the local corporation contradict the law, whilst the *interventor* intervenes in the budgetary process, observing whether legal requirements are taken into account. Other local officials are either members of a specific *corps*, and recruited locally, such as architects and economists, or are contracted employees who do not have the status of *functionario*.

Not all *grand corps* are of the same strength and or capacity to influence. At different points in the evolution of the state, different *corps* have dominated the top positions in political appointments. During Franco's regime, the central administration was mainly controlled by those *corps* involved in juridicial matters (Alba, 1984), including public prosecutors, attorney generals, judges, notaries and university professors, especially from legal faculties. Lawyers, members of the military and diplomats were also important in an autarkic state, whose major concerns, in the absence of a welfare state, were establishing and maintaining the state's legitimacy.

With the advent of democracy, political decentralization and entry into the EU, there has been an increase in the number of economists in the top political positions of central government. Measured by the possession of university degrees, in 1993, economists represented 31 per cent of GDs and jurists 37 per cent (MAP, 1994a), compared with 11 per cent and 61 per cent respectively in 1973 (Alba, 1984). The most important *corps* today are: economists and commercial technicians of the state (7 per cent);

finance comptrollers (14 per cent); civil administrators (18 per cent); diplomats (13 per cent); and university professors (15 per cent) (MAP, 1994b). Interestingly, after five years' service, members of a *corps* are allowed to leave the civil service to work in private industry. They can stay out of the public sector for up to 15 years and still return to a job at the same grade.

Politics and Administration

During the Franco era the relationships between the administrative and political spheres were blurred. The period is characterized by strong executive power (Tamames, 1988), when Spain was dominated by bureaucratic styles of administration (Alvárez, 1984; Alba, 1981; Baena *et al.*, 1984). Most political posts were occupied by members of the major *corps* – ministers 80 per cent, undersecretaries 92 per cent, and GDs 90 per cent (Alvárez, 1984). Bureaucrats also controlled the *Cortes*, the House of Parliament, installed by Franco in 1943 (Linz and Miguel, 1975; Bañón, 1978). Bureaucrats also held a variety of positions in public and private enterprises at the same time (Baena, 1977). This helps to explain the great power of bureaucrats who embodied the core of a power élite (Mills, 1956). It also explains the inefficiency of public servants, if they shared their time amongst different posts.

In the post-Franco era each central government ministry is headed by a minister, supported by the chief of the minister's private office. The second tier is the secretary of state, also a political appointee, plus the undersecretary and general secretary who are political appointments. The third tier of general directors are also political appointees. These appointments are technically made by the Council of Ministers, though recommendations for appointment or promotion are usually made by officials at one level higher than the one concerned. The GDs in charge of a specific administrative area of work act as a link between professional civil servants and politicians within the department.

There are four different named posts at this tier in the hierarchy: general director (GD); chief of the minister's private office (CMP); technical general secretary (TGS); and president of an *Organismo Autónomo*. The CMP and the TGS are involved in advising on political and technical matters respectively, although only the CMP depends directly on the minister. The GDs manage public resources to deliver services and participate actively in decision-making, especially in implementation procedures. Eighty per cent of GDs are drawn from the ranks of the civil service.

The system of Spanish public administration under dictatorship was highly centralized, based upon administrative law, and designed by the specialist *corps* in juridicial matters. They dominated the top political and administrative posts but had a low service orientation. Politics and bureaucracy were thus inextricably linked.

DEMOCRATIZATION AND ADMINISTRATIVE REFORM

In 1994 there were 2.3 million public employees almost equally distributed between Central Administration and other public bodies (see Table 12.1). Personnel policy is established by central government, although the AACCs are allowed to approve their own laws governing civil servants. Measures adopted by Socialist governments after 1982 attempted to achieve a personnel policy based on a professional, administrative career

Table 12.1 *Employment in the public sector in Spain, 1994*

Units and levels of government	Numbers	Percentage
1 Universities		
Professors	26 509	2.1
Administrative staff	12 461	1.0
2 School teachers	138 616	11.0
3 Social security	46 065	3.6
4 Prisons	14 143	1.1
5 Post and Telegraph	54 056	4.3
6 Tax Agency	26 906	2.1
7 Ministries and OOAA	163 278	12.9
8 Labour contracts in armed forces	36 608	2.9
9 Health institutions	140 962	11.2
10 Police and others	117 958	9.3
11 Armed forces	73 327	5.8
12 Justice administration	40 688	3.2
13 Public entities	72 971	5.8
14 Public enterprises	299 672	23.7
15 Central Administration	1 264 220	55.6
16 Autonomous Communities	639 874	28.1
17 Local corporations	371 456	16.3
Total	2 275 550	

SOURCE: MAP, 1994b.

divorced from party political sympathies (Ortega, 1992). Careers were to rest on merit, performance was to be measured and elements of performance-related pay were to be introduced.

The aim was to undermine the strength of the *corps* and encourage the emergence of new public managers at all levels. This objective could only be achieved if both organizational structures and the budgetary system were reformed at the same time. Legislation, introduced in 1984, attacked the practice of colonizing administrative posts, without recourse to a competitive *concours*. The original intention was to weaken the *grand corps* through introducing a 'post' system of appointment, grouping posts into grades (7 to 30) and setting down educational requirements for entry into those grades (see Figure 12.2). Up to grade 29, posts are filled through merit *concours,* whilst offices at level 30 are filled from amongst existing *fonctionnaires* by politicians, and the incumbent must leave the post at the will of the recruiter or an incoming superior post-holder. The civil servant, at this level, may be downgraded to an inferior post but still retains grade 30 status, if he or she had been in post for at least two years.

Jobs are no longer automatically assigned to a *corps*. Each civil servant within the required group – A, B, C, D, E – can compete to hold that par-

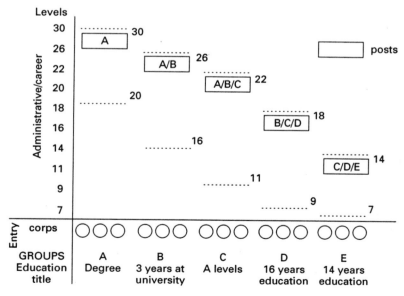

Figure 12.2   *Corps and post system in Spain 1984–95*

ticular post. Payment relies mainly upon the post held and not upon the *corps*. There are four main components of the payment system: basic salary, rank complement, specific complement and a productivity component similar to the concept of performance-related payment. For all levels, the first two elements are set down in the Annual Budgetary Law, whilst the latter elements are determined by each ministry. In reality, however, the productivity or performance element is normally agreed upon with the relevant trade union for each administrative level and only in extreme cases will the superior deny the productivity complement to a public servant.

The 1984 Act was a first step to introducing rationality into the promotion system but it failed because the *corps* continued to supervise advancement, whilst the strongest *corps* have not lost their informal powers over appointments. Another important issue dealt with by legislation was regulating the ability of civil servants to hold two or more jobs. The presence of bureaucrats in public and private enterprises, as well as membership of the *Cortes* permitted under Franco was outlawed in 1984 (*Ley 53 de Incompatibilidades*). Civil servants cannot hold more than one public-sector job and restrictions are also placed on holding posts in the private sector. Only secretaries of state and ministers, who are not civil servants, are allowed to simultaneously hold positions in the executive and the Senate.

The Impact of Decentralization on the Civil Service

In the past, only three historical regions, Galicia, Catalonia and the Basque Country, had demanded a differentiated status with autonomy from the centre. The Constitutional Law of 1978 accepted a diversity of territorial units, according to the functions that each one could execute. Although there are differences among the Autonomous Communities (AACCs) regarding the amount of services they currently deliver, decentralization has been introduced everywhere. One of the greatest difficulties in this process was the transfer of personnel needed to manage services (Escuin, 1986).

Civil servants in the highest grades normally opted to work in Madrid, since the best posts are in the centre, and did not want to be transferred to the capital of an Autonomous Community. As a result, incentives were offered to less-qualified civil servants of ministry delegations in the provinces to work for Autonomous Communities. The AACCs, especially the historical ones, were reluctant to receive civil servants who had served under a centralist, anti-democratic regime. Pressure to deliver services devolved from the centre created problems in the short term. Patronage prevailed over recruitment by merit as the authorities had to rely on labour hired on short-term contracts and civil servants who came, unwillingly, from central government. Civil servants who obtain the highest marks in competitive examinations get first choice of postings and tend to prefer Madrid or their own region.

An initial assessment of this situation demonstrated that the most qualified civil servants remained with the Central Administration, and the civil service of the AACCs was made up predominantly of inexperienced public workers or lower grade civil servants transferred from the centre. These were not ideal conditions to establish a new public management. It was a lost opportunity, due to the resistance of the strong *corps* who preferred to work for the state administration in the regions rather than for the AACCs.

Although the 1984 Act regulates the basis of the civil service at AACC level, they can create their own Acts, which give AACCs some freedom to organize their own public services. Because top people did not want to transfer to the regions, AACCs had opportunities to break the mould and develop a new public manager cadre. However, the absence of a pool of public managers waiting to be recruited constrained any such change.

Decentralization and Local Officials

Local government in Spain consists of two tiers: 52 provinces (*provincia*) and about 8000 municipalities (*municipio*). The large number of towns in Spain gives rise to great diversity of local authorities. Although local government has evolved in the last two decades as a consequence of democratization, Spanish administration is still centralized, in spite of 17 Autonomous Communities. These 17 regions have taken on most of the services delivered previously at national level, and local authorities have experienced an increase in the level of services they have to provide as a consequence of the growth of the welfare state.

The services that local authorities must provide are specified in Acts of Parliament. National legislation is uniform in nature and does not recognize local diversity. In 1986, 43 per cent of towns had less than 2000 inhabitants and accounted for only 8 per cent of the population (Carrillo, 1991). Delivery of services is difficult in these small municipalities, due to limited resources and lack of professional staff. As a result, the provinces take over delivery of services. At the same time there are a small number of large towns and cities which provide a more extensive range of services. Although central government sets the national framework for service provision, recent legislation aims to reduce detailed intervention in the delivery of services (Morell, 1988).

There are 371 000 local government employees in Spain, around 2 per cent of the active population and 16 per cent of total public-sector employment. Only 10 per cent possessed a degree in 1989 (Carrillo, 1991) and only 10 per cent of public expenditure is financed by local taxes (Carrillo, 1994). Local services are provided by elected local authorities alongside those provided by the different delegations of Central Administration, public enterprises and other autonomous agencies. Nationally recruited local civil servants, such as the *secretario*, enjoy considerable power in the authority.

Local administration has become more complex since the creation of the Autonomous Regions and their field offices in the localities (*Consejeros*). The mayor is no longer designated by the centre. In the new system, elected councillors elect the mayor. The full council (*Ayuntamiento*) and a range of advisory committees monitor the activities of the local executive. The executive is composed of the mayor, government commission (appointed by the mayor from among the councillors) and delegated councillors who manage the different departments of the local authority. They are responsible for delivery of the services. Such a structure is typical of a municipality with a population of more than 20 000. In this new situation, the power of local civil servants recruited nationally has weakened. Now the struggle for power lies in the relationship between elected councillors and officials recruited directly by the local authority. The *secretario*, chief of the administration, does not have much say in the delivery of most services.

THE MODERNIZATION PROGRAMME AND MANAGERIALIZATION

The Modernization Programme (MP) was launched in the late 1980s, with the aim of introducing more efficient and effective delivery of public services and goods to citizens. The ultimate objective of the MP was the introduction of a 'new managerialism'. It was envisaged that 'new public managers', responsible for the execution of state programmes, would be *in situ* at the end of the modernization process. This involved organizational redesign, introducing budgeting by objectives and human resources reorganization. However, the attempt to reinvent government has failed and only some organizations have overcome bureaucratic rigidity to provide more efficient services.

Organizational Restructuring

One of the most important tasks envisaged in the MP was to reorganize the internal structure of ministerial departments and address the need to give Autonomous Organizations more freedom from central bureaucracy. The complex structure of Spanish public administration owes more to political pragmatism than administrative rationality. Nevertheless, across decentralized functional units – commercial OOAAs, administrative OOAAs, Entities of Public Management (EPMs), Public Enterprises (PPEEs), linked either to Central Administration, AACCs or local authorities – there is a uniformity of internal structure.

Three weaknesses were highlighted by official analyses (MAP, 1990). First, there was a mismatch between structures of operational units within the department and tasks performed. Second, financial and human resources were managed by Common Services (a staff function) and were not controlled by the civil servants responsible for operational units. Third, the establishment of OOAAs had failed to overcome the rigidity of central bureaucracy. The solution to these obstacles was an organization based upon accountable units or 'cost centres' defined by their state functions, with autonomy to manage human and budgetary resources. Managers responsible for particular units have to accomplish predetermined objectives and deploy appropriate resources to achieve them, without detailed control by central units over the allocation of money and personnel. Both ministerial units and the OOAAs could fit into this model (MAP, 1990).

The unit proposal implied the decentralization of the tasks of the horizontal departments engaged with personnel (Ministry for Public Administration) and finance (Ministry of Economy and Finance) into the ministries, and further deconcentration within the ministries themselves (MAP, 1991). A further implication might be the deconcentration of responsibility with the elimination of the political post of undersecretary, giving GDs a stronger managerial role as heads of department. However, it does not seem that the fourth Socialist Government elected in 1993 will undertake this radical reform of ministerial units. The unit philosophy has been strongly opposed by horizontal departments, especially the Ministry of Economy and Finance, which resisted a loss of power. Finance Comptrollers located in this ministry do not accept their loss of budgetary control of the service (*La Gaceta de los Negocios*, 1990)

Human Resources

The most important proposals in the MP documents were decentralizing human resources management and integrating the *corps* and post system.

Taken together, the *corps* and appointment-to-post system do not function effectively and are impeding the creation of public managers. The post system can be used, theoretically, to allocate human resources in a more rational way by promoting on merit. However, there are two major aspects still controlled by the *corps*. First, the *corps* is still effective in obtaining favourable initial posts for their members. Members from Group A normally enter at level 20 but in strong *corps*, such as civil administrators, diplomats and finance comptrollers, level 26 or 28 is common. Second, the *corps* lobby effectively to obtain posts with special salary allowances for extra responsibilities (specific complements). Perhaps the solution would be to abolish the *corps*. However, that is unrealistic, bearing in mind the key role of members of the *corps* in drafting the MP proposals in the first place. The MP attempted to combine both traditional public administration with aspects of private management. The aim was to achieve equilibrium between innovation, such as introduction of the post system, and continuity as represented by the *corps* system.

Budgeting

In theory, ministries use budgeting-by-objectives, employing the programme budget as the focus for resource allocation. In practice, the programme does not really act as a mechanism for assigning financial resources (Zapico, 1989). There are two reasons for this (MAP, 1990). First, the new system is more complex than the old, where incremental budgeting was applied. Second, there is a lack of co-ordination between the programmes and the budgetary process. The government has tried to introduce budgeting based on objectives, to accompany the unit philosophy, but neither have so far taken root in Spanish public administration.

Implementing Modernization

The failure to reform government does not mean total paralysis towards a more effective public sector. The initiation of the MP put administrative reform on the agenda, and some minor projects have been implemented, albeit unrelated to the central themes of the Government's modernization documents. Given the intense debate that surrounded the MP, government had to be seen to be doing something.

In 1992 the Government agreed on the implementation of 204 projects in all ministerial departments. The projects were grouped into two phases (MAP, 1993). The first phase involved enhancing communications with citizens, improving quality of services and increasing the effectiveness of internal management. Reduction of costs and productivity increases were added in the second phase (MAP, 1994c). The projects did not result in the creation of accountable units but focused on better service delivery. Early evaluation of the projects suggests that in some services, such as passport and identity card issue, there is evidence of improved service. The most relevant aspect of the second phase concerns the production of Employment Plans (*Ley* 22, 1993). Departments must project their staffing needs and any plans for the redeployment of surplus staff must be put to the *Ministerio para las Administraciones*. Only then can new vacancies be filled as a result of competitive examination. Such reforms are not being centrally co-ordinated or planned, thus progress is piecemeal.

Other reforms include a new Act of Parliament to improve relationships between citizens and the Administration (*Ley de Régimen Jurídico y del Procedimiento Administrativo*, 1992), the restructuring of the territorial services of the state and the establishment of an 'Observatory' to measure the quality of public services (MAP, 1994a).

If a stable Government, lasting over 12 years, was not able to implement the modernization project, then the chances of the new minority government of achieving success are small, given the unstable alliances that must be forged by the Aznar administration. However, the modernization idea has spread throughout the public service and there is some evidence of a development of a new administrative culture. Some top civil servants clearly see themselves as managers with responsibility to deliver services and not merely administrators applying the law.

New Agencies

A number of state functions have been transferred to separate agencies, which enables them to evade the traditional dependence upon the ministry and public law. They can operate more autonomously, using civil and commercial law and employing the unit philosophy. They have the status of Autonomous Agencies. Examples can be found among the 204 projects mentioned in the Modernization Plan of 1992. These include Social Security, Post and Telegraph, the Sports Council and Traffic. Only Post and Telegraph became an agency. Such agencies act as 'private' companies and are seen as a step towards privatization (Garrido, 1994). The new OOAA wants effectiveness and efficiency in the delivery of public services.

THE NEW PUBLIC MANAGERS

If the MP had succeeded, then most civil servants holding posts at level 30 would have been rapidly converted into public managers. If the unit philosophy had triumphed, and if the GDs had become accountable managers at the head of the civil service, they would have been the top public managers of the new administrative cost centres. As the modernization proposals did not materialize in the way intended, the incumbents of level 30 and GD posts cannot be labelled public managers as such. They do, however, possess two features of new public managers as defined in the EGPA research project: they are appointed to post for a limited period of time and they are line managers, not policy advisers. Nonetheless, they lack the most important characteristics: they do not have personal responsibility for the execution of a programme, they are not evaluated by their results according to well-defined criteria and they do not have freedom of action over resource allocation.

Successful introduction of new public managers requires not only the development of new recruitment policies but also broader structural changes in public administration. Even the most performance-oriented and citizen-oriented civil servants are insufficient, unless management techniques, departmental structures and resource management issues are addressed. The fiscal crisis of the state and the poor standard of many public services, due to the rigidity of management, still give cause for concern. Even the OOAAs, operating within a special administrative legal framework since the 1950s, have experienced the same inadequacies which characterized the work of traditional general directors in central ministries. Many reasons underlay the creation of such autonomous entities, but greater effectiveness in delivering public objectives was never realized.

The creation of a new breed of agencies in the 1990s has begun to transform the public sector. These agencies operate according to private civil or commercial law rather than administrative law, although they remain in public ownership. The shift in legal status is designed to give greater freedom to manage and thus enhance performance. A number of agencies have opted for this new status: post and telegraph services, tax competences, coin and notes manufacture, railways, ports, institutes for energy and technological development, national enterprises of buses, airports and air traffic, the tourist organization and the sports council. It is these organizations that are most likely to provide a suitable habitat for the new public managers.

These agencies have been set up through the annual budgetary law drafted by the Ministry of Economy and Finance. In normal circumstances, an Act of Parliament is required for the creation or transformation of a public organization. This governmental manoeuvre has had two consequences. First, it reduces parliamentary scrutiny of the creation of such agencies. Second, it has enabled government to evade opposition from pressure groups and political parties who may have resisted such change (Baena, 1994). It is too early to evaluate the impact of the above changes in status on public managers. However, there are some specific initiatives where they can be seen to be emerging. There are three examples of OOAAs which are attempting to overcome bureaucratic rigidity, namely the Tax Agency, some universities and schools and the Institute for the Social Security System. In addition, there are also examples of change in local government, notably in the province of Valencia.

The Tax Agency

The creation of the Tax Agency was designed to give greater freedom from control by Central Administration. This autonomy gives managers more freedom to manage human and financial resources and collect taxes in a more efficient way (*Agencia Tributaria*, 1992). In the absence of central control, the contracts of employees and their salaries are based upon the needs of the service. In the first year, such flexibility produced good results (*Agencia Tributaria*, 1992), although there was much criticism of salary increases of financial comptrollers (*Dinero*, 4 October 1993). The Tax Agency is still accountable to the Minister of Finance and Treasury and all civil servants of the agency may be demanded to answer parliamentary questions.

The agency outlined a strategic plan to face the challenges of the future, but it failed to find support among the strongest *corps* of the Agency, the finance comptrollers (*La Gaceta de los Negocios*, 1993). The agency, under the GD Abelardo Delgado, wanted to fuse the different *corps* dealing with tax competencies but the finance comptrollers rejected and opposed this measure (*Expansion*, 24 March 1994; 11 April 1994; *La Gaceta de los Negacios*, 1994). One year after his appointment, Delgado resigned and the Government appointed the third GD in the four years of the life of the agency, as a result of the strong opposition of finance comptrollers to the strategic plan (*Cinco Dias*, 3 September 1994).

The resistance of the *corps* in the agency was not opposition on party political grounds. Generally, political party affiliation among civil servants, although permitted, is relatively low. Even at GD level, which are political appointments, only a third were PSOE party members between 1982 and 1991 (Parrado, 1995). Rather, the opposition of the *corps* can be explained by their desire to preserve their professional autonomy.

The Institute for Social Security

The public management revolution began in 1987–88 in the Institute for Social Security (ISS) when its General Director (GD), Constantino Méndez, decided to introduce programme budgeting and management by objectives. In order to deliver the service more effectively and efficiently, the GD set objectives in advance to be achieved by all DgDs and provincial directors (PDs). Performance indicators were established on a monthly basis and checked against targets. The previous year's performance acted as the baseline for improved objectives for the following year, so that if in 1986 the achievement was 92 per cent, in 1987 the target might be 93 per cent and so on. This national average takes into account the results in all 52 provinces. From the centre, the DgD for Management imposes targets to be obtained in each province. DgDs receive productivity pay only if the provinces perform at the level of service required.

Management by objectives has been accompanied, since 1990, by a performance-related payment system, composed of three levels of achievement: normal, above normal and below normal. These levels are applied collectively to all staff in the province, by the centre, and individually by the provincial director. The attitude of the *grand corps* involved, namely that of the Social Security Technicians, has been to co-operate in this scheme. Most of the senior members of the ISS belonged to that *corps*.

The Universities

The need for a more efficient management of resources is also seen in the education sector. The introduction of managers to replace professors in the tasks of administering universities is a relatively new phenomenon, dating from the early 1980s. The *gerente* (general manager) is normally appointed by the Rector and cannot simultaneously teach at the university, depending on its regulations. The *gerente* plays a key role in administering the resources of a university. The existence of a new public manager, with a focus on achieving clearly stated objectives, is important in attracting private investment into public universities. The traditional Spanish university was not market-oriented and did not have links with the private sector, unlike in parts of the UK. The pioneer universities in this field are Carlos III (Madrid) and Autonoma and Politecnica (Barcelona). Other universities are still far away from this new philosophy.

The *gerente* is subject to the pressure of the traditional *corps* in a university, that is the professors, especially department directors and deans and vice-deans. The *gerente* is also directly responsible to the rector and vice-rectors, who, as a political body, do not really set objectives to be achieved by the *gerente* and the administrative staff. They have the freedom to set their own performance targets. Otherwise, the productivity element of their pay is determined as it is elsewhere in the public sector, and it is not awarded if there is very poor performance.

Local Authorities

There is great diversity across the range of *municipio*, in that relationships between local politicians and officials vary and that traditions of strong central legal and administrative control have only been broken down since 1985 (*Ley de Bases del Réqimen Local* (LBRL) 1985). Decentralization of more services to local level, combined with fiscal pressures, are forcing local authorities to manage more efficiently and, in at least three cases, to create the posts of 'city manager'. Similarly, increased demands for services are leading to a customer-oriented approach in some authorities. The use of 'one stop shops' and the creation of city managers in Valencian local authorities are the first signs of a new managerial approach.

However, such innovations are not widespread outside Valencia. This is because the representative role of elected politicians dictates the organization of local authorities: political accountability is above managerial accountability. Councillors actively seek a 'hands-on role' in the daily management of local matters, in what has been referred to as 'representative management' (Morell, 1988). The mayor keeps the councillors of his political party content by appointing them to run a service. Sometimes, the services are split if the number of councillors is large. This politicization of the structure means that the political domain grows at the expense of the administrative sphere. In large authorities, councillors are paid to be part of the executive, see themselves as professionals and tend to resist any movement towards stronger management by officials.

Officials possess mainly juridical functions and do not act as city managers. They are more like the old town clerks in the UK (Carrillo, 1994). A city manager who centralizes human and finance resources under the direct supervision of the mayor is a threat to councillors. However, the *corps* are not well organized as pressure groups at local level. This leaves more scope for the development of public managers at local level, rather than at Central Administration level where the *corps* are well organized.

A recent study by the *Valencia Federation del Municipes e Provinces* (FVMP) showed that only five of the 539 local authorities in the Valencia region in 1994 had a city manager. In four cities, the manager reports directly to the mayor, whilst in one city he reports to an administrative departmental director (FVMP-IUOG, 1994). The five local authorities are in a group of 41 which have populations between 20 000 and 100 000 persons (FVMP-IUOG, 1994). It is only these medium to large size authorities that have the capacity to establish a manager in charge of local services. In smaller towns, there is less scope for a city manager, because of the small number of paid staff and the relatively larger number of elected councillors. Where managers exist, they are hired and fired by the mayor. Once again, their small number can be explained by the threat they pose to elected politicians (Carillo, 1994)

CONCLUSION

There is general consensus that the old public administration has not yet given way to a new public management in the Spanish public sector. The MP, designed to introduce a new public management, has not succeeded. The failure of the MP is due to a number of factors. First, there was no clear plan to implement the proposals. The Socialist Government enjoyed continuous power for 12 years with a majority in parliament and in most of the regional authorities but, despite this, their grand plans yielded few results. Second, the organizational culture of the public sector was not ready for such radical reforms. Third, the opposition of the *grands corps* to their loss of autonomy and pre-eminence within the career structure of the civil service has been firm and effective. Reform of top management is necessary, if the Government's objectives to devolve responsibility for the managing of resources, and to become more responsive and sensitive to consumers and the environment, are to be achieved.

Although the general reform movement has largely failed, the pressure of citizens for better services has not been silenced. There have been improvements in the social security system, Tax Agency, and postal service, although not all of these agencies have created public managers. They have become more efficient in spite of their administrators. Some of these units have opted for autonomy in order to have freedom in managing resources. The Tax Agency, in particular, has emerged as a new model for tax administration. However, its attempts to introduce a management culture have so far failed, due to the opposition of the professional *corps* of tax controllers who wish to retain autonomy over their own performance. Only in the ISS has the drive for efficiency and effectiveness also been accompanied by a new managerial culture set by senior management. There are still only a handful of managers in Spain who meet the criteria of 'public managers'. Politicians at both central and local levels are still very reluctant to relinquish power over human and budgetary resources. Devolving such authority to senior civil servants, even at Level 30, or to senior local officials, is seen as a threat to their political power.

The movement towards new public managers is moving very slowly in Spain but is shifting in the same direction as in other countries. The economic, financial and political pressures, which are common features of the 'new public management' (Hood, 1991), provide the context for change. The public law tradition and the administrative culture, in particular the power of the *corps*, are some of the variables explaining the current outcomes of the modernization process.

References

Agencia Tributaria (1992) *Balance del primer año de gestión*, Agencia Tributaria.
Alba, C. (1981) 'The organization of authoritarian leadership: Franco's Spain' in R. Rose and E.N. Suleiman (eds) *Presidents and Prime Ministers*, Washington, American Enterprise Institute for Public Policy Research, pp. 256–83.
Alba, C. (1984) 'Bürokratie und Politik: Hohe Beamte im Franco-Regime, 1938–1975' in Waldmann Bernecker and Lopez-Casero (eds) *Sozialer Wandel und Herrschaft im Spanien Francos*, Munich: Ferdinand Schöningh.
Alvárez Alvárez, J. (1984) *Burocracia y poder político en el régimen franquista*, Madrid: INAP.
Baena, M. (1984) 'La elite española y la presencia en ella de los burócratas' en *Documentación Administrative*, No. 200.
Baena del Alcázar, M. (1993) *Curso de Ciencia de la Administracíon*, vol. 1, Madrid: Tecnos.
Baena del Alcázar, M. (1994) 'Organizacíon, régimen, jurídico y sector público estatal: La incidencia de las leyes de presupuestos' in A. Perez (ed.) *Administración Instrumental. Libro homenaje a Manuel Francisco Clavero Arévalo*, Madrid: Civitas, pp. 73–102.
Baena del Alcázar, M. (1977) 'El poder económico de la burocracia en España' *ICE*, 522, 12–21.
Bañón, R. (1978) *Poder de la burocracia y Cortes franquistas 1943–1971*, Madrid: INAP.
Beltrán, M. (1985) *Los funcionarios ante la reforma de la Administración*, Madrid: Centro de Investigaciones Sociológicas.
Carillo, E. (1991) *Guestión de Recursos Humanos, Presupuestación y Hacienda Local en España*, Madrid: Instita de Estudios Fiscates, monografia no 97.
Carillo, E. (1994) '*El gobierno y la administración local en el Estado de las Autonomías*' (*mimeo*).

Clegg, T. (1987) 'Spain' in Page, E. and Goldsmith, A. (eds) *Central and Local Government Relations: a Comparative Analysis of West European Unitary States*, London: Sage.

Derlien, H-U. (1990a) 'Wer macht in Bonn Karrierre?', *DöV.* 8, 311–19.

Derlien, H-U. (1990b) 'Continuity and change in the West German federal executive elite 1949–1984, *EJPR* 18, 349–72.

Escuin, V. M. (1986) *El accesso de personal y la provision de puestos de trabajo en la Administracion del Estado y de las Communidades Autónomas*, Madrid: INAP.

FVMP-IUOG (1994) *Bianuario estadístico sobre el Gobierno y la Administración local en la Comunidad Valenciana*, Valencia: FVMP.

Garrido, F. (1994) 'Orígen y evolución de las entidades instrumentales de las Administraciones públicas' in A. Perez (ed.) *Administración Instrumental: Libro homenaje a Manuel Francisco Clavero Arévalo*, Madrid: Civitas, pp. 27–45.

Heclo, H. (1977) *A Government of Strangers: Executive Politics in Washington*, Washington: Brookings Institution.

Hood, C. (1991) 'A Public Management for all Seasons?' *Public Administration* 69, 1 Spring, pp. 3–19.

Linz, J.J. and De Miguel, J.M., (1975) 'Las Cortes españolas: 1943–1970', *Sistema*, 8 and 9.

MAP (1990a) *Reflexiones para la modernización de la Administración del Estado*, Madrid: MAP.

MAP (1990b) *Estudio Delphi. La modernización de los procedimientos de actuación en la Administración Pública*, Madrid: MAP.

MAP (1991) *La modernización de la Administración del Estado: Los Servicios Communes*, Madrid: MAP.

MAP (1993) *Plan de modernización de la Administración del Estado*, Madrid: MAP.

MAP (1994a) *Directores Generales en la Administración del Estado*, Madrid: MAP.

MAP (1994b) *Funcionarios de carrera con nivel 30 en la Administración del Estado*, Madrid: MAP.

MAP (1994c) *Plan de modernización de la Administración del Estado: Segunda fase*, Madrid: MAP.

Mills, C.W. (1956) *The Power Elite*, New York: Oxford University Press.

Morell, L. (1972) *Estructuras locales y ordenación del espacio*, Madrid: IEAL.

Morell, L. (1988) *El régimen local español*, Madrid: Civitas.

Nieto, A. (1988) *La organización del desgobierno*, Barcelona: Ariel.

Orteqa, L. (1992) 'La reforma de la alta burocracia en España', *Sistema*, 107, 5–20.

Parrado, S. (1995) 'Las élites politico-administrativas de Estado central en España (1982–91)' PhD dissertation, Camplutense University, Madrid.

Perez, A. (ed.) (1994) *Administración Instrumental: Libro homenaje a Manuel Francisco Clavero Arévalo*, Madrid: Civitas, vol. 1, p. 11.

Tamames, R. (1988) *La República: La era de Franco, Historia de España*, vol. 7, ed., Miguel Artola, Madrid: Alianza Editorial.

Zapico, E. (1989) *La modernización simbólica del presupuesto público*, Bilbao: IVAP.

Part III
Conclusion and Assessment

13 Public Servants in Transition?

Roger Depré, Annie Hondeghem and Jean-Luc Bodiguel

In this concluding chapter we offer some general observations about new public managers in Europe. This will contribute to the on-going debate about the major changes taking place in public administrative systems around the world and particularly the NPM which most OECD countries are embracing.

ORIGINS OF THE NEW PUBLIC MANAGERS

It is evident from the national studies that the main impetus for the changes occurring in the organization and management of government is an economic one. In almost all cases, rising government expenditures in the 1980s were seen as a problem, as public budgets were increasingly out of balance and, as a result, public debt was growing. The proportion of GNP absorbed by the public sector was generally perceived as being too high. In order to solve this problem, governments had to curb expenditure, increase the efficiency and effective use of resources and ensure better value for money.

This economic situation was accompanied by a changing political climate. With the election to power of President Reagan in the USA and Mrs Thatcher in Britain, neo-liberalism became the dominant political ideology in the Western world. In several countries, there was an anti-government movement challenging any further growth in state activity and demanding privatization. Free enterprise, the market and competition were seen as alternatives and panaceas, capable of solving all the economic and social problems confronting governments. The idea was that the public sector should follow the example of the private sector in order to increase productivity and its responsiveness to community needs.

In several countries, government was also confronted with a problem of legitimacy. Citizens expected answers to problems such as unemployment, rising crime and poverty but lacked confidence in governments' ability to provide answers. Because of better standards of education, citizens had also become more critical of politicians and more demanding of the political authorities. They wanted quality in service delivery, more influence over what was provided, and challenged traditional bureaucratic structures. Most public services, however, were still organized in accordance with the classical bureaucratic model, with strong emphasis on legality and fulfilment of regulatory functions. Since a service-oriented public administration needs a different organizational approach, with more flexible and innovative structures, there was a growing consensus that organizational structures had to be revised. Therefore, organizational factors are also important in explaining the transition towards a more business-like approach to public administration.

It is also significant that in several country studies reference is made to the influence of international organizations, such as OECD, the EU and World Bank, and on the changes taking place. These international bodies have been not only a major source of ideas and pressure for change but also an important source of legitimation of NPM. Changes, including cutbacks in public expenditure, were presented as if they were imposed by international agreements such as IMF conditions for financial support in Britain, or the Maastricht norm in the member states of the EU. International consultancy organizations have also been important in spreading NPM. They have been invited by governments to apply their generic models to different countries and have been important disseminators of new ideas, language and managerial thinking.

One conclusion we draw is that new public managers have been introduced under external financial and economic pressures. This affirms Crozier's classical theory that bureaucracy only changes in crisis situations and that change is introduced by agents from outside the system. However, there is also evidence in the national studies that the new values of efficiency and client orientation have been internalized by the new public managers who have accepted and enthusiastically implemented the changes externally imposed upon them. They see themselves now as managers rather than as administrators. As a result, an internal dynamic is operating. Public managers have themselves become agents of change, and this makes the transition towards NPM all the more irreversible.

NUMBERS AND LOCATION OF NEW PUBLIC MANAGERS

The question of how many new public managers there are is difficult to answer. First, the national studies were not all based on original empirical research but on documentary and secondary analyses of existing research work. Second, there were problems in defining who public managers are, raised in Chapter 1. This resulted in some inconsistencies in what was measured. Belgium, which adopted the strict EGPA model and defined new public managers in terms of its seven criteria (see Chapter 1), only found 32 top public servants who could be classified as new public managers. France, in contrast, identified public managers as those civil servants with a positive orientation towards the government's modernization policy. Several hundreds were identified on this basis. In Finland, the link between public managers and budgetary arrangements again produced figures in the hundreds. A third reason why it is difficult to quantify the number of public managers is that in most countries the number is changing all the time. Today's figures can be completely out of date tomorrow, as the reform process continues.

Instead of giving exact figures, therefore, we have constructed a framework within which the degree to which new public managers are found in each country can be assessed. There are clear differences amongst countries, not only in the number of new public managers, but also in the pace of change, the areas where public managers are found, the organizational levels where they are located, the form that the NPM is taking and therefore in the role of public managers. A brief overview of each country illustrates these points.

The first country in the study where the principles of NPM were introduced was Britain. The appointment of Margaret Thatcher as Prime Minister in 1979 saw the beginnings of a transformation of the public sector. Since then, public bureaucracies have been changed into public businesses, the powers of professionals reduced and public services managerialized. This started at central level, but the same policies have been imposed on local government, so that NPM is a feature of the whole public sector, with public managers found at every level.

In Finland, the reform of public-sector management, which started in the late 1980s, has spread rapidly throughout all levels of government. NPM was identified within 134 organizations. Most public managers are located in three types of organizations: result-budgeted and net-budgeted agencies; institutions with business action plans; and public enterprises and state-owned companies. These are concentrated in industry and trade, communications and training, and public utilities.

In the Netherlands, the modernization process began in the mid-1980s with the 'great efficiency operations'. New organizational structures were created – such as agencies – new management tools were introduced to enhance efficiency and effectiveness and the role of the public servant was reshaped. Those trends are seen at all levels of the public sector.

Modernization in Belgium started at the end of the 1980s. New public managers are found in public enterprises, such as the Post and the Railways, but there are also clear trends towards NPM in other sectors such as ministries. This trend is more pronounced in the Flemish part of Belgium than in Walloonia.

The modernization programme in France started at the end of the 1980s and has not involved any institutional reforms or changes in the legal status of higher civil servants. New public managers, identified as those committed to modernization, are found in all ministries and functions but are far more frequent in field offices than in central departments. They are particularly common in sectors undertaking a quasi-commercial or a technical activity, such as the Ministry of Infrastructure, France Telecom and the Postal Service.

In Ireland, there is a trend towards NPM but it is slow. There has been no fundamental structural change in the machinery of government, only a shift in organizational climate towards a more result-oriented approach. At present, NPM is located mainly in the state-sponsored public enterprises, the local authorities and, to a lesser degree, in the health boards.

Italy is the most recent country to embark upon public-sector reform. A legislative decree of 1993 is resulting in a totally new concept of public personnel management. Top civil servants are considered as public managers, with significant autonomy in organizing work. However, new rules and regulations are being applied in their entirety only to the administrative corps of central government ministries. They provide, however, an outline for a model which could be applied to other branches of public administration in the future.

In Germany, the term public manager is, at this moment, used only in state enterprises. The core administration at federal, state and local level is still dominated by classical bureaucrats. The impetus of change is coming mainly from the local sector where many larger cities, and some towns, have started to transform their traditional bureaucratic structures into more management-oriented systems. There is also some movement at state level, Baden-Württemberg, for example, but change is slow and there is no central direction.

The Spanish modernization programme, launched in the late 1980s, has largely failed. Only some minor projects have been implemented. A new administrative culture is slowly developing, but currently new public managers can only be found in Social Security, the Tax Agency, some universities and some local authorities in the Valencia Autonomous Community.

This overview shows that, although there is a transition taking place in all the countries studied, there are significant differences amongst them. First, there is a difference in pace. In some countries NPM started in the early 1980s; in others it has only just begun. Second, there are differences in areas where the new public managers are found. In Britain and the Netherlands they are fairly universal, whilst in Ireland and Germany they are located only in organizations on the borderline between the public and private domains, such as public enterprises or local government. Third, there are differences in organizational levels affected. In some countries, the transition is restricted to the top of organizations, whilst in others we find new public managers at all levels. Fourth, there are differences in the form that the NPM is taking. In all countries, NPM involves the use of managerial techniques, but only some have embarked on organizational restructuring, changing people and developing new organizational cultures. Examples of new managerial techniques include: financial management information systems; performance appraisal; strategic plans; and monitoring systems. The creation of agencies and decentralization are examples of changes in organizational structures. When external persons with a business approach are recruited for management functions, it is possible to claim that new public management applies to people. And when public servants have a new, more business-oriented conception of their role, there is a change in organizational culture. Where countries demonstrate significant changes in all four areas, then the degree of transition to NPM is high. These countries are characterized by a high profile of new public managers. Those countries displaying some degree of movement on all four variables may be rated fairly highly. Countries showing developments in only some of the four variables receive a lower rating, whilst those with very little transition in any of the variables are rated as low.

Table 13.1 broadly classifies the Study Group's sample of nine countries into four categories, according to the degree of transition from traditional public administration to NPM and from public administrators to public managers. Although this classification could be challenged, its purpose is to stress that whilst the shift towards new public managers is a general trend, there are still dissimilarities amongst countries. Group one is made up of countries where the principles of NPM have been introduced over an extended period of time; all areas of the public sector and all management levels are involved; and there has been extensive change in managerial techniques, organizational structures and culture. Our conclusion is that transition in this group is well advanced and irreversible. Britain clearly fits into this group.

Table 13.1   *Degrees of transition to NPM*

GROUP 1	Britain	HIGH
GROUP 2	Finland Netherlands	
GROUP 3	Belgium France Ireland Italy	MEDIUM
GROUP 4	Germany Spain	LOW

Group Two includes countries well along the road to transition, scoring highly on at least three of the four dimensions of NPM. Netherlands and Finland fall into this group. Although in both countries the time period over which NPM has been introduced is relatively short, there is evidence of change in all other categories.

Group Three includes countries displaying some of the characteristics of NPM, but where change is limited in all four dimensions. This is the case in Belgium, France, Ireland and Italy.

Group Four countries are low in the continuum of change. New managerial tools are being introduced but there is no structural or people change, with only a slight modification of organizational culture. In this group, which includes Germany and Spain, traditional systems of public administration and traditional public administrators still dominate. The process of change is probably not irreversible.

These differences amongst countries, which are all experiencing similar economic pressures and environmental changes, have to be explained. Several factors are clearly significant. These include consitutional, legal, political and cultural variables. First, it is clear that constitutional and legal arrangements in individual countries have a bearing on the ease with which changes in their administrative systems can take place. The introduction of NPM in Britain was probably facilitated by the fact that it has an unwritten constitution and no tradition of administrative law. Unlike continental European States, there is no special procedure required to change the machinery of government and no constitutional court to pronounce on the constitutionality of the action. Change in Britain takes the form of either ordinary legislation or executive order. In Germany and France, in contrast, authority to change central or local government requires constitutional amendment and weighted majorities.

Second, continental countries with traditions of administrative law, and in particular established civil service structures such as the corps, are faced with further hurdles to initiate and implement change. In France and in Spain, for example, the corps system, entrenched in the law, has been a major impediment to the transition to NPM.

Third, the political context and priorities on the political agenda are also important factors. In Britain, the introduction of NPM was easier because of a strongly centralized state, dominated by the executive, and because an ideologically committed government, with a large majority in parliament, was in office for more than 17 years. In several countries, NPM is not the first priority on the political agenda and weak governments, or frequent changes of government, have slowed the process down. In Belgium, for instance, modernization of administration was slowed down in the 1980s by the federalization process. In Germany, reunification dominated the political agenda for almost a decade and restricted reforms there.

A further important factor in explaining the receptiveness of countries to NPM is the degree to which public organizations are exposed to the market and consumers. In almost all countries NPM started in the public enterprises and spread to areas in contact with the public directly. This can explain why the impetus for change in Germany is coming from local government, since, as they are responsible for welfare activities, local authorities have to deal directly with the problems of their citizens.

Fourth, cultural perceptions of the welfare state are another significant variable. In some countries public services, such as education, health and social housing, are carried out by semi-governmental or private organizations, which are partly or totally funded by public means. In the Netherlands, the concept of the welfare state is based on the Protestant principle of sovereignty within its own circle. In Belgium and Germany it is based on the Catholic principle of subsidiarity and abstinence of government in the delivery of social services. In those countries, there is less need to privatize public services, as important areas are already managed by private welfare organizations. In others, such as Britain, with virtually monopolistic provision by the state of welfare services, more radical structural and attitudinal change was required to achieve a transformation.

Fifth, it is clear that the Anglo-Saxon states are more oriented towards NPM than continental Europe. This can be explained by cultural factors and language. The literature on NPM, which is almost entirely written in

English, is more widely disseminated in countries in northern Europe than in the south. This also creates separate networks through which ideas and practice can be exchanged.

These observations do not exhaust other possible explanations. They warn us, however, that although there is a common 'economic' drive for NPM, this has to be placed in the context of constitutional, legal, political, cultural, social and historical variables.

CHARACTERISTICS OF NEW PUBLIC MANAGERS

The new public managers are almost all men, certainly at the top. In several countries, however, the number of female public managers increases at the lower levels. Most public managers are middle-aged. In those countries where the NPM has been introduced without recruiting outside staff, the average age is higher. This is particularly the case in Italy, where the new public managers are the same people as the higher civil servants who were in post before the law of 1993.

Educationally there is no significant difference between old style administrators and new style managers. Many of the latter, however, have undergone considerable additional training in management and managerial practices. Although private management training programmes have become more popular in the public service, there is a growing consensus that these are not sufficient. Public managers must be effective not only managerially but also in their political sensitivity. There is, therefore, a need for specific management programmes for the public sector to develop the sort of instrumental and value competencies identified by Virtanen (see Chapter 3).

Most new public managers come from inside their organizations. The number of outsiders, however, is rising and in several countries the recruitment of public managers from the private sector is no longer an exception. More attention is now paid to clear job and person specifications, and new selection techniques, such as the use of biodata, assessment centres and extended interviews, are now being used during recruitment.

As to their legal status, there appear to be three categories of new public managers. Most of them still have the status of a civil servant. This implies that they are career civil servants, have permanent full-time employment and privileged conditions of service. This is certainly true in France, where all the new public managers identified in Rouban's research (Chapter 7) have the legal status of higher civil servants. A growing number of new public managers, however, are appointed on fixed-term contracts. In Ireland, managers in local authorities, since 1991, are appointed for a seven-year term. In Britain, all chief executives of the new civil service agencies have fixed-term contracts and this was extended to other members of the senior civil service in 1996. Managers in public enterprises and local government are also on fixed-term but renewable contracts. A third legal status is the mandate system. This means that a civil servant can be temporarily appointed to a managerial position. At the start of the mandate, clear management objectives are set down and performance is evaluated at the end. Only if the objectives have been achieved is the mandate renewed. This system has already been applied in some public organizations in Belgium, such as the autonomous public enterprises, and there are plans to extend it to all top positions in the federal government.

In most countries studied, new instruments of modern human resources management have been introduced. Traditional systems of staff appraisal are being replaced by performance evaluation. In some countries, the new public managers are evaluated on the basis of predetermined personal objectives and in others on the performance of their organization. Performance-related pay (PRP) has been introduced in some countries, although it is mostly restricted to public managers in public enterprises, except in Britain where it is used throughout the civil service and in local government. There is still a lot of resistance to these new personnel systems, especially from unions and the *corps*. PRP in particular is seen as threatening one of the basic principles of traditional public administration, namely the equal treatment of all employees in the same grade.

Mobility of public managers is still very low, both within the public sector and between the public and the private sectors. The trend is likely to be towards more mobility as fixed-term contracts are extended. The closed career system, which is an important feature of traditional public personnel systems, will come under pressure, as open competition at all levels, but especially at the top, becomes the norm rather than the exception. This will lead to a convergence of pay systems in the public and private sectors in order to attract outsiders into public service. The pantouflage, which has until now been a French phenomenon, is appearing in other countries. Experienced civil servants are moving out into other parts of the public sector and the private sector. Commitment to a lifelong career in the same organization has diminished and there is a greater readiness to contemplate career change. In Britain, 46 per cent of higher civil servants stated that they would leave for a better-paid job if other terms and conditions of employment were similar. Thus, an important challenge for public organizations in the future will be to make their managerial jobs attractive in a competitive labour market.

AUTHORITY, RESPONSIBILITY AND ACCOUNTABILITY

The classical bureaucratic model of public administration is based on the concept that policy should be determined by politically elected people and that implementation of policy is the responsibility of civil servants. Civil servants must serve ministers, or local politicians, who are accountable to the parliament or the town council. In the ministry, there is a clearly defined hierarchy from the minister to the bottom, through the various ranks. In order to guarantee their professional and technical competencies, civil servants are protected against the excesses of political intervention by security of tenure. In exchange, they are expected to be loyal to the 'minister'. In most countries in continental Europe, these principles are anchored in the constitution and regulated by law. This model is now under pressure.

First, there is a trend to decentralize management responsibilities to more autonomous bodies, such as public corporations, which often have their own executive boards, responsible for policy-making and monitoring the organization. Public managers are accountable to the executive board, not the minister. In some countries, like Belgium, these executive boards have extensive powers.

Second, there is another trend towards making new public managers directly accountable to parliament. In Britain, the new public managers of the executive agencies, though still accountable to the minister, are at the same time answerable to the House of Commons and its select committees and they may be called to account before the Public Accounts Committee. They are also increasingly involved in responding to letters from politicians and other bodies concerning the running of their organization.

Third, public managers are increasingly directly answerable to the users of public services. In almost all countries, institutions such as ombudsmen have been created, whilst Citizen's Charters have enhanced the rights of consumers.

Fourth, in all countries there is a shift in responsibility between politicians and public managers. In the new managerialist model, politicians are responsible for setting down guidelines and monitoring the results, whilst public managers are empowered to handle operational and administrative activities. The political authorities decide on general strategies, political objectives, performance standards and budgets, whilst public managers are responsible for carrying out the political programme. They have freedom of action concerning the resources of the organization, financial as well as human, in order to perform efficiently and effectively.

There is an increasing use of contracts or framework documents, with the result that the relationship between the political body and the management corps is no longer hierarchical but complementary. Government by contract is replacing government by administrative hierarchy. This style of management is facilitated by the fact that public management is concentrating primarily on the use of resources and not on policy. In contrast with the past, public managers are engaged more in managing than in policy-making, and this trend is supported by structural changes. In several countries, there is a trend towards concentrating policy determination in so-called 'core ministries' and leaving policy execution to autonomous agencies.

As a result, two types of top civil servants are emerging: those dealing with ministers, whose main concern is policy-making, and those heading executive agencies whose main preoccupation is policy implementation. The new public managers are found in the latter. The structural differentiation of policy-making and policy implementation could be an indication that NPM is reaffirming the old policy–administration dichotomy, but that is not yet clear. The role of new public managers is definitely broader than the role of traditional public administrators in the Weberian model. They not only have more power over the resources of the organization, but also can influence organizational policy to a large extent, through the negotiation process on the management contract. Therefore it is probably better to speak of a 'new' model instead of a replication of the old policy–administration dichotomy.

We conclude that public managers operate in an environment which is radically different from that of the past. The traditional doctrine of ministerial or political accountability, however, remains in place. It is important that questions of authority, responsibility and accountability, which have become increasingly unclear, are re-examined in the future.

PUBLIC MANAGERS AND POLITICS

The relationship between politicians and public managers hinges on power. Whether NPM has changed the power balance remains an open question. On the one hand, the power of the new public managers has increased because they have more discretion to implement programmes and manage resources. On the other hand, the position of politicians is strengthened as they can formulate and control well-defined targets regarding client groups, prices, quality and quantity of services.

The power of the politicians, however, is relative. First, their control over new public managers depends on their ability to measure performance, and the presence of sets of valid output indices. Compared with the private sector, both of these are weak in the public sector. Second, there is a fear that, as in the old bureaucratic model, the new public managers have accumulated such expertise that they can hardly be controlled by politicians. This is most likely when politicians are not engaged in full-time politics as in local authorities. This fear is expressed very well in the German chapter (see Chapter 7).

> There are considerable doubts whether local politicians in council can exercise effective control over the chief executive officer and his professional staff. Similar doubts exist at the federal and state level with regard to the role of members of parliament. In practice the position of top administrators in the present system is extremely powerful.

There is evidence to suggest that the fundamental democratic problem of control by elected politicians is not solved by NPM. In fact new public managers present more of a threat to democracy because of the managerialist culture.

A second issue concerning the relationship between politicians and public managers is politicization. Politicization refers to three practices: the political engagement of public servants; the political role of public servants; and the influence of politics in the appointment of public servants. The case studies have shown that the introduction of NPM has not fundamentally altered the situation of politicization in each country. As to the political engagement of public servants, the situation remains almost the same. In some countries it is possible for public managers to participate in elections and become members of parliament or local councils. This situation is widespread in Germany, where more than 50 per cent of state parliaments and 35 per cent of the federal parliament are civil servants. In Britain, in contrast, where there is a tradition of political neutrality, senior public servants are expected to keep aloof from politics.

As to the political role of the public managers, it could be argued that their role has been depoliticized as they are concentrating more on the use of resources than on policy. But in government, ends cannot totally be divorced from means, nor policy from management. Moreover, public managers are involved in formulating political objectives through negotiating management contracts. As the new public managers are more and more directly answerable to parliament and to the public, their role has become more politicized.

As to political appointments, the most important change is that appointments based on mere nepotism and patronage have diminished and more attention is now paid to the competencies of public managers. In some countries, like Italy and Belgium, this trend has been enforced by the Council of State, by requiring clear motivations for each appointment. Another important change is that in several countries the appointing authority is no longer vested in a political body but in top management, with the exception of the top managers themselves. This is the case for agencies in Finland, the Flemish administration in Belgium and agencies in Britain. This delegation of power can support a process of depoliticization.

Political influence on the appointment of top managers, however, has not altered. Even in Britain, with its tradition of political neutrality, governments have become more concerned with top appointments, with top managers being expected actively to support government policy. In the Belgian administration, top positions have always been politicized. Politicization is an instrument to maintain the traditional equilibria – political, philosophical and linguistic – in Belgian society. Therefore, not only are the appointments of top managers politicized but also those of the members of executive boards. Even the existence of a management contract between ministers and the autonomous public enterprises is not a guarantee of depoliticization.

GENERAL CONCLUDING REMARKS

Although we see in all the countries studied a transition from the traditional public servant to new public managers, there is still a lot of resistance. Resistance comes from politicians, top civil servants, lower-level managers and public servants in general. In some countries, Spain for example, politicians are reluctant to relinquish power over human and budgetary resources, and devolving such authority to senior civil servants is seen as a threat to their political power. Another fear is that new public managers have too narrow a focus on management and lack sensitivity towards the world of politics and interest groups. This could create a climate of tension and conflict and be a hindrance in a democratic society.

Higher civil servants sometimes feel threatened and fear that NPM will relegate their role to that of budget-holders. As NPM calls for a clear-cut separation of political duties and management tasks, this separation is difficult to implement in countries where the higher public service has always had an important role in defining policy and protecting the interests of the state. In Germany and France, top civil servants are particularly opposed to NPM because they see their role as policy-makers becoming restricted and their special status threatened. In both countries there is an important osmosis between the political world and the world of administration, and the number of civil servants in both parliament and local government is very high. This makes any real separation between politics and administration difficult to realize in these countries.

Resistance to NPM is sometimes located at middle-management levels where officials fear for their jobs and positions, promotion possibilities, security of tenure and employment privileges. But this is true for public servants in general. To overcome this resistance it is important for information and communication processes to be developed. Changes are often created and implemented at the top of organizations, whilst those lower down the organization stay unaware. The motivation and the mobilization of lower personnel, however, is one of the success determinants of NPM. Staff must be convinced that NPM will improve the productivity and the quality of the public services they are providing.

A second determinant of success relates to performance measurement. If the performances of new public managers cannot be measured, political control will be very difficult. There is a need to measure not only quantity of output but also quality. There are boundaries to performance measurement and one has to avoid figure-fetishism: figures must be instruments not goals in themselves.

A third determinant of success is the relationship between politics and public managers. NPM has strengthened the position of public managers who now constitute a new and potentially powerful professional group. In order to maintain equilibrium, it is necessary to strengthen the position of elected politicians. Mechanisms have to be found to reassert the primacy of politicians over public managers. One solution is for politicians to concentrate on important strategic issues, which have been neglected in the past, as political bodies were too much involved in matters of implementation.

A fourth determinant of success relates to the ethics of new public managers. As public managers are responsible for the results of their organizations, they are becoming 'entrepreneurs', permanently in search of ways to improve results. The attitudes of entrepreneurs, however, are totally different from those of traditional public servants. There is a danger that, in order to enhance efficiency and results, new public managers will neglect some fundamental values of the public sector. These values constitute a code of ethics which expects civil servants to be impartial, correct, honest and loyal to their democratically elected political masters. One of the challenges of NPM is to evolve a code of ethics for the public managers, allowing them to operate in an efficient and effective way but also respecting the traditional values of the public sector and public servants.

Finally, we would like to make a warning against the phenomenon of NPM. It is sometimes seen as a panacea for all the problems of the public sector. The idea is that if the public sector applies the same principles and methods as the private sector, and if public servants behave in the same way as private managers, all these problems can be resolved. Public management, however, cannot be reduced to private management. Public management deals not only with the question 'how can things be done in an efficient and an effective way?' It is also concerned with the question 'what are the best things to do for society?' 'Management' alone will not solve the major problems of society, such as combating discrimination, unemployment, poverty, inequality and injustice. These are fundamental political issues which require political solutions. Maybe, after the emergence of 'new' public managers, the emergence of 'new' politicians will follow.

Index